SOCIOLOGY OF SANITATION

"SOCIOLOGY OF SANITATION
TEXT BOOK SERIES"

under the aegis of

Sulabh International Centre for Action Sociology

in close collaboration with

Sulabh International Social Service Organisation

SOCIOLOGY OF SANITATION

Mohammad Akram

KALPAZ

ISBN: 978-93-5128-156-6
Price: ₹ 750/-

First Published 2015

Published by

Kalpaz Publications
C-30, Satyawati Nagar,
Delhi —110052
E-mail: kalpaz@hotmail.com Ph.: 9212142040

Laser Typesetting : Rajender Vashist, Delhi
Printed at : G. Print Process, Delhi

Cataloging in Publication Data–DK

Courtesy: D.K. Agencies (P) Ltd. <docinfo@dkagencies.com>

Akram, Mohammad, 1971- **author.**
Sociology of sanitation / Mohammad Akram.
pages cm. -- (Sociology of sanitation text book series)
Includes bibliographical references and index.
ISBN 9789351281566

1. Sanitation--Social aspects--India. I. Title. II. Series: Sociology of sanitation text book series.

DDC 363.720954 23

Dedicated to

Dr. Bindeshwar Pathak, Sociologist,Social Reformer and Founder, Sulabh Sanitation Movement, who gave the theory of "Sociology of Sanitation" to be included in the universal domain of Sociology, for teaching and research in the Universities of India, and across the globe. It will not only enlarge the scope of sociology, but will also be helpful in solving the problems of society in relation to sanitation, social deprivation, water, public health, hygiene, poverty, gender equality, welfare of children and empowering knowledge for sustainable development. This will strengthen sociological quest for knowledge on sanitation.

Dr. Pathak has given his entire life to the cause of sanitation, and in emancipation of scavengers with dignity and mainstreaming them. He has invented "Sulabh Shauchalya" as a tool of social change, which has revolutionised the field of sanitation.

Dr. Pathak has propounded the theory of Sociology of Sanitation, which is as follows:

"Sociology of Sanitation is a scientific study to solve the problems of society in relation to sanitation, social deprivation, water, public health, hygiene, ecology, environment, poverty, gender equality, welfare of children and empowering people for sustainable development and attainment of philosophical and spiritual knowledge."

Truly, he is founder and father of Sociology of Sanitation.

Contents

Foreword

Dr Mohammad Akram, in this pioneering book, *Sociology of Sanitation* has used intensive sociological imagination to uncover the wide range of the underlying structures and mechanisms of Indian society to present the not so obvious trajectories of sanitation and insanitation conditions in developing countries. This work reminds me of the classical work *The Sociological Imagination,* written by the celebrated author C.W. Mills in 1959. The phrase, 'sociological imagination' as used by C.W. Mills, is a reflection of a qualified and distinct imagination while dealing with the 'normal' and 'routine' affairs. Renowned sociologist Anthony Giddens, in his book *Sociology* (6th edition, 2009: 6) says: "The sociological imagination requires us, above all, to 'think ourselves away' from the familiar routines of our daily lives in order to look at them anew". Dr Akram has vividly used his sociological insight to address the sanitation issues in India and used his trained mind to develop a paradigm including several postulates and conceptual formulations for constructing a sociological framework which can be used to study sanitation situation anywhere in the world. This intellectual craft will definitely give Sociology of Sanitation a distinct recognition.

Dr Akram's treatment with the contents of the book is afresh at every level. He has given a very comprehensive definition of sanitation and very impressively included the values of equality, fraternity and social justice in it. He has quoted several definitions including the definitions given by World

Health Organisation (WHO) and Government of India, and I agree with his treatment to the subject. The inclusion of democratic and humanitarian values in the definition of sanitation recognises not only the rights of the citizens but also the rights of the very vulnerable scavenging castes, a social category for which I have worked all through my life and have established that given human treatment and equal opportunity, they are no way less capable than the greatest achievers of the age.

Another big contribution of the author is identification of objectively definable 'attributes' of sanitation. For him, sanitation is a 'conscious', 'collective' and 'realistic' social act. Sanitation needs social engagement in the forms of socialisation and social control. He sees sanitation as an integral component of development processes and claims that no real development can be attained without appropriately developing sanitation standards. He is seeing the centrality of sanitation not only in the context of economic, social or sustainable development but also in the structuring of individual and public health trajectories.

The author is very methodological in identifying the hidden and underlying structures and mechanisms which collectively produce sanitation or insanitation culture in any society. He builds up his framework in the first chapter of the book and gives sound and informative arguments to support his views in the remaining seven chapters. His second chapter locates sanitation within the health and environmental contexts and gives nuanced details of the causation of multiple types of diseases due to inadequate sanitation. The author identifies the relationship between technology and sanitation in the third chapter of the book and says that increasing industrialisation, urbanisation and concentration of human population in urban areas have increased the technological requirements for sanitation. Dr Akram identifies the cultural bases of sanitation in the fourth chapter and argues that the notion of pollution and purity is detrimental to the growth of public sanitation. The notion of pollution and purity, within the caste system, created a caste of scavengers. The growth of the service latrine is a result of this practice.

The remaining chapters of the book talk about the

development interventions carried out in the field of sanitation. The book makes an assessment of the sanitation programmes and policies like 'Central Rural Sanitation Programme' (1986), 'Total Sanitation Campaign' (1999), 'Nirmal Gram Puraskar' (2003), 'National Urban Sanitation Policy' (2008) and the functioning of the Village Health, Sanitation and Nutrition Committees under the National Rural Health Mission and finds that government interventions are half-hearted. Dr Akram has used the terms policy deficit, implementation deficit, and development deficit to describe these situations. Further, contestation deficit causes the maintenance of status quo and the other deficits are never addressed socially. A social mobilisation can combat the contestation deficit also.

The author has included the *Sulabh* experiences as the last chapter of his book and demonstrates how vision with commitment can bring the desired change in any walk of life and especially in the sanitation field. *Sulabh* International Social Service Organisation, a non-profit voluntary social organisation came into existence in 1970 with a dedication to Gandhian ideology of emancipation of scavengers. *Sulabh* has been working for the removal of untouchability and social discrimination against scavengers, a section of Indian society condemned to clean and carry human excreta manually. *Sulabh* is noted for achieving success in the field of cost-effective sanitation, liberation of scavengers, social transformation of society, prevention of environmental pollution and development of non-conventional sources of energy. While trying to solve the problem of sanitation in the country, it also seeks to rehabilitate scavengers and their family members into the mainstream. This is done by providing them with education and training for several types of jobs. *Sulabh* movement is a practical demonstration of the work initiated by Mahatma Gandhi and Babasaheb Ambedkar.

I must acknowledge, before I close this foreword, that I am personally very impressed with the sociological treatment of this book. I would love to see Sociology of Sanitation, taught and practiced not only in India or developing countries but also in the developed part of the world. The students of Sociology need to play very important role in the contemporary age of globalisation. As students of Sociology, we should not keep ourselves confined to understanding the global problems only, we should move forward and come out with the global solutions. I am doing my part. I must acknowledge that Dr Mohammad Akram has taken his responsibility well. The readers of this excellent book should read this message and get ready to play their roles. The Prime Minister Mr Narendra Modi has also shared his vision of 'Swacch Bharat'. Let us make sanitation a reality. Together, we can.

Dr Bindeshwar Pathak
Ph.D., D. Litt.
Founder
Sulabh Sanitation Movement
and
Social Reforms Movement

Preface

An author, trained in sociology, needs to be very clear about few questions when he/she attempts to write something new. The questions are: What does the author intend to write? Why does he/she intend to write? Who are the potential readers and why do they need to study this work? How does the work intend to satisfy the queries of the readers? Which methodological and ontological traditions the author has followed in the work? I will share my understanding about these questions at the very outset.

I will answer the first question by stating that I intend to write an introductory book rooted in the traditions of Sociology and exploring the potential to treat Sociology of Sanitation as a sub-discipline of Sociology. It intends to go beyond a sociological study of sanitation and aims to develop conceptual and theoretical framework which can be applied to study the sanitation situation in any society. It begins with giving a sociological definition of sanitation and develops the concepts like 'sanitation deficit', 'sanitation culture', 'sanitation standards', 'insanitation', 'societal arrangements', 'social contestations', 'technological deficit', 'development deficit', 'policy deficit', 'cultural deficit', 'compounding deficit' and many more. It defines the 'attributes' of sanitation and develops postulates related to causation of 'insanitation'. It explores the dimensions of sanitations and uncovers the hidden factors producing 'culture of insanitation'. It locates how 'contestation deficits' maintain 'sanitation deficits' and why multifaceted social mobilisation is necessary to attain 'sanitation culture'. In brief, I intend to write a book which will make sanitation studies systematic and broad based.

I intend to write this book due to three main reasons: the importance of the topic, my interest in it and an immediate inspiration. Sanitation is an integral aspect of private and public life of human beings world over. It is embedded in the social, cultural, economic, political and environmental dimensions of social life. It is intermingled with the values of equality, freedom, justice and fraternity. It is a core component of development. My interest in the topic finds its academic roots in my efforts to understand the health and development trajectories in India. Sanitation is one of the most important social determinants of health as well as development. I have written one chapter on 'sanitation and environment' in my book *Sociology of Health* and few papers on sanitation programmes in India. But an immediate inspiration for writing a book on *Sociology of Sanitation* came from Dr Bindeshwar Pathak, the founder of Sulabh International Social Service Organisation. This book shares Dr Pathak's vision to educate younger generations about sanitation and make necessary interventions to achieve the goals of social justice and equity in India.

This book has the potential to address the academic needs of students coming from diverse backgrounds. It also has the potential to widen the understanding of policy-makers, administrators, social activists and amateur readers. Any student or person who has any of the following queries in his/her mind is a potential reader of the work: (i) Can Sociology of Sanitation improve our common sense understanding about sanitation infrastructure, technology and practices related to open defecation? (ii) Does social background of individuals/groups influence their sanitation behaviour? (iii) What are the factors that cause insanitation? (iv) Can we develop some theoretical postulates related to causation of insanitation? (v) What are the various dimensions of sanitation and insanitation behaviour? (vi) What is the relationship between sanitation and health? (vii) How does culture, religion or caste influence sanitation behaviour and goals? (viii) Is there any relationship between scavenging and caste? (ix) Is caste or religion a factor in preserving open defecation behaviour? (x) Is sanitation related with the values of equity and social justice? (xi) Is sanitation deficit a result of planning and development deficit in India? (xii) Why did various government policies and programmes related with sanitation fail to achieve the desired goals in India? (xiii) Can we attain sanitation reforms through social movements in India? (xiv) What other measures are required to achieve the goals of sanitation for all? (xv) Can we achieve the goals of economic, social or human development without bringing sanitation reforms in India? One needs to go through this book to get logical and sociological answers of these and many more such queries.

This book presents very lucid and informative contents in a very systematic way. It presents a 'sociology of sanitation' framework which thematically integrates all the above questions and answers them, one by one, without deviating from the main theme. For me, the postulates developed in the first chapter will work like a paradigm. These postulates lead us to the various dimensions of sanitation and insanitation. All the eight chapters of this book are appropriately titled and the readers can identify the possible contents just by going through the titles of the chapters.

The last question related to methodology and ontology is the most important question for any scientific study. The arguments developed in this book are methodologically sound and rooted in core sociological traditions. I will explain the methodological and ontological dimensions of this book first so that the readers understand its logic of inquiry and can move further during their own research in Sociology of Sanitation. I will also include the other logics of inquiry, in brief, here as they can be equally productive for this sub-discipline.

Sociology is a scientific and systematic study of social experiences. As a discipline, it is not keeping itself confined to 'what' questions but goes further and answers the 'why' and 'how' questions also. Different ontological traditions address these 'what', 'why' and 'how' questions and the various sociological perspectives use these ontological traditions singularly or in different combinations to provide logical and scientific answers. The 'what' type questions are generally answered by the 'inductive' or 'abductive' research strategies.

The inductive studies, based on positivist traditions study the existing social patterns and believe that the objectively studied patterns reflect the social realities. The founding fathers of sociology like August Comte, Emile Durkheim and generations of their followers used these traditions. Such studies are also identified as quantitative studies because of use of statistical and other quantitative methods in them.

The 'abductive' research strategy also tries to answer the 'what' questions but uses the subjective methods. Instead of recording the social patterns, the abductive strategy focuses on the meaning given by the social actors and studies the orientations and experiences of the social actors. Among the founding fathers, Max Weber made a significant attempt to understand the meaning attached to social action (later identified as interpretivism). At a later stage, phenomenological and ethnomethodological approaches widened Weber's approach. In contemporary world, post-modernist approach also shares this strategy at some level. Both inductive and abductive studies are often identified as exploratory studies by students of sociology. Very often these traditions are used to give descriptions also and in this mode, they are known as descriptive studies.

The 'why' questions need a different kind of understanding of the multi-layered social realities. The positivistic traditions suggest 'deductive' research strategy for answering the why questions and follow the 'hypothesis-testing' methods to identify the causation of a social pattern. At some level, this research strategy begins with the recorded patterns and test whether they can be validated in specific situations. The deductive strategy is not necessarily positivistic always and can use the non-positivistic methods such as descriptions to test or validate certain hypotheses. The deductive strategy is often followed by the later generation of sociologists to test the conclusions arrived at by the early generations or to see their validity in different socio-cultural contexts. The deductive strategy shares some of the assumptions of the inductive strategy in the sense that it also believes that social realities can be observed by studying the behaviour of people and the 'why' questions can be answered by studying the social experiences. The abductive studies can also explain the 'why' questions depending upon the methods adopted.

However, the fourth research strategy, known as 'retroductive' research strategy is very different from all the other strategies as it believes that social realities are multi-layered and cannot be directly observed. It believes that there are 'underlying' realities or mechanisms which operate as underlying forces and the individual or social actors are not necessarily aware of them. Such underlying realities cannot be studies by studying the group patterns or individual experiences only and need to unearth those underlying structures or worldviews which structure or construct realities.

The retroductive research strategy does incorporate some of the influences of the inductive or abductive research strategies but goes beyond them and digs out the unexplored larger underlying structures or mechanisms and explains the unexplained or the major differences identified through the other research strategies. The structuralists identified the importance of the underlying structures and the constructivists identified the importance of the various underlying behavioural mechanisms in understanding the social realities within the retroductive strategy.

The advantage of the retroductive research strategy lies in identifying the hidden or invisible aspects of human societies. It attempts to answer not only the 'what' questions but also explains the 'why' and 'how' questions. It also relates the observable human experiences with the larger social environment and studies the influences of the later in structuring or constructing the earlier.

This book has used the data collected through inductive strategy (the survey reports) and abductive strategy (the case studies) and analyses them to understand the larger patterns and the subjective orientations. But, it mainly follows the retroductive strategy and uses critical realism to go beyond the obvious. It builds up paradigms and examines them in specific contexts. The dimensions of sanitation are identified using this strategy only. The issues like planning, policy making, governance, technology, environment, pollution, urbanisation, development etc., are examined as underlying structures or mechanisms for causing culture of insanitation or sanitation in any society.

However, I do not underestimate the importance of pure inductive, deductive or abductive studies for carrying out future research in this sub-discipline. In fact, some of the postulates developed in this book needs to be tested through deductive studies. Further, more and more abductive studies are required to understand the varied sanitation experiences of different social groups in different contexts. The framework developed here can be used to broaden the scope of identifying the various determinants of sanitations and factors producing insanitation. I also want to acknowledge here that the research strategies mentioned here are not very nuanced and are presented to inform the readers about my own methodological orientations.

I feel very thankful to Dr Bindeshwar Pathak for encouraging me to undertake this important assignment. I am not in a position to judge the quality of my work. I hope the responses of the students and fellow teachers will help me to understand the worth of my work. The purpose of writing this work will be served if it succeeds in widening our sociological imaginations and improves our understanding about sanitation. I have great faith in the potentials of the younger generations. I hope that my readers will not keep the understanding developed after reading this book confined to their examination rooms or research thesis only; I hope that they will carry the understanding to their practical lives; I hope that they will use it to change the prevailing discourses and will become the agents of change. I will always wait for their feedback and friendly responses.

I must acknowledge that I have quoted Dr Bindeshwar Pathak at several places. Chapter eight is completely based on the information and the images provided by Sulabh Websites. I have quoted from my own published works also. I have mentioned the appropriate references at all such places. I have presented the summaries of the contributions of some well known academicians. Besides, I have also included the views of Mahatma Gandhi and Dr. B.R. Ambedkar at some relevant places. I have alsol included. 'The Prohibition of Employment as Manual Scavengers and their Rehabilitation Act, 2013' in a simple format as an Appendix for making the readers aware of the Act. I must acknowledge that any lapse in citing the appropriate references or summarising the views of the prominent thinkers is a mistake on my part and I apologise for that.

I must express my gratitude to all those who helped and encouraged me in different capacities in completing this challenging work. I feel very thankful to Prof A K Sharma, IIT Kanpur, Prof P S Vivek, Bombay University, Mumbai and Prof Madhu Nagla, M D University, Rohtak for giving their valuable advices as and when I needed. I am always thankful to Prof Mohan Advani for inculcating in me a temperament to say yes to all the academic challenges. I am equally thankful to my research students Mr Zulufkar Ahmad Khanaday, Ms Mubeena. O and Ms Nadiya Muzaffar for helping me in every possible way. They read the manuscript several times very carefully and corrected me whenever I was out of track.

The love and affection of my father Mr Mohammad Naimuddin and mother Mrs Noor Dana Khatoon is always a source of moral courage and strength for me. They always want me to do a little extra to achieve the greater values in life. I am always thankful to my wife Dr Firdousi Begam who takes extra pain so that I complete my assignments in time. I appreciate my son Arshad Amaan and daughter Alveena Firdaus for their readiness to help me in every possible way.

I am indebted to Aligarh Muslim University, Aligarh for providing excellent work atmosphere without which any academic exercise is never possible. I am equally thankful to all my colleagues at the Department of Sociology for maintaining a very academic environment always. I am extremely thankful to Kalpaz Publicatons and Sulabh International for undertaking the publication of this book.

Dr Mohammad Akram

Aligarh Muslim University, Aligarh

akram_soc@yahoo.co.in

1

Sociology of Sanitation: An Introduction

Introduction

'Sociology of Sanitation' is a new sub-discipline of sociology emerging in India. The sub-discipline intends to study the social, cultural, political, economical, historical, ecological, environmental, technological, spiritual, medical and other possible institutional as well as structural dimensions of issues related to sanitation by applying the concepts, approaches, theories and methodological perspectives embedded in sociology. Unlike the growth of several sub-disciplines within sociology in 20th century, sociology of sanitation has to face several specific challenges at the very outset. The first challenge is related to defining the concept of 'sanitation' itself. Any definition of 'sanitation' is myopic and narrow unless it addresses all the underlying and interwoven dimensions of social life imbibed in the understanding of sanitation. The second challenge is related to situating 'sociology of sanitation' amidst various other sub-disciplines of sociology. The third challenge is to develop a consensus on subject matter of sociology of sanitation. The fourth challenge is to articulate the various sociological approaches to understand and examine the various issues related to the sub-discipline. The fifth challenge is to establish the academic distinction of the sub-discipline in terms of its theoretical and empirical relevance in contemporary and future societies. Besides these, many other challenges will emerge during the course of forthcoming discussions. The book intends to address all these challenges.

It is important to address here why these challenges are specific. The growth of a discipline or sub-discipline takes shape in several contexts. Often a discipline finds its emergence as an intellectual response to seminal contributions in the field of knowledge production. Otherwise, a discipline also emerges as a response to the efforts to understand existing realities and new revelations. The sub-disciplines which develop within some mother disciplines have specific advantages. The sub-disciplines emerge to address some new realities or some new approaches to understand the existing realities. They have the advantage of having the seminal contributions, larger theoretical and methodological frameworks, established readers and critics and above all established channels for dissemination of knowledge.

Sociology of sanitation, as a sub-discipline, cannot boast of having all the advantages that many other sub-disciplines of sociology had. The concept of sanitation has not been defined by any of the classical or contemporary sociologist. Further no specific sociological theory addresses the various intermingling dimensions of sanitation. Most of the problems associated with sanitation are typical to third world and less developed countries and hardly seek the attention of sociologists socialised in western paradigms. To make the situation further complicated, sociology of sanitation has to compete and even contest with other sub-disciplines of sociology like 'sociology of development', 'sociology of health', 'urban sociology', 'industrial sociology', 'sociology of policy and planning', 'sociology of stratification', 'sociology of marginalised groups' and many more because of the interrelatedness of some of the 'underlying issues' of sociology of sanitation with the subject matter of the named sub-disciplines. Different 'texts' and 'discourses' already exist which do talk about 'purity', 'cleanliness', 'pollution', 'disease', 'health', 'environment' etc., but the constructed and implied meanings are not the same as these may have when seen from 'sociology of sanitation' perspectives. Hence, a deconstruction of the constructed meaning is also a challenge.

Sanitation is an integral aspect of human life. Sanitation generally refers to hygienic behaviour and practices related to our day-to-day activities such as maintaining cleanliness, taking bath, washing hands, proper defecation and maintaining scientific distance from pollutants. Lack of sanitation is an important factor in causation and spread of several infectious diseases. Increasing concern for public health facilities and the need to control the spread of communicable diseases have necessitated the concern for sanitation in personal and public life. The sanitation movement started almost one hundred fifty years back in most of the industrialised societies. But the third world countries lagged behind in initiating such movements. India is one such country which could not initiate a sanitation movement at the mass level till now. Therefore, India is paying a heavy price for its sanitation deficit.

Sanitation, although related to several aspects of human life but seen more exclusively in relation to human defecation and safe disposal of the human faeces. Human defecation is as important as other biological necessities like sleeping, reproduction or consumption of food. The defecation-engagements such as availability of private space, necessary tools and infrastructure, availability of water, hygiene and safety concerns, disposal of the urine and faeces, concern for the people engaged in disposal processes, maintenance of the ecological sanctity etc., are some of the very common concerns of human life. Learning the toilet habits is a very important dimension of socialisation of a child. Toilet habits are often considered as important reflection of ethnic, socio-cultural and economic backgrounds of the individuals.

Elke Müllegger, Günter Langergraber, and Markus Lechner (2011) have suggested certain estimates regarding sanitation situation at global level. There are 2.6 billion people living without adequate sanitation of which the vast majority in India, China and Africa. Progress in provision of sanitation services is struggling to keep up with population growth and Africa is lagging behind the most. Within 20 years, it is expected that an additional two billion will live in towns and cities demanding sanitation. The challenge is obvious, already today sanitation-related diseases and poor hygienic conditions cause 2.2 million deaths annually (mostly children under the age of five). Other consequences are the massive pollution of water and soil, the loss of innumerable school-(mainly girls) and working days, losses in tourism income, prevention of economic growth, etc. Along with these, there are equally important social and human concerns for the population who are deprived of these basic human living conditions, even now, in democratic and welfare oriented countries. The perpetuating conditions of insanitation, in their civic and social life, are bound to bring more deprivations for them. In Indian context, the concern further extends to the interests of the social categories who remained engaged with the traditional occupation of 'scavenging'. Sanitation is not only confined to the human acts related to cleanliness and hygiene; it also extends to the collective aspirations related to liberty, equity freedom and above all social justice.

According to the India Human Development Report (IHDR) 2011, sanitation coverage, which ought to be a way of life to safeguard health, is inadequate in India. Access to sanitation facilities is a challenge—almost 50 per cent of households have no toilets (NSS 65th round). Whatever toilets are available also do not fulfil the complete sanitation requirements. The Trench Latrines, popular in several parts of rural India are unhygienic and create distraction. It consists of a shallow pit, a wooden or bamboo plank having a hole in the middle and covered from three sides either by a tin or thatchet. The site of the trench latrine has to be changed after every six months when it is full. It could not eliminate fly-breeding and odour. People prefer open defecation than to have trench latrines because of the more visible negative consequences of the trench latrines.

The practice of Open Defecation (OD) in India remains a major challenge for achieving the Millennium Development Goals (MDGs), which include reducing by half the proportion of people without access to basic sanitation by 2015. According to the IHDR, 'within South Asia, India has a larger proportion of the population using improved sources of drinking water than all South Asian countries (except for Pakistan, which is at par). At the same time, India, along with Afghanistan, is the worst performing South Asian country, next only to Nepal, when we look at the percentage of population using improved sanitation facilities. India is on track for achieving the MDG target of sustainable access to improved sources of drinking water, but sanitation is still a challenge for almost half the population of the country' (IHDR, 2011:171).

The latest NSS (69th round) data covering the time period from July, 2012 to December, 2012 and published in 2013 reveals that 59.4 per cent and 8.8 per cent households in rural India and urban India respectively had no latrine facilities. If one considers the corresponding estimates across rural areas of bigger states, it is observed that during 2012, Jharkhand had the highest (90.5 per cent) proportion of households that had no latrine facilities, much higher than the all India proportion (59.4 per cent). Other states among the bigger states where the estimated proportion (among rural households) was higher than the corresponding all India figure include Tamil Nadu (66.4 per cent), Karnataka (70.8 per cent), Bihar (72.8 per cent), Rajasthan (73.0 per cent), Uttar Pradesh (75.3 per cent), Chhattisgarh (76.7 per cent), Madhya Pradesh (79.0 per cent) and Odisha (81.3 per cent). The same pattern is also observed in urban areas of these states.

The report also shows that during 2012, 31.9 per cent and 63.9 per cent households in rural India and urban India respectively had exclusive use of latrine facilities. If one considers the corresponding estimates across rural areas of bigger states, it has been observed that during 2012, Kerala had the highest (92.7 per cent) and Jharkhand, the lowest (7.5 per cent) proportion of households having exclusive use of latrine facilities. In urban areas of most of the bigger states, more than 55 per cent of household had exclusive use of latrine except in Bihar (44.3 per cent), and Odisha (49.6 per cent).

The figures related to availability of latrines do not necessarily talk about availability of 'state-of-the-art' or 'modern' sanitation facilities. In most of the cases, they merely talk about availability of some basic arrangements in the names of sanitation facilities. An important aspect of the sanitation facility is whether the households have access to 'improved source of latrine' — this is an MDG indicator. Here 'improved source' of latrine includes sources such as 'flush/pour-flush to piped sewer system/

septic tank/pit latrine', 'ventilated improved pit latrine', 'pit latrine with slab' and 'compositing toilet'. The data related to 'improved source' shows number per 1000 households having access to 'improved source' of latrine.

The NSS data (69th round) reveals that during 2012, 38.8 per cent and 89.6 per cent households in rural and urban India respectively had access to 'improved source' of latrine. If one considers the corresponding estimates across rural areas of bigger states, it has been observed that during 2012, Kerala had the highest (96.9 per cent) and Jharkhand, the lowest (8.9 per cent) proportion of households having access to 'improved source' of latrine. In urban areas of each of the bigger states, more than 75 per cent of households had access to 'improved source' of latrine and it was highest (98.8 per cent) in Kerala and lowest (74.9 per cent) in Chhattisgarh.

Besides latrines, an important component of sanitation is bath and hence availability of bathrooms is also important sanitation requirement. The NSS (69th round) data has estimated the availability and non-availability of bathrooms in Indian households during 2012. The data shows that 62.3 per cent and 16.7 per cent of households in rural India and urban India respectively did not have any bathroom facility. Among rural areas of bigger states, Jharkhand had the highest (89.4 per cent) and Kerala, the lowest (9.7 per cent) proportion of households without any bathroom. This situation is relatively better in urban areas. Among all bigger states in urban areas, Bihar had the highest (39.0 per cent) and Uttarakhand, the lowest (2.4 per cent) proportion of households without any bathroom.

The situations discussed definitely reflect the inadequacy of sanitation facilities in Indian society. An important component of such inadequacy is the fact that the availability of such facilities not only depends upon economic factors, but also upon socio-cultural, spatial and politico-administrative factors. Inadequate sanitation facilities are reflections of poor human and social developments. Lack of sanitation infrastructure promotes insanitary practices like open defecation. Open defecation is not only socially stigmatised but causes health, safety and security threats. A personal and private space for sanitation-needs is a core requirement for females.

Hence, lack of sanitation facilities is also an indicator of subjugated status of women. A society where women have subjugated status cannot dream a harmonious and humane life conditions. The subjugation prevailed even in the caste system as those castes that were at the bottom of the ritual hierarchy, historically, had a traditional occupation associated with cleaning and disposing the human excreta. Hence, understanding sanitation within social context is an urgent need. The proposed sub-discipline of sociology of sanitation is intended to fill this gap.

Definition of Sanitation

The definition of sanitation given by the World Health Organisation (WHO) states that sanitation refers to the provision of facilities and services for the safe disposal of human urine and faeces. The WHO also adds that sanitation also refers to the maintenance of hygienic conditions, through services such as garbage collection and wastewater disposal.[1] Improved sanitation, according to the WHO/UNICEF Joint Monitoring Programme for Water Supply and Sanitation refers to the management of human faeces at the household level. The WHO definition of sanitation looks at it from health point of view only and keeps sanitation narrowly confined to safe disposal of human urine, faeces or garbage. It is a narrow approach and does not talk about many underlying constructs. It does not define what is meant by 'safe disposal'. It does not talk about the possible 'adverse effects on others' while enjoying the sanitation facilities by many. The service latrines and similar variants, popular in third world countries, have been considered as 'safe disposal' of human urine and faeces by the users although they create unsafe and unhygienic ecologies and maligning, unjust and inhuman conditions for those who are manually engaged in carrying the human excreta.

Elke Müllegger, Günter Langergraber, and Markus Lechner (2011) are of the view that the term 'sanitation' comprise all interventions which aim to protect and promote human health by providing a clean environment and breaking the cycle of disease. It refers to the principles and practices relating to the collection, treatment, removal or disposal of human excreta, household wastewater and refuse as they impact upon people and the environment. This definition also looks at sanitation from a 'disease' and 'physical environment' perspective.

In World Health Organisation and United Nations Children's Fund's Global Water Supply and Sanitation Assessment 2000 Report, sanitation was defined to include connection to a sewer or septic tank system, pour-flush latrine, simple pit or ventilated improved pit latrine, with allowance for acceptable local technologies. The excreta disposal system was considered adequate if it was private or shared (but not public) and if it hygienically separated human excreta from human contact (NSS 69th round, 2013:24).

The Macmillan English Dictionary for Advanced Learners (2009) defines sanitation as: *The conditions and processes relating to people's health, especially the systems that supply water and deal with human waste*. This definition of sanitation looks at it from people's health point of view. It also defines the word 'sanitise' which means 'to make something clean and healthy, especially by killing bacteria'. However, the dictionary gives another meaning of the word 'sanitise' also which explains it as 'to take out from information, writing etc., parts that might be offensive or unpleasant, usually in a way that makes them less interesting and less useful' (2009: 1257). However, the word 'sanitise' has been used in its first sense only in the present context.

The US National Sanitation Foundation defines sanitation in much broader context and looks at it from the 'quality of life' perspective. According to it, 'It is the quality of living expressed in clean homes, clean farms, clean neighbourhoods and clean community. Being a way of life, it must come from people, nourished as it is by knowledge and it grows as obligation and ideal in human relations.'[2]

The Total Sanitation Campaign (TSC), a Government of India sponsored programme started in 1999 to achieve total sanitation in rural India, has adopted a specific and contextual definition of sanitation. According to an evaluation study on Total Sanitation Campaign (TSC), a study conducted in 2013 by Programme Evaluation Organisation, Planning Commission, Government of India, 'The concept of sanitation, which was previously (before the launch of the TSC) limited to the disposal of human excreta by cess pools, open ditches, pit latrines, bucket system, has now (within the TSC) been expanded to include liquid and solid waste disposal, food hygiene, personal, domestic as well as environmental hygiene' (Planning Commission, 2013:12).

Contrary to the above definitions, Dr Bindeshwar Pathak, the founder of Sulabh International Social Service Organisation has given a further broad definition of sanitation. According to him, 'Sanitation includes water supply, safe disposal of human waste, waste water and solid waste management, control of vectors of diseases, domestic and personal hygiene, food, sanitation, housing etc.' Keeping in mind the broader implications of sanitation in personal as well as public life, Dr Pathak also adds, 'The obvious fact is that the future of the country largely depends on sanitation which is the most important thing, next to population control. We have to accept this fact in order to raise production and create a clean and civilised society which India has always been.'[3]

Keeping in mind the merits and limitations of the above definitions of sanitation, a more comprehensive definition of sanitation is given by the present author. By sanitation, I mean adopting the principles, practices, provisions, or services related to cleanliness and hygiene in personal and public life in such ways that one enjoys the beneficial impact on physical, mental, moral and spiritual well-being at personal as well as community levels and ensures that no one else get adversely affected, directly or indirectly, by the negative impacts of human excreta, household wastes, garbage and other pollutants. Sanitation is not just meant for attaining ritualistic purity in individualistic ways; it is meant for the protection and promotion of individual and collective well-being at the personal level and maintaining the harmonious social fabrics in judicious and humane ways at societal level. The judicious treatment requires that sanitation facilities should reach to all sections of human population in an equitable way. The humane consideration requires that it is also related to the principles, practices, techniques and infrastructure relating to prevalence of safe and non-maligning ways of collection, treatment, removal, disposal or recycling of human excreta and other wastes.

Locating Sanitation in Social Life

Although little documented records are available about the sanitation practices and facilities prevailing in private and public spheres during the ancient periods, the classical scriptures suggest that sanitation in personal and public lives of individuals were highly valued. Sanitation, at the individual level, was related to ritualistic or religious requirements of purity. Human faeces and other excreta were considered as impure and physical distance was maintained. In several religions, a purification bath was required after defecation. In the Varna system prevailing in India, various social categories (castes or *jatis*) belonging to the fourth Varna—namely the Shudra (located at the bottom of Varna hierarchy) were considered as impure and were assigned the occupation related to the impure work. There was also a social category identified as 'scavenger' responsible for cleaning the human excreta.

The widely dispersed shifting or agrarian economies and the simple life styles of people during ancient or medieval periods, in several other parts of the world, might not have called for the necessity to look for sanitation requirements beyond the personal domains of the individuals or the families. People used to defecate close to the water sources (river banks) or other open/forested places. The need of specific sanitation spaces emerged with the growing needs of privacy and security. The need for specific sanitation space and infrastructure became a social requirement in the industrialised and urbanised societies.

In contemporary world, sanitation is a massive issue. The 'sanitation phase' of the mid-nineteenth century was an important phase of the 'public health movement' in the industrialised countries. It characterised concentration on issues such as housing, working conditions, the supply of clean water, hygiene and the safe disposal of waste. In most industrialising countries over the last 150 years, public health regulations and health and safety legislation have been enacted to provide safeguards for the industrial workforce, to control pollution levels in rivers, and to ensure proper sewerage and drainage. In nineteenth century England, sanitary reformers and radical politicians argued, on economic grounds, for ill health prevention through public policy interventions. The need for effective public health services in the developed countries was also triggered by military concerns, since army casualties from disease were far higher than from battle.

In India, sanitation is a challenging issue. It has rarely attracted the imagination of the reformers or the rigour of the policy-maker-administrators during the colonial period. Although the socio-religious reform movements, in early twentieth century, addressed the issues related to untouchability, subjugation of women, backwards castes (including those who were at the bottom of the hierarchy), cultural awakening, etc., but sanitation as a societal issue could not attract the imagination of the political and social leadership. Mahatma Gandhi, the father of the nation, took initiative for personal engagement in cleaning of the defecation places; but such initiatives had limited impacts. Even at the public health level, there were hardly enough initiatives which could have translated into a sanitation movement in India. The Constitution of India declared the practice of untouchability as unlawful. But notion of impurity or polluted continued to prevail. Consequently, the sanitation related problems took the shape and size of a demon or a monster in India.

Although the Government of India had initiated few sanitation programmes in last few decades [the Central Rural Sanitation Programme (CRSP) in 1986; the Total Sanitation Campaign (TSC) in 1999; Village Health and Sanitation Committee (VHSC) under National Rural Health Mission (NRHM); Nirmal Gram Puraskar (NGP); Jawaharlal Nehru National Urban Renewal Mission (JNNURM) etc] and some individual level initiatives were taken by the founder of 'Sulabh Sauchalaya', Dr Bindeshwar Pathak since 1970s (Pathak 1991), but the sanitation needs of the country are yet to be addressed comprehensively. A study conducted by World Bank's 'South Asia Water and Sanitation Unit' estimated that India loses Rs 240 billion annually due to lack of proper sanitation facilities. According to it, premature deaths, treatment for the sick and loss of productivity and revenue from tourism are the main factors behind the significant economic loss.[4] Poor sanitation is something that not only affects the economic development of the country, but also affects the social and human development of the nation. In fact, women are most adversely affected by the hazards of lack of proper sanitation. For instance, in India majority of the girls drop out of school due to lack of toilets. Only 22 per cent of them manage to even complete class ten.

On economic grounds, according to the Indian Ministry of Health and Family Welfare, more than Rs 12 billion is spent every year on poor sanitation and its resultant illnesses (see also Akram: 2013, 2014a).[5]

The India Human Development Report (IHDR) 2011 gives specific information about the differential distribution of sanitation facilities in India. The report provides specific information (on the basis of National Sample Survey (NSS) 58th and 65th Rounds) about the social composition of the population which is adversely affected by the inadequate sanitation facilities in India. In India, only 40 per cent of households had access to sanitation facilities in 2002, which increased to 51 per cent in 2008–9. In Bihar, Chhattisgarh, Jharkhand, Madhya Pradesh, Odisha, Rajasthan, Tamil Nadu, and Uttarakhand over 60 per cent of households were without toilets, and thus there was a greater possibility of Open Defecation (OD) in these states. In 2008–9, the North-Eastern states were better off than most of the remaining states in terms of access to sanitation facilities. Making a comparison between rural and urban parts of the nation, the report finds that in both 2002–4 and 2008–9, the proportion of households with toilet facilities was significantly higher in urban areas than rural areas. It should be noted that in rural India as many as 65 per cent of households were without toilets. Thus, it is not surprising that in the rural areas the population has many health problems. Except for Rajasthan, Tripura, Bihar, Jharkhand, and Assam, the rural areas of all the states showed a rise in access to sanitation facilities.

Further, the proportion of households without toilets is much above the national average of 49 per cent for all the three social groups— Scheduled Castes (SCs), Scheduled Tribes (STs), and Other Backward Classes (OBCs). However, OBC households were relatively better placed compared to SCs and STs, with around 54 per cent of OBC households without toilet facilities as against 69 per cent ST households and 65 per cent SC households. Among major religious communities, Hindus were the worst off as 50 per cent of households lacked toilet facilities, compared to 36 per cent for Muslims. The relatively higher access to toilet facilities among Muslims is probably explained by the fact that a higher proportion of Muslims (than Hindus)

Table 1: Per cent distribution and social background of the households without latrine in various states (2008–9)*

States	*Over all*	*Rural*	*Urban*	*STs*	*SCs*	*OBCs*	*Others*	*Hindus*	*Muslims*	*Census 2011*	*Census 2001*
Andhra Pradesh	47.5	64.3	11.2	70.9	60.1	51.4	27.4	50.0	28.4	48.0	67.0
Bihar	74.1	79.8	27.7	69.1	83.9	73.3	41.7	71.0	57.8	75.8	80.8
Chhattisgarh	72.9	82.3	31.5	81.9	73.4	75.2	21.2	73.8	14.4	74.0	85.8
Jharkhand	74.7	84.1	24.5	84.1	71.5	70.6	31.1	60.8	63.9	77.0	80.3
Karnataka	51.5	75.2	11.3	70.0	71.5	55.8	30.9	54.3	35.4	45.0	62.5
Madhya Pradesh	70.2	85.3	24.3	90.2	84.4	69.0	38.3	72.6	39.3	70.0	76.0
Odisha	78.7	88.2	29.1	91.9	87.5	78.4	54.8	78.8	56.0	76.6	85.1
Rajasthan	63.6	82.1	12.6	92.6	75.3	67.3	32.2	65.8	45.7	64.3	71.0
Tamil Nadu	46.6	73.5	16	54.3	72.8	40.8	5.6	49.3	19.7	45.7	64.8
Uttar Pradesh	42.5	53.5	-	73.2	84.1	68.3	42.1	71.4	46.8	63.0	68.6
Uttarakhand	65	79.2	14.2	28.1	67.8	36.1	36.5	44.6	21.4	33.1	54.8
All India	49.2	65.2	11.3	69.1	65.0	54.2	26.2	52.5	35.8	49.8	63.6

*Source: NSS 58th and 65th Rounds.

live in urban areas. Septic tanks and pit latrines have together been classified as improved sanitation by the NSS (2008–9). Going by this definition, access to improved sanitation has increased over time (IHDR 2011: 171).

Thus, sanitation forms a very important place in the social life of India. The need to study the sanitation situation of India sociologically finds its justification with this realisation of location of sanitation problems of the country within the social life of the population. A sociological approach towards sanitation makes us understand that sanitation is not equivalent to having toilets or latrines in the households or public spaces only. Toilets or latrines which are technologically not scientific or hygienic also produce conditions of insanitation. In India, several variants of prevailing latrines produce more insanitation than sanitation. Further, the issues related to 'bath', 'wash', and all other uses of water are equally important. The sanitation issue related to women during their menstrual cycle are also no less important. The use of sanitary napkins and their several ethnic (often very unhygienic) 'equivalents' by women during their menstrual periods are also having sanitation dimensions. The socio-cultural 'taboos' associated with women during their menstrual cycles pose serious health and life threatening challenges. Hence, there is a felt need to study the situations more systematically and scientifically. Consequently, there is an advocacy to have a new sub-discipline in sociology titled as 'Sociology of Sanitation'.

The 'Sociology of Sanitation' conference organised by 'Sulabh International Centre for Action Sociology' and 'Sulabh International Social Service Organisation' and inaugurated by Hon'ble Smt. Meira Kumar, Speaker, Lok Sabha on January 28th and 29th, 2013 at New Delhi is the biggest milestone in the direction of a sociological study of sanitation. The founder of 'Sulabh International Centre for Action Sociology' and 'Sulabh International Social Service Organisation' and social reformer Dr Bindeshwar Pathak stated that a multi-faceted approach is required to deal with the plethora of issues embodying sanitation. He proposed 'Sociology of Sanitation' as a sub-discipline of Sociology and the galaxy of sociologists present on the occasion approved the proposition. According to Pathak, 'Sociology of sanitation is a scientific study to solve the problems of society in relation to sanitation, social deprivation, water, public health, hygiene, ecology, environment, poverty, gender equality, welfare of the children and empowering people for sustainable development and attainment of philosophical and spiritual knowledge to lead a happy life and to make a difference in the lives of others' (Pathak 2013).

Sociology of Sanitation

The crisis related to sanitation in India is related to several visible and invisible factors. Some of these are identified and the governments are trying to address them by taking several institutional initiatives. But many of the underlying factors causing perpetuation of insanitation are existing beyond the comprehensive imaginations of policy-makers or the leadership. A comprehensive academic exercise is the need of the hour to unfold the various interwoven and interconnected dimensions of sanitation in India. The sanitary environment of India is not a replica of the sanitary environment prevailing in western industrialised countries because of differences existing in historical, cultural, political, administrative, technological, geographical and several other factors. The effort of the present author to develop a 'sociology of sanitation' approach to understand the various underlying and embedded issues while studying sanitation in India should be seen in this context. It is an effort to widen the academic imaginations related to issues of sanitation and insanitation and construct and deconstruct the discourses built upon historical, cultural and even on administrative worldviews.

Theoretical Framework for Sociology of Sanitation

Sociology of sanitation, according to present author, needs to trace the state of 'sanitation culture' in human societies through unfolding the dominant 'societal arrangements'. The 'societal arrangements' refers to the interconnectedness and embeddedness of various mechanisms and agencies within societies and their creation of the living situations operating within different domains of human social life. It includes the biotic and abiotic conditions surrounding human life as well as the non-material realities imbibing human life. But the societal arrangements are not necessarily humane and evenly accepted.

There is always a possibility of conflict of interest and misrepresentation of societal aspirations. Hence along with the understanding of 'societal arrangements' there is also the need to understand and identify the 'social contestations' associated with them. The 'social contestations' include such underlying as well as expressed conflict of interests inherent within the prevailing or even dominant discourses related to the societal arrangements and a social mobilisation to combat them.

The interplays between the 'societal arrangements' and the 'inherent contestations', both at the individual and the societal levels shape the macro culture of the society and the specific dimensions related to sanitation or insanitation produce 'sanitation culture' at a larger level. 'Sanitation culture', thus, includes habits, practices, customs, traditions, worldviews, taboos, sanctions, prescriptions, norms, values and all underlying institutional or non-institutional mechanisms and grounded or floating realities which together or separately facilitate or restrict building up of private or public trajectories generally understood as 'moves' from the state of 'insanitation' to the state of 'sanitation' or even the vice-versa. Sanitation culture plays important role in deciding the sanitation act and behaviour of people at large. Sanitation culture is not static. Since the societal arrangements change and the nature and degree of contestations also change—sanitation culture does change.

Attributes of Sanitation

Sociology of sanitation, as a sub-discipline of sociology, needs to understand the state of sanitation culture and the various structural, cultural, institutional or even non-institutional factors and mechanisms associated with it. The theoretical framework, as discussed in earlier paragraphs, cannot be properly explained without some postulates which can explain the causation of insanitation in various societies. Our examinations, based on these postulates, will reflect that the state of sanitation is a state of synergetic combination among various components and dimensions of sanitation. Insanitation, on the other hand, is not simply a complete absence of 'sanitation culture' but a lack of attainment of the desired coordination between the various components or dimensions of sanitation.

Sanitation is a desired state of attainment; the failure in attaining it is insanitation. The failure in attaining sanitation may be a manifestation of failure of one or more components because insanitation is socially contextualised. However, before proposing the postulates, we need to specifically understand the attributes of sanitation.

1. Sanitation is a conscious and deliberate social act in modern industrial societies.
2. It is related with health and well-being of individuals as well as communities.
3. Individual acts of cleanliness can contribute to sanitation but cannot completely define sanitation; sanitation is collectively attainable goal.
4. Sanitation is not ritualistic or symbolic; it is realistic.
5. Sanitation needs social engagement through the processes of socialisation and social control.
6. Sanitation needs technological and environmental/ ecological compatibility.
7. Sanitation has social, cultural, economic, political and other related dimensions.
8. Sanitation is an integral component of all desirable forms of human progress and development.
9. Sanitation is a dynamic equilibrium within and among all biotic, abiotic and non-material components of the macro environment.
10. Sanitation is a value in general but needs defined standards.

Postulates Related to Causation of Insanitation

Human societies have multiple dimensions. Societies often maintain status quo and often change; the state of the society depends upon the cumulative effects of combination of several internal and external factors. However, several specific stimuli create specific effects within human societies. While exploring the state of sanitation culture in any society, we need to identify the factors which work together to construct the state of sanitation deficit or insanitation in that society. Such factors may vary from society to society in their relative importance but do play an important role in production of sanitation culture. In the following section, we will identify the factors causing insanitation and will emphasise upon the need of addressing them for attaining sanitation for all.

Sanitation Deficit

Rationalisation, technological growth, democratisation, secularisation, planned change, development, urbanisation, humanitarianism, harmonisation, social justice etc., are some of those important processes which play very important role in the production of sanitation culture in any society. The outcomes of each of these processes or mechanisms depend upon the existing societal arrangements of the society and the degree or the level of contestation they may face. The outcomes influence several facets of human life including sanitation. Very often, these processes or mechanisms do not create consistent change and cause some kind of disruption or negative developments because of their differential interface with the prevailing cultural or even structural patterns which may contest these changes. When seen from the perspective of a normative or aspired situation, the negative developments or the deficiencies appear to be some kind of deficits contributing to sanitation deficit. The conceptualisations of normative or aspired situations in the present discourse find their conditionings from the requirements related to sanitations needs of the society. Very often, many of these deficits influence human living conditions together. Insanitation, for the present author, is a compounding manifestation of such deficits working together. It is important to mention here that some of these deficits may have a universal applicability. However, when many of these deficits conglomerate (in the context of specific space or community), they invariably create multiple deficit leading to an absolute sanitation deficit or a culture of insanitation.

Technological Deficit

Industrial revolution changed human life very comprehensively in societies where it originated. Industrialisation and urbanisation not only changed production-consumption patterns but also changed the civil, social, cultural, religious, political, and other related dimensions of human life. Technology engrossed human life to the extent that almost all aspects of human life needed state-of-the-art or developed technologies. However, dissipation of technology was not uniform. In the developed countries, technology almost uniformly touched all dimensions of life and modified the material bases of life. But the less developed countries like India which also had a colonial past experienced a selective exposure towards technology. Consequently, adoption of technology was never in totality. For example, railways were adopted as modern means of transport in India but the toilets provided in the trains were not technologically upgraded or modern. Industries were established in several cities but sewerage systems were not developed. This created technology deficit societies. Lots of abnormality and incoherence is caused because of the 'technology deficit' imbedding the civic life of people. This technology deficit is an important causative factor for insanitation.

Public Health Deficit

The technological growth helped in rationalisation of human mind and his need fulfillment mechanisms in most of the industrialised societies. The developments in medical sciences improved human life in a significant way. The morbidity, mortality and fertility patterns changed dramatically after popularisation of modern medical and health sciences. Modern healthcare and especially the public healthcare have almost revolutionary changes not only in biological aspects of human life but also in the socio-cultural aspects. Healthy and hygienic life style became a cultural aspiration. Sanitation, as a requirement of healthy life style, got great impetus from the public health movement popularised in western industrial societies in mid-nineteenth century. The public health infrastructure supported the sanitation movement and further got supported by that. But the third world countries, including India, missed a thrust for the public health movement for several reasons till late twentieth century. The 1978 Alma Ata declaration popularised the goal of 'health for all' in most of the developing countries and made an advocacy for strong primary healthcare. However, the public health facilities could not develop the way it should have for several reasons. Even in India, public health could not capture the imagination of the government the way it has captured the imaginations of governments in western societies. There is a huge shortage of public healthcare institutions in several states of India. The shortfall of trained health staff is further worsening the situation. This public health deficit is prevailing in India and has huge consequences for causation of sanitation deficit.

Equity Deficit

The nature of political governance also changed in most of the societies during last three centuries. The growth of sovereign nation-states, intrusion, penetration and even expulsion of colonialism, the emergence and vanishing of dictatorial regimes, the distribution of power through centralisation and federalisation, the upsurge of political and cultural nationalism, the clashes of communities and civilisations, and the growth of different levels of local bodies for the governance of urban and rural spaces through decentralisations caused differential absorbing of the human and humanitarian values like justice, equality, liberty and freedom within the framework of democratisation creating different types of administered societies.

Within these societies, emerged the trajectories of development as well as deprivations. Several political revolutions, cultural reforms, social movements and even constitutional innovations (like social justice, protective discriminations etc) were operationalised to attain the liberal humane and humanitarian values. Amidst these discourses of justice, equality, freedom, liberty, empowerment, emancipation and many more similar liberating values, several social categories could not find similar treatments. Societies often attained the aspired liberating values but without equity. Democratisation of societies, aiming to achieve equality and equity, simultaneously created equity deficits for several sections of population. The deprivations, besides being a construction of historical, economic, political, geographical and even cultural inappropriation, are manifestations of widely prevailing 'equity deficits' in the governance and administration. The equity deficits (or inequities) often create incoherent and uneven societies. The deprived sections of the societies get lesser share in all the benefits and facilities including the sanitation facilities.

Implementation Deficit

Governance and administration are also closely associated issues related to sanitation situation in contemporary societies in general and India in particular. Ensuring availability of sanitation infrastructure is an important responsibility of the government. In India, the union government has responded to the sanitation needs of people in the past three decades. The 'Rural Development Department', Government of India had initiated India's first national programme on rural sanitation, the 'Central Rural Sanitation Programme' (CRSP) in 1986. The CRSP interpreted sanitation as construction of household toilets, and focused on the promotion of a single technology model (double pit pour-flush toilets) through hardware subsidies to generate demand. The programme could not become very successful for several lapses. The Government of India launched the 'Total Sanitation Campaign' (TSC) in 1999 with the goal of achieving universal rural sanitation coverage by 2012. The responsibility for delivering on programme goals rested with local governments (Panchayati Raj Institutions — PRIs) with significant involvement of communities. The state and central governments had a facilitating role that took the form of framing enabling policies, providing financial and capacity-building support, and monitoring progress.

Further, to give a fillip to the TSC, the government introduced an innovative incentive programme known as Nirmal Gram Puraskar (NGP) in 2003. The NGP offers a cash prise to motivate Gram Panchayats (GPs) to achieve total sanitation. In addition, the NGP is an attractive incentive as winners are felicitated by the President of India at the national level and by high-ranking dignitaries at the state level. The TSC has recently completed a decade of implementation (1999-2009) and the NGP has completed five years of operation (2005-10). Since its launch, the programme framework of the TSC and NGP has been based on a common national guideline whereas implementation has been decentralised to the state and district levels. The government launched National Urban Sanitation Policy in 2008 and identified 100 per cent sanitation as a goal during the 11th Five Year Plan. However, despite such initiatives of the government, the implementation and administration is not very rewarding. The implementation of these programmes is not very successful and we can trace several instances of implementation deficits in them (Akram, 2014b). Thus, together with the equity deficit inherent in contemporary political systems, there is an additional burden of implementation deficit.

Urbanisation Deficit

The divide of the world between the capitalist and socialist models of development (or under development) in the twentieth century furthered different kinds of convergences as well as divergences in the production-consumption patterns at global as well as regional levels actualised through different kinds of planning. Such planning accorded differential roles to the upcoming intervention mechanisms like system of institutional governance and bureaucratisation, patterns of socialisation and social control, opportunities of social mobilisation, expressions of legitimate and legal formulations, articulations and manifestations of collective interests, growth of urban spaces and cities, etc. The divides also got manifested in terms of the natures of the agencies identified to bring the planned changes. The fallacious components of the newly designed instruments of 'planning' and 'social policy' failed to deliver the desired results at both sides of the divides. These planning models continued with some inherent deficits and manifested themselves in causing other deficits. Gradually such deficits got formalised and even structured. The problems related to lack of sewerage systems, absence of waste disposal mechanisms, shortage of toilets in public spaces, disposal of waste water in rivers, lack of houses, growth of slums, etc., are reflections of shortages or omissions in urban, industrial or even metropolitan planning and exhibit such urbanisation deficits.

Planning and Policy Deficit

Further, the sectoral planning became very popular and the development trajectory, instead of remaining comprehensive and integrated, became fragmented and compartmentalised. The federal planning divided the responsibilities of the governments between the 'unions' and the 'federal units' (say, states in India). Sectoral planning focused on different sectors like health, education, employment, industry, transportation, food, water, sanitation, rural development, urban development, power, environment, human resource etc., at different levels 'separately' and the basic structural continuity amidst all these components of contemporary civic life got disturbed and ruptured. Each of these sectors started functioning almost independently under different kinds of political leaderships without necessary coordination and consequently, the necessary links among them got sabotaged. The environmental problems, pollution, population explosion, over urbanisation, uncontrolled and often undirectional migration, urban degradation, and even emergence of slums and other contemporary problems are results of such planning deficits. The unfinished tasks within each of these sectors and the unrecognised interplays between these sectors gradually lead to creation and perpetuation of insanitary environment. The missing of initiative to ensure public health or sanitation needs at grass root levels is an unfortunate consequence of such departmental or sectoral exclusions and hence an outcome of planning and policy deficits.

Development Deficit

A political expression of the 'wish' to borrow the best from both the capitalist and socialist models of development become visible in the growth of synchronisation of the two models in the form of 'welfare governance' in the third world countries—the societies which imbibed the goals of maximisation of development and minimisation of deprivation simultaneously (at least theoretically) in the post-second world war era. The 'designs for development' aiming to attain the 'welfare of the governed' are numerous. In fact every nation-state developed or adopted its own path selecting combination of desired interventions. However, the role played by 'market', 'leadership', 'activists', 'vested interests', 'elites', etc., as 'interest group', 'pressure group' or even 'civil society groups' within the 'welfare paradigms' differed from society to society and the outcomes also varied. Such outcomes varied even more at the level of the masses. The meaning, context and paradigms of development varied. Societies witnessed different forms of development like economic, social, cultural, human, political and even sustainable developments. Amidst the varying notions of development, the discourses adopted are not always coherent or synchronised. Often the cultural patterns contest and even confront the economic or even rational patterns of development. Thus, within the larger parlance of positive changes or development, few dimensions do not change. Several people in rural and even in urban India continue to have households without toilets and practice open defecation although they can very well afford construction of toilets. The lack of toilets in such households is not only caused because of the economic factors; this is also caused because of continuation of a traditional outlook. People have adopted the symbols of development 'selectively'. This is a situation which can be labeled as development deficit (Akram, 2013). The continuation of sanitation as a low priority for economic investment and the consideration of situating toilets inside or close to household as a cultural taboo are the worst consequences of adopting poor development trajectories causing development deficits.

Moral and Ethical Deficit

Moral and ethical values play very important roles in promoting humanism and humanitarianism. The humanitarian values often provide the basis for erection of the edifices of the civic societies. Knowledge, science, information, etc., along with education or general learning propagate mechanisms for ethical standardisation. Civil and societal consciousness both at the personal or public levels do get regulated by these humanitarian values. Corruption, self-centricism and other fissiparous tendencies create situations which can be identified as moral and ethical deficits. Such moral and ethical deficits play negative roles in creating civil societies or productive public spheres. Public spiting, keeping neighbourhood and public spaces unclean, not following civil society or municipal rules, corruption in public life, etc., reflect moral and ethical deficits. Such moral and ethical deficits construct social environments in which even the responsible citizenship roles are compromised and even avoided. Poor sanitation at public spaces is also a consequence of such moral and ethical deficits. The lack of sanitation standards at the societal level and the poor legitimating of sanitation laws to govern the regulation of public or even private sanitation behaviours are also reflections of moral and ethical deficit prevailing at the level of collectivity.

Cultural Deficit

Amidst the diversity of the mechanisms and the plurality of the agencies causing change in attitudes and behaviours of people at large, the 'structured patterns' of the societies and their 'temporal-institutional manifestation' in terms of cultural practices, customs, traditions, norms, values, etc., continue to express their specific constructions at individual, group and societal levels through different processes. The stratification systems caused by class, gender, race, ethnicity, religion, caste or other structured patterns differ in different parts of the world and continue through different cultural formulations. The cumulative and the compounding historical and cultural divides confluence with the discrete, integrated, grounded and upcoming forces and finds their social expressions in diverse ways. The convergence of structural inequalities with the failures in dissemination/attainment of development goals present different patterns of cumulative deprivations often understood as inequality, deprivation, discrimination, exclusion, marginalisation etc. These structural and institutional patterns which keep certain social categories as 'deprived' are cultural constructs as well. The emergence and sustenance of such cultural constructs are reflections of cultural deficits.

Within the larger environment of contestation deficit, those who are most deprived are forced to work at the bottom level even within the hierarchy of occupations. The so-called 'outcastes', within the varna and caste systems prevailing in India, were continued to be forced to work in occupations associated with cleaning the human faeces or dead animals. The secularisation of occupations and the modernisation of minds of the liberated social categories hardly had any impact in changing the attitude or behaviours related to treating the disposal of human faeces at societal level as 'polluting'. The continued physical distancing of certain social categories from their own faeces for maintaining their ritual purity sustained the practice of not having toilets close to their dwelling places. This so-called preference for cultural purity created and sustained the practice of assigning the work of carrying and disposing human faeces to the 'others'. This is the continued manifestation of the 'cultural deficit'.

This created a worldview in which sanitising behaviour itself became a stigma. Consequently, the sanitation engagements at the public sphere and to a great extent even at the private sphere continued to remain the burden of few social categories identified as scavengers. Those who got adversely affected by these societal arrangements could not protest or contest such situations because of the cultural and structural patterns prevailing historically.

Contestation Deficit

The deficits discussed above are relevant universally. Any society, which is facing problems related to sanitation, can apply these 'constructs' to understand the underlying dimensions. As discussed in earlier pages, the sanitation culture prevailing in any society is not immune from the societal arrangements and the social contestations against them. While studying sanitation environment in India, we witness a specific type of deficits which can be articulated as 'contestation deficits'. We know because of our understanding related to the prevalence of varna and caste systems and the practice of untouchability that the society in India was divided among four varnas namely—the Brahmin, the Kashtriya, the Vaishya and the Shudra. The four fold varna system historically gave birth to caste system. However, the four-fold division remained preserved even within the caste system. Within varna (and even within caste) system, the notion of pollution and purity was the benchmark to decide the ritual positioning of the varnas (also castes). The top three varnas were considered as pure; the Brahmins were at the top of the ritual hierarchy followed by the Kashtriyas and the Vaishyas respectively. Many social categories among the Shudra and other outcastes were considered as untouchable and were assigned the occupations of serving the higher varnas and castes. Historically, several caste groups, considered as polluted, were assigned the occupations considered as polluted. Gradually, there is coming into existence of a social category, known as scavengers, who were socially and ritually assigned the role of cleaning and carrying the human excreta. It was an inhuman practice but got social acceptance. The practice continued historically and still prevails in different forms. No revolutionary social protest erupted against such practice till the early

20th century. Social practices, no matter how malign they are, continue to prevail unless contested at massive level. When contested, they create alterations in the societal arrangements and change the overall culture. In the field of sanitation, this is an absolute case of contestation deficit.

Infrastructure Deficit

The deficits discussed above together cause infrastructure deficits. In case of India, the deficits related to infrastructure is also massive. India has a population of almost 1.2 billion people. Fifty five per cent of this population (nearly 600 million) has no access to toilets. Most of these numbers are made up by people who live in urban slums and rural areas. A large populace in the rural areas still defecates in the open. Slum dwellers in major metropolitan cities, reside along railway tracks and have no access to toilets or a running supply of water.[6] According to Harshal T. Pandve (2008), most cities and towns in India are characterised by over-crowding, congestion, inadequate water supply and inadequate facilities of disposal of human excreta, wastewater and solid wastes. No major city in India is known to have a continuous water supply and an estimated 72 per cent of Indians still lack access to improved sanitation facilities. Besides this, the 63 per cent of urban population in India is without proper sanitation. Further, the waste disposal and sewage treatment plants are missing in most of the cities. Most of the wastes are disposed in rivers, canals or outskirts of the cities (Kumar, Kar, and Jain, 2011). Thus, caused by other deficits, the infrastructure deficit makes the situation worst.

In India, the situations related to sanitation and the larger prevalence of the insanitation is a compounding manifestation of 'multiple' deficits. The technology deficits, equity deficits, policy and planning deficits and development deficits cumulatively constructed social spaces in which the societal arrangements remained unchallenged. These are the excluded and the marginalised spaces in different contexts. Technologies could not reach there because of the policy deficits, policies could not address them because of the design deficits, the designs could not accommodate them because of the equity deficits. The trajectory is never the same in all such cases of exclusion and marginalisation. There is a vicious circle; any of these deficits can cause any other and continue to prevail together. The 'contestation deficits' could not create an environment in which the 'cultural deficits' could have been challenged and the cultural practices of exclusion and exploitation continued. The infrastructure deficit is the cumulative manifestation of the existence of multiple deficits.

The silver lining is the fact the issues related to sanitation is now attracting the imaginations of the activists, social reformers and intellectuals. For the present author, 'sociology of sanitation' is an effort to construct and deconstruct the discourses and the texts, the ideologies and the fantasies, the realities and the myths and the structured and the structuring patterns surrounding the world of sanitation. The imaginations may appear narrow in some contexts and may go beyond the disciplinary boundaries of an emerging sub-discipline in other contexts; but the purpose is humble to understand the different patterns of human behaviours centred around the practices and processes widely termed as 'sanitation' and 'insanitation'.

Dimensions of Sanitation

The sanitation phase was an important component of the 'public health movements' which took place in the mid-nineteenth century in the industrialised countries to control spread of communicable diseases, epidemics, premature mortalities and improvement in quality of life in general. The sanitation movement in western and industrialised countries originated with public health concerns at a larger level and characterised concentration on issues such as housing, working conditions, the supply of clean water, hygiene and the safe disposal of waste. The motivating force for these public health movements was definitely improvement in health conditions of people but there was also a concern with economic efficiency and better social cohesion between the working class and other sectors of society. Sanitation movements were supported by improvement in technology, public health, planned development, democratic governance and urban planning. Increasing population concentration in industrial and urbanised societies necessitated the desired sanitation reforms in those societies. The developments related to sewage treatment, waste water management, safe disposal of industrial pollutants, recycling and environmental sanitation supported the sanitation movement in industrial societies.

However, the third world countries in general and India in particular have additional dimensions of the sanitation situation. Sanitation issues in these countries have additional dimensions related to the traditional division of labour, religious sanctions and power relations among castes and communities. Within the four-fold Varna division of the society, the Shudra were considered as the untouchables for their association with polluted work and the caste divisions largely maintained the Varna prescriptions in traditional Indian society. Hence, sanitation practices on the one hand created cleanliness for the upper Varna castes and on the other hand created inhuman conditions for those who were engaged in sanitising occupations. The birth-based division of occupations created the situations worst as those who were labelled as untouchables were not allowed to come out of this inhuman circuit. The sanitation issue in India needs to take into consideration the deeper structural and cultural dimensions of the society also.

Thus, sanitation, as we defined it earlier in this chapter, has several components and dimensions engrossed in it. For a broader understanding of the issues involved, we need to understand the multiple dimensions of sanitation. It is related to the structural and cultural patterns of the societies and cannot be considered as a static notion. Because of its association with technology, the notion of sanitation may change very fast in some of the societies. Contrary to it, it may also remain static in some other societies because of its cultural roots. Hence, meaning of sanitation will keep changing or evolving depending on the contexts.

Sociology of sanitation looks at the sanitation situation from the perspectives of various underlying factors involved in it. To begin with, sanitation issue has a health and well-being dimension. Sanitation is indispensible because of its health and well-being impacts. The absence of public health concern has created poor concern for sanitation. Further, sanitation has a technological dimension because the operationalisation of all sanitation requirements is completed through technologies. Because of the specific infrastructure needs, sanitation is also associated with economic conditions of a society.

The economic hiatus prevailing within a society may reflect differentially within the sanitation practices. There is a political dimension of the situation as contemporary societies are administered societies and political governance is very important in deciding the nature of the society. Besides, sanitation is situated in people's attitudes, behaviour, culture, customs, practices and over all structural patterns. Hence sanitation has a social dimension. Further, sanitation behaviour is also governed by cultural prescriptions and inhibitions, taboos and stigmas, preferences and denials etc. Thus, the cultural dimension of sanitation is also very important. Behaviour of individual is also governed by his moral and ethical considerations. The compliances of civil rules largely depend upon the moral and ethical standards of the societies. Hence, sanitation has an ethical and moral dimension also. Thus, by applying the sociology of sanitation approach we can understand the sanitation situation at a larger level. We will discuss various dimensions of sanitation in succeeding chapters.

Notes

1. http://www.who.int/topics/sanitation/en/(accessed on January 16, 2013)
2. quoted in Sulabh International's website, see http://www.sulabhinternational.org/content/sanitation (accessed on March 9, 2013)
3. Sulabh International's website, http://www.sulabhinternational.org/content/sanitation (accessed on March 9, 2013)
4. http://articles.timesofindia.indiatimes.com/2010-12-21/india/28213388_1_indian-economy-world-bank-poor-sanitation (accessed on January 16, 2013)
5. http://theviewspaper.net/public-sanitation-a-hazard-not-so-trivial/(accessed on January 17, 2013)
6. http://www.youthkiawaaz.com/2011/02/sanitation-in-india/ (accessed on January 17, 2013)

References

Akram, M. (2013). 'Sanitation, Health and Development Deficit in India: A 'Sociology of Sanitation' Perspective' , Paper presented *at National Conference on Sociology of Sanitation-Environmental Sanitation, Public Health and Social Deprivation*, Organised by Sulabh

International Centre for Action Sociology at Mavalankar Hall, New Delhi, (January 28-29, 2013).

Akram, M. (2014a). *Sociology of Health*, Jaipur/New Delhi: Rawat Publications.

Akram, M. (2014b). 'Sanitation Needs of India and NRHM: A Strategic Assessment' in *NRHM: An Unfinished Agenda,* edited by Sharma, S. and Joe, W., New Delhi: Bookwell Publications.

Giddens, A. (with Philip W. Sutton). (2009). *Sociology: 6th edition*, New Delhi: Polity and Wiley India Pvt. Ltd.

IHDR. (2011). *India Human Development Report 2011*, Institute of Applied Manpower Research, Planning Commission, Government of India, New Delhi, Oxford University Press.

Kumar, G.S., Kar, S.S. and Jain, A. (2011). 'Health and environmental sanitation in India: Issues for prioritising control strategies', *Indian J Occup Environ Med.* Sep-Dec; 15(3): 93–96.

Macmillan English Dictionary for Advanced Learners (2009). International student Edition, Macmillan Publishers India Limited.

Mills, C. W. (1970). *The Sociological Imagination*, Harmondsworth: Penguin.

Müllegger, E., Langergraber, G. and Lechner, M. (2011). 'Sustainable Sanitation Practice, Planning Tools: Sustainable Sanitation Practice', EcoSanClub, Issue 7, 04/2011.

NSS 58th round. Ministry of Statistics and Programme Implementation, Government of India.

NSS 65th round. Ministry of Statistics and Programme Implementation, Government of India.

NSS 69th Round (2013). July 2012-December 2012, Ministry of Statistics and Programme Implementation, Government of India.

Pandve, H.T. (2008). 'Environmental Sanitation: An Ignored Issue in India', *Indian Journal of Occupational and Environmental Medicine*, 12(1): 40.

Pathak, B. (1991). *Road to Freedom: A Sociological Study on the Abolition of Scavenging in India,* Delhi: Xtreme Office Aids Private Limited.

Pathak, B. (2013). *Inaugural speech delivered at National Conference on Sociology of Sanitation-Environmental Sanitation, Public Health and Social Deprivation*, Organised by Sulabh International Centre for Action Sociology at Mavalankar Hall, New Delhi, (January 28-29, 2013).

Planning Commission. (2013). *Evaluation Study on Total Sanitation Campaign (TSC)*, Programme Evaluation Organisation, Planning Commission, Government of India.

2

Sanitation, Health and Environment

Lack of sanitation or insanitation is responsible for causation and spread of several diseases and illness conditions. Disease caused by germs and worms in faeces, wastes and pollutants are constant source of discomfort for millions of people and animals. These diseases can cause many years of sickness and can lead to other health problems such as dehydration, anaemia, malnutrition and even mortality. Severe sanitation-related illnesses like cholera can spread rapidly, bringing sudden death to many people. Children have a high risk of illness from poor sanitation. While adults may live with diarrheal diseases and worms, children die from these illnesses.

Diseases, including cholera, can be largely prevented if contamination of waterways, groundwater and drinking water supplies are prevented through effective sanitation and water treatment measures. There have been five main cholera outbreaks and pandemics since 1825. In London alone, the second cholera outbreaks killed 14,137 people in 1849, and the third cholera outbreaks took 10,738 lives in 1853-54.[1] In 1849, the English physician John Snow published a paper *On the Mode of Communication of Cholera*, in which he suggested that cholera might be waterborne. During the 1854 epidemic, he collected and analysed data establishing that people who drank water from contaminated sources such as the Broad Street pump died of cholera at much higher rates than those who got water elsewhere. According to *The Global Water Supply and Sanitation Assessment 2000* by the World Health Organisation, 40 per cent of the global population does not have access to "good" "excreta disposal facilities"—they live mostly in Asia and Africa.[2] There are efforts being made to design simple effective squat toilets for these people.

Sanitation is an important social determinant of health. Social determinants are the social circumstances in which people live, from their birth to death. Life style, food, water, housing, sanitation, social harmony, justice, social integration etc., are important social determinants of health, morbidity and premature mortalities. These social determinants are strongly influenced by the economic and cultural conditions of the population. Sanitation, as an important social condition of life is embedded with the class, occupation, religion, caste, ethnicity and spatial conditions of life. Consequently, people associated with lower economic or occupational statuses are witnessing more negative consequences of poor sanitation. The health impacts of insanitation are more adverse on people coming from poor socio-economic background. Thus, the negative impacts of insanitation are harsher for the people living in slums or villages than those living in posh colonies.

For understanding the relationship between sanitation, diseases and health, we need to understand the notions of health, disease and healthcare at a deeper level. The notions of 'health', 'disease', 'illness' or 'healthcare' are popularly defined from the 'bio-medical perspectives'. The bio-medical perspectives on health or healthcare generally remain silent on social determinants of health. Hence, even at the professional or academic levels, there is little realisation about the social determination of health or diseases conditions. For having a deeper understanding about causation of health, disease or premature mortalities and for exploring the interplay among them, a sociological understanding of these notions is very important. At the same time, the macro environmental conditions also play very important role in causation of disease. In this chapter, we will examine all these concepts sociologically and will see their relationship with sanitation.

Disease

Disease is a departure from the state of health. Disease is a state of not being well or being unwell. The notion of disease is cultural. The understandings related to wellness and unwellness are both objective and subjective depending upon the larger understanding of biological, physiological, psychological, social, medico-technological and cultural factors. Oxford English dictionary defines *disease* as 'a condition of the body or some part or organ of the body in which its functions are disrupted or deranged'. Webster's dictionary defines *disease* as 'a condition in which body health is impaired, a departure from the normal state of health, an alteration of the human body interrupting the performance of vital functions'. The World Health Organisation (WHO) has defined health, but not disease. Disease is also multidimensional and may refer to different states of being but the complete well-being. Disease may refer to a state of malfunctioning, over-functioning, under-functioning or non-functioning of one or more organs or mechanisms of the body or in the perceived understanding of the functioning of the body with a larger cognizance that the alteration may take place instantly, intermittently, continuously or even simultaneously. From a sociological point of view, disease is considered as a social phenomenon, occurring in all societies and defined and fought in terms of the particular forces prevalent in the society.

According to Cockerham and Ritchey (1997: 34), 'disease is considered an adverse physical state consisting of a physiological dysfunction within an individual, as compared to an illness (psychological awareness of a disease) or a sickness (a social state)'. For the bio-medical approach, disease is a state of bio-physical dysfunction or infirmity within an individual. It is a phenomenon characterised by altered functioning of a body as a biological organism. Biomedical model of disease regards it as the consequence of certain malfunctions of the human body.

Diagnosis of a disease is made by correlating the observable signs or symptoms of a disease with knowledge about the functioning of the human organism (Coe, 1970). Thus, understanding of disease depends upon observations of altered, abnormal states of the human organism. These signs may be objectively observed and even measurable, such as elevated body temperature or skin rash or they may be subjective symptoms, such as pain in the back etc. many of the signs are not directly observable and it has been one of the basic sources of the success of modern medicine to have found methods for taking "readings" of bodily function which allow a skilled observer to pick up signs which he would ordinarily not be able to sense.

Agents of Disease

According to Park (2009), disease 'agent' is defined as a substance, living or non-living, or a force, tangible or intangible, the excessive presence or relative lack of which may initiate or perpetuate a disease process. A disease may have a single agent, a number of independent alternative agents or a complex of two or more factors whose combined presence is essential for the development of disease. Disease agents may be classified broadly into following groups:

Biological agents: These are living agents of disease, viz, viruses, fungi, bacteria, protozoa and metazoa. These agents exhibit certain "host-related" biological properties such as: (i) **infective:** this is the ability of an infectious agent to invade and multiply in a host; (ii) **pathogenicity:** this is the ability to induce clinically apparent illness, and (iii) **virulence:** this is defined as the proportion of clinical cases resulting in severe clinical manifestations. The case fatality rate is one way of measuring virulence.

Nutrient agents: These can be fats, proteins, carbohydrates, vitamins, minerals and water. Any excess of deficiency of the intake of nutrient elements may result in nutritional disorders. Protein energy malnutrition (PEM), anaemia, goitre, obesity and vitamin deficiencies are some of the current nutritional problems in many countries.

Physical agents: Exposure to excessive heat, cold, humidity, pressure, radiation, electricity, sound etc., may result in illness.

Chemical agents: (i) **Endogenous:** some of the chemicals may be produced in the body as a result of derangement of function, e.g., urea (uraemia), serum bilirubin (jaundice), ketones (ketosis), uric acid (gout), calcium carbonate (kidney stones), etc: (ii) **Exogenous:** Agents arising outside human host, e.g., allergens, metals, fumes, dust, gases, insecticides etc. These may be acquired by inhalation, ingestion or inoculation.

Mechanical agents: Exposure to chronic friction and other mechanical forces may result in crushing, tearing, sprains, dislocations and even death.

Social agents: It is also necessary to consider the social agents of disease. These are poverty, smoking, abuse of drugs and alcohol, unhealthy lifestyles, social isolation and maternal deprivation and environment of insanitation etc.

Social Causes of Disease and Death

An important realisation about causation of diseases in the second half of the twentieth century is related to social causation of disease as the movement, spread, appearance and control of the 'agent' causing disease depends upon the social factors. According to Gabe, Bury and Elston, 'Within medicine, the turn towards the social causes of disease rather than medical intervention was based on work such as Thomas McKeown's (1979) analysis of the nineteenth-century decline in mortality in England and Wales. He argued that medical interventions such as drug therapies and vaccinations had made, historically, little contribution to the decline in mortality from infectious disease. Rather, increasing life expectancy was the result of improving social conditions, smaller family sizes, better nutrition and a healthier environment' (Gabe, Bury and Elston, 2004: 234). However, people get sick and die also due to natural causes. One person may have a genetic predisposition to cancer. Another may come in contact with the deadly Ebola virus in the environment. However, over and above such natural causes of illness and death, we can single out some of the social causes also (Brym and Lie, 2007).

Lifestyle factor: Cigarette smoking, excessive use of alcohol and drugs, poor diet, lack of exercise, and social isolation are associated with poor health and premature death. Official statistics seemed that the best available estimates for the United States suggest that the three leading background causes of death in 2000 were tobacco use; poor diet and physical inactivity and alcohol consumption. One-third of the people who smoke are likely to die prematurely from smoking-related illnesses. This amounts to about 435,000 Americans *annually*. About 30 per cent of all cancer deaths in the United States result from tobacco use, and smoking is also a leading cause of heart disease. Many experts believe that poor diet and physical inactivity will soon overtake tobacco as the leading background cause of death. Today, poor diet and physical inactivity are responsible for about 400,000 American deaths every year. They are leading causes of heart disease and are implicated in about 35 per cent of all cancer deaths. Poor diet and physical inactivity is especially big problems in poor neighbourhoods.

Social situation: Social isolation too affects one's chance of becoming ill and dying prematurely. Social class, caste, ethnicity etc., define an individual's social situation. Many a time, social situation may lead to isolation and marginalisation. Social isolation is a particularly big problem among elderly people who retire, lose a spouse and friends, and cannot rely on family members or state institutions for social support. Such people are prone to fall into a state of depression that contributes to ill health.

Public health system: The public health system is composed of government run programmes that ensure access to clean drinking water, basic sewage and sanitation services, and inoculation against infectious diseases. The absence of a public health system is associated with high rates of illness, disease and low life expectancy. The health-care system is a component of the public health system. It is composed of a nation's clinics, hospitals and other facilities for ensuring health and treating illness. The absence of a system that ensures access by citizens to a minimum standard of healthcare is also associated with high rates of disease and low life expectancy. Exposure to all three sets of social causes of illness and death is strongly related to country of residence, class, race and gender.

Basic Health Goods (BHGs): Nutrition, food, safe drinking water and sanitation are the basic needs of every human being and the present author categorise them as Basic Health Goods (BHGs). The BHGs have huge bearing on the health condition of the individual and community. Lack of availability, accessibility and affordability of the BHGs is an important cause of prevalence of disease among various social categories in different parts of the world, including India. A crisis caused by lack of BHGs gradually gets translated into malfunctioning of the human body in several possible forms. There are evidences that such malfunctioning, over a period of time, take the form of disease. Sometimes, such effects become chronic or even get genetically transmitted. Lack of availability of food, nutrition, potable water or sanitation is important cause of disease and premature death. However, the social environment (along with the political and economic system) is more responsible for such causation of disease or death than the individual or the community. Government's inability to provide BHGs to its people is '*dehealthism*'; a term coined and defined by the present author (see Akram, 2012; 2014).

According to the India Human Development Report (IHDR) 2011, 'access to safe drinking water and sanitation reduces the incidences of waterborne diseases like diarrhoea that are a major cause of death of millions of children and adults each year' (IHDR, 2011: 170). Sanitation, hygiene, availability of water and other quality of life factors play very important role in control of diseases and especially the communicable diseases. The impact of medical care and medicine also depends upon the availability of these social determinants.

Classification of Diseases

Diseases and health problems can be classified in several meaningful ways. The public often classifies diseases by organ or organ system, such as kidney disease, heart disease, respiratory infection, and so on. Another method of classification is by causative agent—viral disease, chemical poisoning, physical injury, and so forth. But in community health diseases are usually classified as acute or chronic, or as communicable (infectious) and non-communicable (non-infectious) diseases.

Communicable (infectious) diseases: Communicable (infectious) diseases are those diseases for which biological agents or their products are the cause and that are transmissible from one individual to another. The disease process begins when the agent is able to lodge and grow within the body of the host. The process of lodgement and growth of a microorganism or viruses in the host is called infection. Communicable diseases remain an important concern for communities. Of the 9.2 million cases of TB that occur in the world every year, nearly 1.9 million are in India accounting for one-fifth of the global TB cases. Experts estimate that about 2.5 million persons have HIV infection in India, world's third highest. More than 1.5 million persons are infected with Malaria every year. Diseases like dengue and chikungunya have emerged in different parts of India and a population of over 300 million is at risk of getting acute encephalitis syndrome/Japanese encephalitis. One-third of global cases infected with filaria live in India. Nearly half of leprosy cases detected in the world in 2008 were contributed by India. More than 300 million episodes of acute diarrhoea occur every year in India in children below five years of age (MOHFW, 2010: 14).

Non-communicable (non-infectious) diseases: Non-communicable (non-infectious) conditions and diseases are second only to communicable diseases in terms of their contribution to the disease burden in India. These conditions include cardiovascular diseases, cancers, diabetes, respiratory diseases and mental health diseases. In fact, non-communicable (non-infectious) diseases are those that cannot be transmitted from an infected person to another, healthy one (for details see, Akram, 2014).

Illness

Illness, different from disease, is a subjective phenomenon, pertaining to an individual's awareness of having a disease, symptoms and pain and having an altered state of his/her perceptions of himself/herself. Illness is transformed into sickness when the condition of the ill person becomes socially known through announcement by the affected person, observations by significant others or professional diagnosis. Unlike illness, the amount of sickness varies widely from society to society and reflects the perceptions and responses of society at that point of time.

Kleinman (1988) suggests that disease is a biophysical event and the prime concern of medical practitioners, whereas illness 'refers to how the sick person and members of the family or wider social network perceive, live with and respond to symptoms and disability' (1988: 3). Dingwall argues that there is no such thing as 'essential illness', rather, illness is construed through the meanings and interpretations that are accorded to certain categories of experience and 'there is no necessary relationship to any biological happening' (1976: 26). For Giddens (2006), illness has both personal and public dimensions. When we become ill, not only do we experience pain, discomfort, confusion and other challenges, but others are affected as well. Hence, Sarah Nettleton concludes, 'rather than simply observing illness behaviour, sociologists must endeavour to understand illness action. The former refers to the way people behave given the presence of symptoms, whilst the latter focuses on how people make sense of and interpret their illness experience and, crucially, what it means to them' (1995: 78).

Medical sociologists have identified four dimensions of the illness that influenced the decision to seek medical help: (1) the frequency with which the illness occurs in a given population; (2) the familiarity of the symptoms; (3) the predictability of the outcome of the illness; and (4) the amount of threat and loss that is likely to result from the illness. Mechanic (1978) has identified few other factors also relating to illness that influence help-seeking behaviour. These include the visibility of the symptoms, the perceived present and future seriousness of the symptoms, the extent to which symptoms disrupt social activities, the frequency of symptoms and interpretations of the cause of symptoms and availability of treatment. In addition, Mechanic recognised that the impact that illness had on those caring for the patient was an important determinant of illness behaviour.

Biomedical Model of Disease and Health

The biomedical model of disease finds its origin in the post-industrial era of growth of scientific knowledge and regards disease as the consequence of certain malfunctions of the human body. The biomedical model of disease is based on certain assumptions like: disease is an organic condition; disease is caused by some 'agent' which is defined as a substance, living or non-living, or a force, tangible or intangible, the excessive presence or relative lack of which may initiate or perpetuate a disease process; disease is a temporary organic state that can be eradicated—cured—by medical intervention; disease is experienced by a sick individual, who then becomes the object of treatment; disease is treated after the symptoms appear—the application of medicine is a reactive healing process; medical specialists possess 'expert knowledge' and prescribe the only valid treatment of disease; and, disease is treated in a medical environment—a surgery or a hospital—away from the site where the symptoms first appeared.

Sociological Understanding of Disease and Health

Health and well-being has always been a basic human need. Societies have always created some mechanisms and discourses for responding to the physical, mental or social conditioning of its members. The concepts of health, disease and treatment are related to the social structures of communities. Every culture, irrespective of its simplicity or complexity, has its own system of beliefs and practices concerning health and disease and evolves its own system of treatment to combat disease (Akram, 2007). Definitions and conceptualisation of health may vary systemically among various social groups and it is likely that different accounts of health are drawn according to social circumstances. The biomedical approach which dominated the medical thought till the end of nineteenth century and based on the 'germ theory of disease' views health as an 'absence of diseases'. This approach almost ignores the role of environmental, psychological and other socio-cultural factors in defining health. The ecological approach views health as a dynamic equilibrium between man and his environment. For them, disease is maladjustment of the human organism to environment. The psychological approach states that health is not only related to the body but also to the mind and especially to the attitude of the individual. The socio-cultural approach considers health as a product of the social and community structure (Advani and Akram, 2007).

Sociologists show how diseases could be differently understood, treated and experienced by demonstrating how disease is produced out of social organisation and not merely by the nature, biology, or individual lifestyle choices (White, 2002). A functional definition of health treats health as the ability of a person to participate in normal social roles.

Parsons believed that illness is dysfunctional for both individuals and the larger society (Kendall, 2011). According to functionalist perspective, the sick role exempts the patient from routine activities for a period of time and assumes that the individual will seek appropriate medical attention and get well as soon as possible. Physicians are empowered to determine who may enter the sick role and when patients are ready to exit it and for this they are certified by the society to be 'gatekeepers' of the sick role. Parsonian sociology emphasises the role of medicine in maintaining social harmony.

Marxist approach emphasises the causal role of economics in the production, distribution and treatment of disease. Medicine in a capitalist society reflects the characteristics of capitalism. Medicine is profit-oriented and reproduces the class structure within the medical profession itself. It emphasises on the social, economic, and political forces that affect health, disease and the healthcare delivery system of people in the society. Marxist theorists are interested in issues related to unequal accessibility of healthcare facilities; power relationships between doctors and other healthcare workers; the dominance of the medical model of healthcare; and the role of profit in the healthcare system (Kendall, 2011).

Symbolic interaction perspective focuses on how health, healthcare, and illness of individuals are influenced by meanings, definitions, and labels and how such meanings are learned through interaction with others and through media messages and portrays (Knox, 2008). According to McNeill (1990), symbolic interactionists believe that individuals actively construct understandings of themselves using the evidence that comes from their interactions with others. Some of these interactions may lead them to understand themselves as healthy. In contrast to biomedical and social positivist researchers, interactionists tend to focus on the more subjective aspects of health. Foucault, too, highlights the social role of medical knowledge in controlling populations, and like Parsons emphasises the diffused nature of power relationships in modern society. Also, like Parsons, he sees the professions, especially the helping professions, playing a key role in inducing individuals to comply with 'normal' social roles. For Foucault, modern societies are systems of organised surveillance with the catch being that individuals conduct the surveillance on themselves, having internalised 'professional' models of what is appropriate behaviour (White, 2002).

Health

The Universal Declaration of Human Rights stated in Article 25: 'Everyone has the right to a standard of living adequate for the health and well-being of himself and his family....'(United Nations, 1948). The Preamble to the World Health Organisation (WHO) constitution affirms that it is one of the fundamental rights of every human being to enjoy the highest attainable standards of health. Article 21 of the Constitution of India also identifies health as an integral aspect of human life (Desai, 2007). Health is human being's natural condition; health is his/her birth right. It is the result of living in accordance with natural laws pertaining to the body, mind, and environment. These laws relate to fresh air, sunlight, diet, exercise, rest and relaxation, sleep, cleanliness, right attitude of mind, good habits, and above all lifestyle. Improving health status of the citizens is one of the most important goals of all the modern welfare governments. The Alma Ata Declaration made in 1978 has set the target of achieving the goal of "health for all" by 2000. The target could not be achieved within the stipulated time period and the world had the Millennium Development Goals by the turn of the century.

According to Sen (2006), health contributes to a person's basic capability to function. Capability refers to the freedom of persons or groups to promote or achieve things which they consider valuable and it was used by Sen to attend to the foundational importance of freedom (Alkire, 2003). Hence, health is the most basic requirement for every individual. Denial of health is not only denial of 'good life-chance', it is also denial of fairness and justice. Sen regards functionings as, doings and beings which create a better conceptual space to examine social welfare than utility or opulence. Sen has helped to make the capabilities approach a paradigm for policy debate in human development where it inspired the creation of the UN's Human Development Index.

Health is man's natural condition; health is his birth right. It is the result of living in accordance with natural laws pertaining to the body, mind and environment. These laws relate to fresh air, sunlight, diet, exercise, rest and relaxation, sleep, cleanliness, right attitude of mind, good habits and above all lifestyle. The WHO definition of health states that health is a state of complete physical, mental and social well-being, and not merely an absence of disease or infirmity. Health is multidimensional; three important dimensions of health are reflected in the WHO definition which are: physical, mental and social. (Park, 2009)

Physical Dimension: The state of physical health implies the notion of "perfect functioning" of the body. It conceptualises as a state in which every organ is in perfect harmony with the rest of body. The signs of physical health in an individual are—a good complexion, a clean skin, bright eyes, lustrous hair with a body well clothed with firm flesh, not too fat, a sweet breath, a good appetite, sound sleep, easy and coordinated movements.

Mental Dimension: Good mental health is the ability to respond to the many varied experiences of life with flexibility and a sense of purpose. The signs of a mentally healthy person are that he is free from internal conflicts, he is well-adjusted and has a good self control. Further, he is not overcome by emotions; he is not dominated by fear, anger, jealousy, guilt or worries, he faces problems and solves them intelligently.

Social Dimension: The social dimension of health includes the levels of social skills one possesses, social functioning and the ability to see oneself as a member of a large society. In general social health takes into account that every individual is a part of a family and of wider community and focuses on social and economic conditions and well-being of the 'whole person' in the context of his social network.

Holistic Approach to Health

The basic concept of holistic health is that a human being should be an integrated whole. Health professionals keep refining their definition of health to describe a state of total well-being. The constant interaction between all elements of the body makes it impossible to separate mental health from physical health, social well-being from spiritual well-being, or any one of these elements from the others. Each contributes to the status of the others. According to this total concept, better known as holistic concept as promoted by WHO, a healthy person is one who successfully experiences growth and development in all of these elements more or less at the same time.

Medicine, Medical Care and Health Care

Medicine primarily refers to the scientific interventions made to regain the state of well-being or health from a state of illness and sickness. Curative treatment (medicinal as well as surgical) is seldom offered without the individual's or the society's cognizance of the occurrence of disease through the illness or sickness roles. Globally, different systems of medicines have existed for prescribing such interventions. The modern bio-medical system of medicine (allopathy) has made significant impact on combating the causation and spread of diseases and correcting the complications. Besides this, there are other systems (ayurvedic, homeopathy, unani, yoga, siddha etc) grounded in different principles, developed at different periods of time in different parts of world generally known as traditional medicines.

Medicinal care largely depends on clinical care. This clinical care may be curative or preventive. The impact of the curative care varies from culture to culture even in case of application of same medicines because of the differential availability of the Basic Health Goods (BHGs) (like food, water, nutrition and sanitation) and Social Determinants (like occupation, employment, education, housing conditions, social harmony, justice, social integration, peace etc). The modern allopathic medicine is very successful in industrialised countries not only because of the medicinal value but also because of the positive role of BHGs and social determinants. In the developing countries, the poor availability and accessibility of BHGs and social determinants are the biggest challenges in combating diseases and ensuring medical and healthcare. The developed world has almost controlled the conventional communicable diseases (such as cholera, diarrhea etc) which transmit from an agent to a human. This is made possible because of the availability of potable water, hygiene, and sanitation which together combat the spread of most of communicable diseases. On the other hand, in a country like India, in the absence of the nutrition, proper diet, safe drinking water, sanitation, education etc, communicable diseases are still the largest killer. More specifically, the communicable diseases are directly related with the water and sanitation conditions.

Thus, medical care and healthcare are not synonymous. The medical care is primarily clinical care (as prescribed by different systems of medicines) where as the healthcare is much broader and includes all the associated quality of life factors like food, nutrition, potable drinking water, hygiene, and sanitation (termed as BHGs) and also the favourable social determinants like education, awareness, income level, inclusive society etc., along with the medical care. However, the dominance of the bio-medical system of medicine often creates discourses which build up impressions in which 'medical care' and 'healthcare' are used interchangeably. Official policies, literature, discourses, directives and even common sense understanding, in India, often get trapped in a 'design' which promotes using the two phrases synonymously (for details on this section, see Akram, 2013).

Public Health

The Expert Committee of WHO has defined public health as the "science and art of preventing diseases, prolonging life and promoting mental and physical health and efficiency through organised community efforts for the sanitation of the environment, the control of communicable infection, the education of the individual's personal hygiene, the organisation of medical and nursing services for early diagnosis and preventive treatment of disease, the development of the social machinery to ensure to every individual a standard of living, adequate for the maintenance of health and so organising these benefits as to enable every citizen to realise his birth right of health and longevity" (WHO, 1952).

The Expert Committee of WHO has defined public health as the "science and art of preventing diseases, prolonging life and promoting mental and physical health and efficiency through organised community efforts for the sanitation of the environment, the control of communicable infection, the education of the individual's personal hygiene, the organisation of medical and nursing services for early diagnosis and preventive treatment of disease, the development of the social machinery to ensure to every individual a standard of living, adequate for the maintenance of health and so organising these benefits as to enable every citizen to realise his birth right of health and longevity" (WHO, 1952).

There is a vast discrepancy in access to healthcare and public health initiatives between developed nations and developing nations. In the developing world, public health infrastructures are still forming. There may not be enough trained health workers or monetary resources to provide even a basic level of medical care and disease prevention. As a result, a large majority of disease and mortality in the developing world results from and contributes to extreme poverty. For example, many African governments spend less than US$10 per person per year on healthcare, while, in the United States, the federal government spent approximately US$4,500 per capita in 2000. However, expenditures on healthcare should not be confused with spending on public health. Public health measures may not generally be considered "healthcare" in the strictest sense. For example, mandating the use of seat belts in cars can save countless lives and contribute to the health of a population, but typically money spent enforcing this rule would not count as money spent on healthcare.

Under the constitution of India, public health is a shared responsibility of the central, state and local levels of governments. However, health is essentially a state responsibility. The amount of public health spending is not uniform throughout the country but the state and local governments account for three-fourth of the total public health spending. The responsibility for the central government includes looking at port quarantine, research and specific and technical education. On the other hand, the private healthcare services are provided by herbal healers, modern unqualified or quasi-qualified 'quack', and qualified practitioners of different systems of medicine. Until mid seventies, large private hospitals were not for profit or charitable in nature and for-profit private hospitals were primarily small nursing homes. By 1990's corporate sector came forward to invest in private healthcare and thus expanded this sector. Although most of the healthcare is provided by private sector, there is lack of any regulation and specification of standards for private healthcare. The payment in the private sector is largely fee-for-service and paid out of pocket by the patients. There is no uniform standard for the charge of similar activities (for details see, Akram, 2014).

Public Health Structure and the Shortfalls

The organisation of healthcare services in the country extends from the national level to village level. At the grassroots level, healthcare facilities are available in the form of Community Health Centre (CHC), Primary Health Centre (PHC), and Sub-Centre (SC). One CHC is established for every 80,000 to 1,20,000 population, and this centre provides the basic specialty services in general medicine, paediatrics, surgery, obstetrics, and gynaecology. Further down, there is one PHC covering about 30,000 (20,000 in hilly, desert, and difficult terrains) or more population. Each PHC has one medical officer, two health assistants—one male and one female – and supported by health workers and staff. The most peripheral health facility is the Sub-Centre (SC) manned by one male and one female multipurpose health worker for a population of 5,000 in plains and 3,000 in hilly and tribal areas (for a detailed discussion, see Akram, 2014).

India had its first National Health Policy (NHP) in 1983 and before it only vertical health programmes existed which focused on control and treatment of various infectious diseases. Besides this, family planning and population control programmes were implemented to arrest rising growth of population of India. Health was never seen in a holistic perspective and the focus of health programmes remained on clinical treatment of 'diseases'. The second National Health Policy (2002) came in the aftermath of Millennium Development Goals (MDGs). The Centrally sponsored, National Rural Health Mission (NRHM) was launched in 2005 to ensure participation of the local self-government institutions at village panchayat level in a participatory manner. The NRHM is now redesigned as National Health Mission (NHM) and includes the urban poor and slum dwellers also as the beneficiaries along with the rural population. But despite promising such architectural changes, the public health structure is still plagued with several deficiencies and shortages. Some of these deficiencies exist at the very conceptual or policy level. For example, the notion of primary healthcare is itself ill-defined in India.

(a) Limited Reach and Scope of Primary Healthcare

Primary healthcare is the backbone of the health system in India. The Alma Ata Declaration (1978) has given a very comprehensive definition of primary healthcare. However, most of the elements suggested for primary healthcare in the Alma Ata declaration seldom find any mention in the structuring of 'Primary Health Centres (PHCs)' in India. According to the declaration, primary healthcare includes awareness about health problems and the methods of preventing and controlling them. Factors like food supply and proper nutrition, safe water and basic sanitation, maternal and child healthcare, prevention and control of locally endemic disease, appropriate treatment of common disease and injuries, and, provision of essential drugs are also included but less emphasised in practice. PHCs focus mostly on treatment of common diseases and injuries, immunisation, and provision of essential drugs. If we go back to the Bhore committee report submitted in 1946, we find that many of the radical suggestions made by the committee have never been implemented. The PHCs in India have adopted only the clinical aspects from the Alma Ata's definition of primary healthcare; education about prevailing health problems, food supply and nutrition, adequate supply of safe water and basic sanitation etc., remained beyond the purview of PHCs. Further, the PHCs are understaffed and in majority of States suffer from the problem of absenteeism and lack of physical resources.

(b) Lack of Infrastructure

Lack of healthcare infrastructure is a major problem in India. The shortfall in health infrastructure as per 2011 population in various States of India is presented in Table 1. At the level of Sub Centres, Bihar shows a huge shortfall of 48 per cent. Haryana, Jammu and Kashmir and Jharkhand are other States with massive shortfall. Kerala, Tamil Nadu and Andhra Pradesh are three States with surplus number of Sub Centres. Further, at the level of Primary Health Centres, states like Jharkhand and West Bengal reflect huge shortfall. Even Bihar, Madhya Pradesh and Rajasthan show massive shortfall. At the level of Community Health Centres, states like Bihar and Uttar Pradesh show shortfall of 91 per cent and 60 per cent respectively. These figures suggest that these facilities are almost non-existent in

Table 1: Shortfall in Health Infrastructure as per 2011 Population (Provisional) in India (as on March, 2012)

S.No.	State/ UT	Total Population in Rural Areas	Sub Centres				PHCs				CHCs			
			R	P	S	% Short-fall	R	P	S	% Short-fall	R	P	S	% Short-fall
1	Andhra Pradesh	56,311,788	12283	12522	*	*	2004	1624	380	19	501	281	220	44
2	Assam 3	26,780,516	5841	4604	1237	21	953	975	*	*	238	109	129	54
3	Bihar	92,075,028	18533	9696	8837	48	3083	1863	1220	40	770	70	700	91
4	Gujarat4	34,670,817	9156	7274	1882	21	1433	1158	275	19	358	318	40	11
5	Haryana4	16,531,493	4159	2520	1639	39	657	447	210	32	164	109	55	34
6	Jammu & Kashmir 1	9,134,820	3044	1907	1137	37	456	396	60	13	114	84	30	26
7	Jharkhand	25,036,946	6043	3958	2085	35	964	330	634	66	241	188	53	22
8	Kerala	17,455,506	3525	4575	*	*	586	809	*	*	146	217	*	*
9	Madhya Pradesh	52,537,899	12314	8869	3445	28	1977	1156	821	42	494	333	161	33
10	Maharashtra	61,545,441	13410	10580	2830	21	2189	1811	378	17	547	363	184	34
11	Odisha	34,951,234	8136	6688	1448	18	1308	1226	82	6	327	377	*	*
12	Punjab	17,316,800	3463	2951	512	15	577	449	128	22	144	132	12	8
13	Rajasthan4	51,540,236	15172	11487	3685	24	2326	1528	798	34	581	382	199	34
14	Tamil Nadu2	37,189,229	7555	8706	*	*	1254	1227	27	2	313	385	*	*

contd...

contd...

S.No.	State/ UT	Total Population in Rural Areas	Sub Centres				PHCs				CHCs			
			R	P	S	% Short-fall	R	P	S	% Short-fall	R	P	S	% Short-fall
15	Uttarakhand	7,025,583	2341	1848	493	21	351	257	94	27	87	59	28	32
16	Uttar Pradesh	155,111,022	31037	20521	10516	34	5172	3692	1480	29	1293	515	778	60
17	West Bengal2	62,213,676	13186	10356	2830	21	2166	909	1257	58	541	348	193	36
	India	833,087,662	189094	148366	43776	23	30565	24049	7954	26	7631	4833	3044	40

R: Required; P: In Position; S: Shortfall; *Surplus

Source: (RHS 2012, p .49)

Notes: The requirement is calculated using the prescribed norms on the basis of provisional rural population from Census, 2011and estimated rural tribal population in 2011 using per cent of tribal population out of rural population in 2001. All India shortfall is derived by adding state-wise figures of shortfall ignoring the existing surplus in some of the states.

1. As the entire State is included under Hill Area Development Programme, the total rural population of the State is taken as in the Tribal/Hilly/Desert areas.
2. The rural population of districts included under the Hill Area Development Programme has been added in the rural population under Tribal/Hilly/Desert areas.
3. The two districts in Assam, namely North Cachar and Karbi Anglong are included in the list of districts under Hill Area Development Programme. However, as these two districts are having more than 50 per cent tribal population, no change is made in the rural population under Tribal/Hilly/Desert areas.
4. The rural population of districts included under the Desert Development Programme (DDP) also added in the rural population under Tribal/Hilly/Desert areas.

these States.

(c) Lack of Health Professionals

Table 2 shows the situation related to availability of male health workers in various States of India. The table reflects the

Table 2: Shortfall of Health Worker [Male] at Sub Centres

State/UT	Required1 [R]	Sanctioned [S]	In Position [P]	Vacant [S-P]	Shortfall [R-P]
Andhra Pradesh	12522	7601	4608	2993	7914
Assam	4604	NA	2386	NA	2218
Bihar#	9696	2135	1074	1061	8622
Chhattisgarh	5111	4784	2514	2270	2597
Goa	205	150	137	13	68
Gujarat#	7274	7239	4874	2365	2400
Haryana	2520	NA	1682	NA	838
Himachal Pradesh	2065	2008	1183	825	882
Jammu & Kashmir	1907	1907	541	1366	1366
Jharkhand	3958	NA	957	NA	3001
Karnataka	8871	5853	3148	2705	5723
Kerala#	4575	1399	1285	114	3290
Madhya Pradesh	8869	5300	3733	1567	5136
Maharashtra##	10580	10579	6665	3914	3915
Meghalaya+	397	84	133	*	264
Nagaland##	396	276	234	42	162
Odisha	6688	4729	3827	902	2861
Punjab	2951	2858	1694	1164	1257
Rajasthan	11487	2217	1592	625	9895
Tamil Nadu	8706	2896	1266	1630	7440
Tripura	719	NA	543	NA	176
Uttarakhand	1848	920	184	736	1664
Uttar Pradesh	20521	9080	1729	7351	18792
West Bengal#	10356	9457	4478	4979	5878

Source: (RHS 2012, p. 55) (As on March, 2012).

Notes:

Data for 2011 repeated

+Data for 2010 repeated

NA : Not Available.

*Surplus. All India figures for Vacancy and Shortfall are the totals of State-wise Vacancy and Shortfall ignoring surplus in some States/UTs

1. One per each existing Sub Centre
2. For calculating the overall percentages of vacancy and shortfall, the States/ UTs for which manpower position is not available, may be excluded

vacant positions at the level of Sub Centres and also computes the shortfalls. The States like Uttar Pradesh, Andhra Pradesh, West Bengal, Maharashtra, Karnataka etc., show that huge number of vacant positions exist at the level of Sub Centres. Further, these States also reflect huge shortfalls in terms of availability of male health workers also. States like Uttar Pradesh, Bihar, Madhya Pradesh and Rajasthan present huge shortfalls in terms of their population. Thus, the poor performance of these States in health outcome can be appropriately explained by the huge vacant positions and shortfalls in terms of availability of health workers at the grassroots levels.

(d) Policy Shift and Privatisation

Further, the policy shifts in last two decades favour privatisation of healthcare services in India. It has also paved the path of health tourism for the health consumers coming from abroad. But the policies are almost silent on broadening the base or the scope of public health facilities at the national level. On the other hand, despite tall claims, the total fund allocation for implementing the various health programmes is dismal. Limited budgetary allocation from the central and state governments is a big hurdle. In developed countries, government health spending is more than five per cent of the GDP (Norway —6.9 per cent of GDP, USA —6.2 per cent of GDP, etc.). Even in developed Asian countries excluding India, the average health spending is around three per cent of the GDP (Government Health Expenditure in India: A Benchmark Study, 2006). The low spending on health and the dominance of private sector over the public health sector perpetuates the public health problems in India. Poor awareness for sanitation is also a consequence of poor growth of public health facilities in India.

Millennium Development Goals (MDGs)

The United Nations' Millennium Development Goals (MDGs) are important target set at the turn of the century for the global population. The MDGs include a target to reduce by half the proportion of people without access to basic sanitation by 2015. The United Nations declared 2008 as the 'International Year of Sanitation' in view of the 2.6 billion people in the world who lack even basic sanitation facilities. It was also in recognition of the slow progress being made towards the MDGs sanitation target. Particular concerns in MDGs for sanitation are:

- Removing the stigma around sanitation, so that the importance of sanitation can be more easily and publicly discussed.
- Highlighting the poverty reduction, health and other benefits that flow from better hygiene, household sanitation arrangements and wastewater treatment.

Several research findings suggest that sanitation and hygiene promotion needs to be better 'mainstreamed' in development, if the MDGs on sanitation is to be met. There is a realisation that many institutions should carry out activities to develop better sanitation and hygiene in developing countries. For example, educational institutions can teach on hygiene and sanitation by providing better facilities for them, and health institutions can dedicate resources for promoting preventative works. There is also the need of civil society organisations to provide the necessary infrastructure where national governments cannot do that on their own.

Disease, Health and Environmental Sanitation

The term "environmental sanitation" has been given various interpretations in different countries and at different times. In its most restrictive sense, sanitation has been equated with the safe disposal of human excrement. Environmental sanitation is a major public health issue in India. Recent interventional studies on environmental sanitation in India highlighted the importance of prioritising control strategies. Research related to the appropriate cost-effective intervention strategies and their implementation in Indian context is a big challenge.

Environmental sanitation means the control of all those factors in man's surroundings which cause disease or illness and have adverse effects on his health. The sanitation approach makes an effort towards hygiene of water supply and food supply, hygienic disposal of human and animal wastes, hygiene of housing and control of rodents and other vectors (RSHB). The World Health Organisation (WHO) defines 'Environmental Sanitation' as "the control of all those factors in man's physical environment which exercise or may exercise a deleterious effect on his physical development, health and survival. Environmental sanitation/hygiene includes all the activities aimed at improving or maintaining the standard of basic environmental conditions affecting the well-being of people. These conditions include:

- Clean and safe water supply
- Clean and safe ambient air
- Efficient and safe animal, human, and industrial waste disposal
- Protection of food from biological and chemical contaminants
- Adequate housing in clean and safe surroundings (http://www.healthizen.com/blog/index.php/general/environmental-sanitation/)

According to P.C. Mmom and C.F. Mmom (2011), environmental sanitation comprises disposal and treatment of human excreta, solid waste and waste water, control of disease vectors, and provision of washing facilities for personal and domestic hygiene. It aims at improving the quality of life of the individuals and contributing to social development. It has been defined by the Water Supply and Sanitation Collaborative Council as "Interventions to reduce people's exposure to disease by providing a clean environment in which to live, with measures to break the cycle of disease". Environmental sanitation comprises both a change in behaviour and facilities to form a hygienic environment. However, it is a truism that a significant number of people worldwide lack access to adequate water, sanitation, drainage, and solid waste disposal services. The latest statistics reveal that 1.1 billion people still do not have access to safe drinking water, and 2.4 billion people do not have access to adequate sanitation.

Furthermore, in many urban areas of developing countries, less than 50 per cent of the municipal solid wastes are collected and only an insignificant fraction is disposed of appropriately. This not only increases the rate of diseases and mortality, but also slows down the economic progress of hundreds of millions of people in developing countries. At the same time, the world's natural supply of freshwater is subject to increasing environmental and economic pressure. The urban environmental condition is deplorable in many cities of the developing world. In fact, the problems associated with providing environmental sanitation services are central to the urbanisation phenomena. Urban waste is considered one of the most serious and pressing urban environmental problems. Most cities focus on simply getting rid of their waste 'out-of-sight' and fail to recognise its potential danger when not properly disposed, treated or managed.

In developing countries, waste management often emerges as a problem that endangers human health and the environment. To make matters worse, waste management usually has a low priority on the political agenda of such countries, as they are struggling with other important issues such as hunger, health problems, water shortages and unemployment. In such situations, it is easy to understand why waste problems have a tendency to grow steadily. Several past researches have focused on investigating the cost-benefits of providing safe and convenient living conditions to households in the developing world, especially on housing conditions, notably on the relationship between water, sanitation and disease. These researches observed that water supply, sanitation and health are closely related. It is also evident that each year, poor hygiene, mismanagement of liquid or solid waste, and lack of sanitation facilities contribute to the death of millions of the world's poorest people from preventable diseases. Considering the nexus cleansing/sanitation and health, empirical evidence points to their close linkages. In particular, the relationship could be outlined as follows:

1. As cities continue to grow, the management of solid waste is becoming a major environmental and public health concern in urban areas of many developing countries;
2. Lack of sanitation, unsafe disposal or storage of waste in/around houses and streets, and in undesignated containers may provide habitats for vectors of that cause various infectious diseases including amibiasis, typhoid fever and diarrhoeas;
3. Uncontrolled landfills are a huge danger for the

surrounding environment and are a health risk to the population, causing contamination of the drinking water and soil;

4. More than five million people die each year from diseases related to inadequate waste disposal systems;
5. More than five million people die each year from diseases related to inadequate waste disposal systems (WHO, 2007).

An estimated 88 per cent of this burden is attributed to unsafe drinking water supply, inadequate sanitation, and poor hygiene. These risk factors do not evenly threaten urban districts as slums and informal settlements are more vulnerable to communicable diseases. As per estimates, inadequate sanitation cost India almost $54 billion or 6.4 per cent of the country's GDP in 2006. Over 70 per cent of this economic impact or about $38.5 billion was health-related, with diarrhea followed by acute lower respiratory infections accounting for 12 per cent of the health-related impacts. Evidence suggests that all water and sanitation improvements are cost-beneficial in all developing world sub-regions. Sectoral demands for water are growing rapidly in India owing mainly to urbanisation and it is estimated that by 2025, more than 50 per cent of the country's population will live in cities and towns. Population increase, rising incomes, and industrial growth are also responsible for this dramatic shift. National Urban Sanitation Policy 2008 was the recent development in order to rapidly promote sanitation in urban areas of the country. India's Ministry of Urban Development commissioned the survey, as part of its National Urban Sanitation Policy in November 2008. In rural areas, local government institutions in charge of operating and maintaining the infrastructure are seen as weak and lack the financial resources to carry out their functions. In addition, no major city in India is known to have a continuous water supply and an estimated 72 per cent of Indians still lack access to improved sanitation facilities. The 11th Five Year Plan envisaged 100 per cent coverage of urban water, urban sewerage, and rural sanitation by 2012 (Kumar, Kar and Jain, 2011).

According to study conducted by Environment and Social Development Unit South Asia Region, environmental factors account for about 20 per cent of the total burden of disease in

Andhra Pradesh. Over 90 per cent of this is associated with traditional environmental risks, such as lack of access to a protected water supply and sanitation (73 per cent of AP's population has no sanitation facilities) and indoor air pollution resulting from the use of biomass fuels. The largest portion of the environmental burden of ill-health is borne by people in rural areas, where access to basic infrastructure services (water, sanitation and commercial fuels) is lower and where baseline infant and child mortality rates are higher than in urban AP. In rural areas, environmental factors account for 22–23 per cent of the burden of disease, significantly higher than for urban areas. This burden is almost entirely caused by the lack of access to water and sanitation facilities and by exposure to indoor air pollution (89 per cent of the rural population relies on wood and dung cakes for cooking fuel) and contaminated drinking water. Thus, while modern environmental risks linked to industrial pollution and urban development also exist and are growing, environmental health is still to a large degree a rural health issue in AP—and will continue to be for quite some time. Urban households have much higher levels of access to water and sanitation services and rely less upon dirty cooking fuels. As a result of these and other factors (such as higher levels of income and education), the average burden of disease is significantly lower for the urban population, as is the share of the household environment in the total burden.

India is still lagging far behind many countries in the field of environmental sanitation. According to Harshal T. Pandve most cities and towns India are characterised by over-crowding, congestion, inadequate water supply and inadequate facilities of disposal of human excreta, wastewater and solid wastes. Most of the problems in the country are due to improper environment, which in turn rob people of their health, destroy their livelihoods and undermine their overall development potential. The environmental sanitation is still an ignored issue in India. To raise the overall standard of living the issue of environmental sanitation must be tackled seriously. It is essential to take some stricter steps to raise the current state of environmental sanitation in India. For an example in Nigeria, the state government of Lagos has set up a sanitation court, which will prosecute offenders arrested for violating the state environmental sanitation.

A possible sustainable solution to the problems of insanitation at the community level is ecological sanitation, also known as ecosan or eco-san. Ecological sanitation describes a form of sanitation that usually involves the recycling of water and nutrients contained within human wastes back into the local environment. An ecological sanitation (ecosan) viewpoint sees human waste and wastewater as an opportunity. When properly designed and operated, ecosan systems provide a hygienically safe, economical, and closed-loop system to convert human wastes into nutrients to be returned to the soil, and water to be returned to the land. Alternatively, solid wastes are converted into a biofuel. The primary application for ecosan systems has been in rural areas where connection to a sanitary sewer system is not possible, or where water supplies are very limited. The main objectives of ecological sanitation are: to reduce the health risks related to sanitation, contaminated water and waste; to prevent the pollution of surface and ground water; and, to reuse nutrients or energy contained within wastes. Technological adoption of ecological sanitation can provide a long term solution to the problems of insanitation in most of the affected societies.

Notes

1. Types of toilets: Wikipedia.
2. Types of toilets: Wikipedia.

References

Advani, M. and Akram, M. (2007). 'Health Concerns in India' in M. Akram (edited). *Health Dynamics and Marginalised Communities*, Jaipur: Rawat Publications, 03-26.

Akram, M. (2012), 'Looking Beyond the Universal Health Coverage: Health Inequality, Medicalism and Dehealthism in India', *Public Health Research*, Vol. 2 No. 6, 2012, pp. 221-228. doi: 10.5923/j.phr.20120206.08.

Akram, M (2013). 'Disease, Illness and Health Care: A Sociological Conceptualisation of the Indian Experience' Paper presented in *National Symposium on Health and Illness: Concepts, Issues, Practices and Policy* Organised by Humanities and Social Sciences Department, IIT Kanpur, 11th November, 2013.

Akram, M. (2014). *Sociology of Health*, Jaipur: Rawat Publications.

Akram, M. (ed.) (2007). *'Introduction', Health Dynamics and Marginalised Communities*. Jaipur: Rawat Publications.

Alkire, S. (2003). *Valuing Freedoms: Sen's Capability Approach and Poverty Reduction*, New Delhi: Oxford University Press.

Brym, R.J. and Lie, J. (2007). *Sociology: Your Compass for a New World: third edition*, United Kingdom: Thomson Wadsworth.

Cockerham, W.C. and Ritchey, F.J. (1997). *Dictionary of Medical Sociology*, London: Greenwood Press.

Coe, R.M. (1970). *Sociology of Medicine*, New York/London: McGraw-Hill Book Company.

Desai, M. (2007). 'Judicial Responses to Health Care', in Akram, M. (ed.) *Health Dynamics and Marginalised Communities*, Jaipur: Rawat Publications, 27-37.

Dingwall, R. (1976). *Aspects of Illness*, London: Martin Robertson.

Gabe, J., Bury, M. and Elson, M. (2004). *Key Concepts in Medical Sociology*, London: Sage Publications.

Government Health Expenditure in India: A Benchmark Study. (2006). New Delhi: Mac Arthur foundation economic research foundation.

IHDR. (2011). *India Human Development Report 2011*, Institute of Applied Manpower Research, Planning Commission, Government of India, New Delhi, Oxford University Press.

Kendall, D. (2011). *Sociology in Our Times: eighth edition*, CA, USA: Wadsworth, Cengage Learning.

Kleinman, A. (1988). *The Illness Narratives: Suffering, Healing and the Human Condition*, New York: Basic Books.

Kumar, G.S., Kar, S.S. and Jain, A. (2011). 'Health and environmental sanitation in India: Issues for prioritising control strategies', *Indian J Occup Environ Med*. Sep-Dec. 15(3): 93–96.

McNeill, P. (1990). *Health*, London: Routledge Publication.

Mechanic, D. (1978). *Medical Sociology*, New York: The Free Press.

Mmom, P.C. and Mmom, C.F. (2011). 'Environmental Sanitation and Public Health Challenges in A Rapidly Growing City of the Third World: The Case of Domestic Waste And Diarrhoea Incidence in Greater Port Harcourt Metropolis, Nigeria', *Asian Journal of Medical Sciences* 3(3).

MoHFW. (2010). *Annual Report to the People on Health*, Ministry of Health and Family Welfare, Government of India, September 2010.

Nettleton, S. (1995). *The Sociology of Health and Illness*, UK: Polity Presses.

Pandve, H.T. (2008). 'Environmental Sanitation: An Ignored Issue in India', *Indian Journal of Occupational and Environmental Medicine*, 12(1): 40.

Park, K. (2009). *Preventive and Social Medicine*, Jabalpur: M/s Banarsidas Bhanat.

RHS (Rural Health Statistics in India) (2012). Statistics Division, Ministry of Health and Family Welfare, Government of India.

Sen, Amartaya, (2006). 'Health Achievement and Equity: External and Internal Perspectives' in Anand, Sudhir, Fabienne Peter, and Amartya Sen (ed.), *Public Health, Ethics and Equity*, New Delhi: Oxford University Press.

United Nations (1948). *Documents*.[online] Available from: http://www.un.org/en/documents/udhr/(accessed on July 06, 2012)

White, K. (2002). *An Introduction to the Sociology of Health and Illness*, London: Sage.

WHO. (1952). *Report of Expert Committee on Public Health Administration*, WHO/SEARO.

Websites

en.wikipedia.org/wiki/Sanitation.

Environment, Water and Sanitation, Irish Aid key sheet, Environment Policy for Sustainable Development, www.irishaid.gov.ie.

Environmental Health in India: Priorities in Andhra Pradesh, (2001), Environment and Social Development Unit South Asia Region, October.

Rural Sanitation and Health Booklet No. 416, Health and Medicine: HMS–2.

sanitationdrive2015.org/.../Sanitation-sustains-clean-environments. pd....health care

whqlibdoc.who.int/publications/a38153_(ch21).pdf.

3

Sanitation and Technology

Sanitation, at a larger level, is a healthy and hygienic action related to most of our day to day activities. Human activities, whether related to the personal/private domains or the larger public sphere, meaningfully contribute to causation of sanitation or insanitation conditions. Open defecation, spitting in public places, disposal of garbage and wastes at open places, water logging, open sewers, household and industrial omissions, open and trench latrines, washing of clothes, animals, vehicles, machines and other physical objects at the water sources and many more such activities cause insanitation. Sanitation is a conscious and desired action of converting all these actions to hygienic and healthy actions. A narrow definition of sanitation, which keeps it confined to only ways and means related to defecations, is perhaps the biggest hurdle in the path of sanitation. Sanitation is related to the technological and cultural bases of human life. Sanitation is related to our worldviews.

Technological factors play very important role in bringing change in human life and culture. Technology is playing equally important role in causation of sanitation. The understanding of hygienic or healthy action collaborates human understanding related to unwellness and wellness. Simple technologies, prevailing in pre-industrial societies, posed lesser threats to human life. The complex technologies pose complex threats to the human beings. The sanitation challenges, in the complex societies are also complex and need collaborative advanced technological support. With the increasing industrialisation, urbanisation and concentration of human population in urban areas, the sanitation requirements increased tremendously. The coming into existence of planned cities with modern sewerage systems and garbage treatment plants is a technological response to the sanitation requirements of modern urban life. The growth of modern flush toilets is also a similar technological improvement.

The spread of such technological innovations or the levels of their engagements at different levels of human life is not evenly spread globally. The spread of sanitation technologies and the collaborative infrastructure is skewed across the states and communities. The economic, political, cultural and even historical factors play important role in causing this skewness or unevenness. The problems related to insanitation, to a great extent, are caused by this limited reach and spread of technology. The cultural factors, which often resist the adoption of such innovative technologies at the community levels, also contribute in enlargement of such problems. This chapter looks at the technological bases of sanitation and explains how western world developed suitable technological solutions to their sanitation requirements. It also explains how India failed to develop or adapt such technological solutions causing a huge technological deficit in the sanitation infrastructure.

Sewerage Systems

Sanitation system in modern urban settlements is using modern techniques and technologies. Such modern techniques and technologies manifest themselves at different levels. One important technology is the use of sewer systems. The objective of sewage treatment is to produce a disposable effluent without causing harm to the surrounding environment and prevent pollution. Sewage treatment is the process of removing contaminants from wastewater, including household sewage and runoff (effluents). It includes physical, chemical, and biological processes to remove physical, chemical and biological contaminants. Its objective is to produce an environmentally safe fluid waste stream (or treated effluent) and a solid waste (or treated sludge) suitable for disposal or reuse (usually as farm fertiliser).

Sewage is generated by residential, institutional, commercial and industrial establishments. It includes household waste liquid from toilets, baths, showers, kitchens, sinks and so forth that is disposed of via sewers. In many areas, sewage also includes liquid waste from industry and commerce. The separation and draining of household waste into grey water and black water is becoming more common in the developed world, with grey water being permitted to be used for watering plants or recycled for flushing toilets. Sewage may include storm water runoff. Sewerage systems capable of handling storm water are known as combined sewer systems. This design was common when urban sewerage systems were first developed, in the late 19th and early 20th centuries. Combined sewers require much larger and more expensive treatment facilities than sanitary sewers. Heavy volumes of storm runoff may overwhelm the sewage treatment system, causing a spill or overflow. Sanitary sewers are typically much smaller than combined sewers, and they are not designed to transport storm water. Backups of raw sewage can occur if excessive infiltration/inflow (dilution by storm water and/or groundwater) is allowed into a sanitary sewer system. Communities that have urbanised in the mid-20th century or later generally have built separate systems for sewage (sanitary sewers) and storm water, because precipitation causes widely varying flows, reducing sewage treatment plant efficiency (for details see Wikipedia).

Sewerage was first introduced in London in 1850, followed by New York in 1860. Calcutta in India was the next city in the world to have this privilege in 1870, yet out of over 7,933 towns/cities in India only 929 have the sewerage system and that too partially. There are only 160 towns having sewerage treatment plant but there is no such facility in the remaining 769 towns.

Drainage System

Drainage is the natural or artificial removal of surface and sub-surface water from an area. Many agricultural soils need drainage to improve production or to manage water supplies. Drainage is also an integral component of modern urban and industrial societies especially for the urban spaces. In construction projects, the civil engineers set out the plans for all the roads, street gutters, drainage, culverts and sewers involved in construction operations. Civil engineers and construction managers work alongside architects and supervisors, planners, quantity surveyors, the general workforce, as well as subcontractors. Drainage options for the construction industry include both Point drainage and Channel drainage. Point drainage intercepts water at gullies (points). Gullies connect to drainage pipes beneath the ground surface and deep excavation is required to facilitate this system. Support for deep trenches is required in the shape of planking, strutting or shoring. Channel drainage intercepts water along the entire run of the channel. Channel drainage is typically manufactured from concrete, steel, polymer or composites. The interception rate of channel drainage is greater than point drainage and the excavation required is usually much less deep. The surface opening of channel drainage usually comes in the form of gratings (polymer, plastic, steel or iron) or a single slot (slot drain) that runs along the ground surface (typically manufactured from steel or iron).

Gupta (2007) has observed that continuing urbanisation, increasing migrations and economic developments in urban areas create pressures on the existing water infrastructure components, namely water supply, drainage systems, wastewater treatment plants and the receiving waters. Almost 25 per cent of the world's population is concentrated in the Indian sub-continent and it is expected that more than 700 million people would be living in urban areas in the Indian subcontinent alone by 2025. These cities are now caught in the vicious circle of increased impervious surfaces–less recharge–more runoff, thus overloading the existing drainage systems. Thus these cities witness water crisis in the summer and floods during the monsoon season.

Gupta further observed that the drains in the town centre had been designed to be separate, but due to growth and developments in the city centre, a large number of cross-connections from the house sewers to the stormwater drains have occurred. The net result has been that they function as combined sewers in the dry season with severe surcharging and local flooding during periods of heavy rainfall. In the suburbs the open stormwater drains receive increasing quantity of sewage and sullage. Due to their reduced capacity, contaminated stormwater from these drains frequently overflows into the informal settlements located on the periphery of the drains. This not only results in unaesthetic conditions, but has grave consequences for urban health and sanitation, which are particularly severe during times of high intensity rainfall (> 100 mm/hr) when overflows result in loss of lives due to flooding and epidemics due to polluted waters. Consequently, outbreak of epidemics is common during the monsoon in urban areas in India (Gupta, 2007).

Besides the sewage and urban drainage systems, which operate at the community or precisely the urban settlements level, the techniques and technologies of sanitation is also related with construction of toilets and use of other sanitation tools. The sanitation crisis is keenly felt in informal settlements across the globe. With no way to safely dispose of either faeces or garbage, around a billion slum dwellers resort to "flying toilets" (plastic bags that are used then thrown away) and to dumping trash in public spaces. This situation is not limited to urban settlements; in impoverished city suburbs, small market towns, large villages, and semi-urban settlements across the developing world, the public environment is full of human waste. The contents of bucket-latrines and pits, even of sewers, are often emptied into the streets, lakes, rivers or coasts. This excrement immediately contaminates the surrounding environment, enters waterways and harms communities (also see, sanitationdrive 2015.org/.../Sanitation-sustains-clean-environments.pd....).

Further, sanitation habits are closely associated and dependent upon availability of water. Continuous and sustainable availability of water is also related to techniques and technologies of ensuring water availability. Water is a sanitation issue to its very core, and constitutes one of the top drivers of development. Managing water supplies is important that they become neither depleted nor polluted and thus providing good sanitation—are central to the health of communities and the environment on which they depend. Poor water provision can affect the sanitation of the entire communities: one person's bad sanitation is the cause of another's contaminated food or water. Even piped systems of supply of water, if poorly managed, can concentrate any "downstream" problems — such as pollution in rivers, lakes and seas — and further degrade wildlife habitats and contribute to human health problems.

Water Supply

Water is the essence of life. Without water, human beings cannot live for more than a few days. It plays a vital role in nearly every function of the body, protecting the immune system – the body's natural defences – and helping remove waste matter. Sanitation is indispensably related to use and availability of water. Over exploitation of water due to industrialisation and urbanisation have created tremendous pressure on natural sources of water. Lack of safe water is a cause of serious illnesses such as diarrhoeal diseases, which kill over two million people every year (the vast majority children, mostly in developing countries). Contaminated water, whether drunk or used to cook food, harms people's health. Water is also essential for hygiene, growing food, keeping animals, rest, exercise and relaxation and for a variety of social and cultural reasons (also see "Right to Water", Health and human rights publication series; no. 3, World Health Organisation 2003, p. 6).

Access to a regular supply of safe water is a basic human right. But as with other human rights, too many people miss out the water rights also. Of the world's population of 6 billion people, at least 1.1 billion do not have available sources of clean drinking-water, such as protected springs and wells. Lack of access to safe water has a major effect on people's health. Poor health constrains development and poverty alleviation. Poor water and sanitation have an impact on education, but when safe water and appropriate sanitation are provided in schools, increased attendance and a reduction in drop-out rates results.

A study in five Indian states found a negative correlation between the provision of household toilets and community level prevalence of communicable diseases including cholera, typhoid/ enteric disease, diarrhoea/vomiting, hepatitis, nematodal infections as well as malaria and dengue.

A 2002 Planning Commission report expressed alarm over the 'rather extensive presence' of fluoride and arsenic in Indian drinking water, which is associated with a number of cancers (of the skin, lungs, kidneys, and bladder). According to the Water and Sanitation Programme, the cost per Disability Adjusted Life Year (DALY) of poor sanitation in urban areas is estimated at 5,400 INR (also see, Akram, 2014: chap 12).

Hand Washing

Sanitation techniques are related to good number of health producing behaviours and habits at individual as well as societal levels. Hand washing is one such sanitation habit. Hand washing for hand hygiene is the act of cleaning one's hands with or without the use of water or another liquid, or with the use of soap, for the purpose of removing soil, dirt, and/or microorganisms. The use of soap or any chemical in hand washing makes the act of hand washing a technical act. Medical hand hygiene pertains to the hygiene practices related to the administration of medicine and medical care that prevents or minimises disease and the spreading of disease. The main medical purpose of washing hands is to cleanse the hands of pathogens (including bacteria or viruses) and chemicals which can cause personal harm or disease. This is especially important for people who handle food or work in the medical field, but it is also an important practice for the general public. People can become infected with respiratory illnesses such as influenza or the common cold, for example, if they don't wash their hands before touching their eyes, nose, or mouth. Hand washing protects people from airborne diseases, such as measles, chickenpox, influenza, and tuberculosis. It protects best against diseases transmitted through fecal-oral routes (such as many forms of stomach flu) and direct physical contact.

Soaps or Detergents

Removal of microorganisms from skin is enhanced by the addition of soaps or detergents to water. The main action of soaps and detergents is to reduce barriers to solution, and increase solubility. Antibacterial soaps have been heavily promoted to a health-conscious public. Further, a hand sanitiser or hand antiseptic is a non-water-based hand hygiene agent. Hand sanitisers are most effective against bacteria and less effective against some viruses. Despite their effectiveness, non-water agents do not cleanse the hands of organic material, but simply disinfect them. It is for this reason that hand sanitisers are not as effective as soap and water at preventing the spread of many pathogens, since the pathogens still remain on the hands. Medical hand-washing is for a minimum of 15 seconds, using generous amounts of soap and water or gel to lather and rub each part of the hands. Hands should be rubbed together with digits interlocking. If there is debris under fingernails, a bristle brush may be used to remove it. Since germs may remain in the water on the hands, it is important to rinse well and wipe dry with a clean towel. After drying, the paper towel should be used to turn off the water (and open any exit door if necessary). This avoids re-contaminating the hands from those surfaces.

The World Health Organisation has "Five Moments" for washing hands

1. before patient care
2. after environmental contact
3. after exposure to blood/body fluids
4. before an aseptic task, and
5. after patient care.

The hand washing behaviour has been shown to cut the number of child deaths from diarrhea (the second leading cause of child deaths) by almost half and from pneumonia (the leading cause of child deaths) by one-quarter. There are five critical times in washing hands with soap and/or using of a hand antiseptic related to fecal-oral transmission: after using a bathroom (private or public), after changing a diaper, before feeding a child, before eating and before preparing food or handling raw meat, fish, or poultry, or any other situation leading to potential contamination. To reduce the spread of germs, it is also better to wash the hands and/or use a hand antiseptic before and after tending to a sick person.

Bathing

Bathing regularly is also an important sanitation act. Bathing is the washing of the body with a fluid, usually water or an aqueous solution, or the immersion of the body in water. It may be practiced for personal hygiene, religious ritual or therapeutic purposes. By analogy, especially as a recreational activity, the term is also applied to sun bathing and sea bathing. Bathing can take place in any situation where there is water, ranging from warm to cold. It can take place in a bathtub or shower, or it can be in a river, lake, water hole, pool or the sea, or any other water receptacle. The term for the act can vary. For example, a ritual religious bath is sometimes referred to as immersion, the use of water for therapeutic purposes can be called water treatment or hydrotherapy, and two recreational water activities are known as swimming and paddling. Public opinion about bathing began to shift in the middle and late 18th century, when it was argued that frequent bathing might lead to better health.

In collecting information on bathroom facilities available to the members of the household in India, the NSS (69th round) collected important information about availability of bathrooms in the households. For collecting data, two categories of bathroom facilities were distinguished for the households that had bathroom facilities, viz., attached bathroom and detached bathroom. A bathing place which does not satisfy the criteria distinguishing a room was not considered as a bathroom. If the dwelling unit had one or more bathrooms attached to the dwelling unit (i.e., with direct access from its rooms, veranda or corridor), it was considered to have an attached bathroom. On the other hand, if the households had a bathroom within the premises but not attached to the dwelling units, they were considered to have a detached bathroom. The NSS data shows that 62.3 per cent and 16.7 per cent of households in rural India and urban India respectively did not have any bathroom facility.

Types of Toilets and their Technological Bases

A toilet is a sanitation fixture used primarily for the disposal of human urine and feces. They are often found in a small room referred to as a toilet/bathroom/lavatory. Wikipedia—the free encyclopedia has discussed the following main types of toilets popular globally.

Urinals

Although it is possible for urinals to be used by females, they were originally designed for males. They are intended for the disposal of liquid waste, not solid waste. Urinals are meant to be used for the convenience of male users in a standing position. They typically have no door or stall enclosure, and thus take up less space. These fixtures are most commonly found in public places, but can occasionally be found in a private home.

Public Toilet

A public toilet, frequently called a restroom, is accessible to the general public. It may be within a building that, while privately owned, allows public access. Access to a public toilet may require a fee, (pay toilet), or may be limited to business's customers. Depending on culture, there may be varying degrees of separation between men and women and different levels of privacy. Typically, the entire room, or a stall or cubicle containing a toilet is lockable. Urinals, if present in a men's toilet, are typically mounted on wall with or without a divider between them. In the most basic form, a public toilet may be not much more than an open latrine.

In more luxurious variations there may be an attendant, towels, showers, etc. A fairly common feature in more modern toilets is an area to change baby diapers. A charge levied in the UK during the mid-20th century was one British penny, hence the generally adopted term "spend a penny" meaning to use the toilet.

Flush Toilets

Flush toilets, which are common in many parts of the world, may be connected to a nearby septic tank or more commonly in urban areas via "large" (3–6 in or 7.6–15.2 cm) sewer pipe connected to a sewerage pipe system. The water and waste from many different sources is piped in large pipes to a more distant sewage treatment plant. With the onset of the Industrial Revolution and related advances in technology, the flush toilet began to emerge into its modern form. A crucial advance in plumbing, was the S-trap, invented in 1775, and still in use today. This device uses the standing water to seal the outlet of the bowl, preventing the escape of foul air from the sewer. It was only in the mid-19th century, with growing levels of urbanisation and industrial prosperity, that the flush toilet became a widely used and marketed invention. This period coincided with the dramatic growth in the sewage system, especially in London, which made the flush toilet particularly attractive for health and sanitation reasons. Flush toilets were widely available from the mid to late 19th century. Various forms of flush toilets have become widely used in modern times (Kira, 1976). The amount of water used by modern toilets is a significant portion of personal water usage, totaling as much as about 90 liters (24 US gal) of water per capita per day (Leeden, Troise and Todd, 1990).

When a toilet is flushed, the water flows into a sewage system and eventually ends in a water treatment plant. Here the water is cleaned, sanitised and possibly re-used. Modern low flush toilet designs allow the use of much less water per flush—6.1 to 4.5 L per flush—but may require the sewage treatment system be modified for the more concentrated waste. The flush handle on these toilets is pushed up for one kind of flush and down for the other. In some places users are encouraged not to flush after urination. Flush toilets, if plumbed for it, may also use greywater (water previously used for washing dishes, laundry and bathing) for flushing rather than potable water (drinking water). Some modern toilets pressurise the water in the tank which initiates flushing action with less water usage.

Squat Toilets

Squat toilets (also known as an Arabic, French, Chinese, Japanese, Korean, Iranian, Indian, Turkish or Natural-Position toilet) are used by squatting rather than sitting and are still used by the majority of the world's population (Kira, 1976). There are several types of squat toilets, but they all consist essentially of a hole in the ground or floor with provisions for human waste.

To use this toilet, one is in a squatting position rather than sitting, by placing one foot on each side of the toilet and squatting over it. Modern versions are in separate stalls when they are in public lavatories, and include toilet tissue rolls for the user's convenience. The squatting method is accompanied by advantages as well as health benefits that connect to easiness of procedures such as child birth (Russell, 1969). The squat toilet is most commonly found in Asia, Africa, and the Middle East but can also occasionally be found in some European (Romania), Mediterranean, and South American countries (Ling, 2011).

Pit Toilets

A pit toilet is a dry toilet system which collects human excrement and urine in a large container or trench and ranges from a simple slit trench dug in the ground to more elaborate systems with seating and ventilation systems. They are more often used in emergency, rural and wilderness areas as well as in much of the developing world. The waste pit or trench, in some cases, will be large enough that the reduction in mass of the contained waste products by the ongoing process of decomposition allows the pit to be used more or less permanently. In other cases, when the pit becomes too full, it may be emptied or the hole covered with dirt. Pit toilets have to be located away from drinking water sources (wells, streams, etc.) to minimise the possibility of disease spread. Army units typically use a form of pit toilet when they are in the field and away from functional sewerage systems. The use of correctly located pit toilets were found to prevent much of the spread of various diseases which used to kill many more soldiers than the bullets and artillery used in pre-1940 warfare.

Chemical Toilets

Chemical toilets which do not require a connection to a water supply are used in a variety of situations. Examples include passenger train toilets and airplane toilets and also complicated space toilets for use in zero-gravity spacecraft. Chemical toilets are used in mobile and many temporary situations where there is no access to sewerage, dry toilets, including pit toilets and composting toilet require no or little water with excreta being removed manually or composted in situ.

Dry Toilets

Dry toilets, which use very limited or no water for flushing include the pit toilet (a simple hole in the ground, or one with ventilation, fly guards and other improvements), the composting toilet (which mixes excrement with carbon rich materials for faster decomposition), the incinerating toilet (which burns the excrement), and the tree bog (a simple system for converting excrement to direct fertiliser for trees).

"The unsanitary 'flying toilet' used in African slums where plastic shopping bags are first used as a container for excrement and are then thrown as far away as possible (Whitaker, 2007)." This practice has led to the banning of the manufacture and import of such bags in Uganda, Kenya, and Tanzania.

A toilet that pays its users has been opened in Musiri, Tamil Nadu, India. It is the first of its kind. The feces it receives are composted, and the urine is used as fertiliser for bananas and other food crops. Users are paid upto the equivalent of 12 US cents a month.

Before the introduction of modern flush toilets it was common for people to use a chamber pot at night and then to dispose of the 'night soil' in the morning; this practice (known as slopping out) continued in prisons in the United Kingdom until recently and is still in use in the Republic of Ireland. Thegarderobe was used in medieval times, and replaced by the privy midden and pail closet in early industrial Europe.

Urine Diversion (UD) Toilet, Urine Diversion Dry (UDD) Toilet and Urine Diversion Dry Toilet (UDDT) System

These toilets have two compartments: one for urine diversion and the other for the feces. A urine diversion toilet, *UD toilet* or *UDT*, flushes one or both compartments with water. A urine diversion dry toilet, *UDD toilet*, or *UDDT* is more similar to a dry toilet. The term UDDT can also refer to a system incorporating a UD or UDD toilet to recover water or utilise wastes as fertiliser or biofuel. Astronauts use a UDDT to recover potable water in the space station.

Portable Toilets

The portable toilet is used on construction sites and at large outdoor gatherings where there are no other facilities. They are typically self-contained units that are made to be easily moved to different locations as needed. Most portable toilets are unisex single units with privacy ensured by a simple lock on the door. The units are usually light weight and easily transported by a flatbed truck and loaded and unloaded by a small forklift. Many portable toilets are small molded plastic or fiberglass portable rooms with a lockable door and a receptacle to catch waste in a chemically treated container. If used for an extended period of time they have to be cleaned out and new chemicals put in the waste receptacle. For servicing multiple portable toilets tanker trucks, often called "Honey Trucks", are equipped with large vacuums to evacuate the waste and replace the chemicals.

High-tech Toilets

"High-tech" toilets include features such as: automatic-flushing mechanisms that flush a toilet or urinal when finished; water jets, or "bottom washers" like a bidet; blow dryers; artificial flush sounds to mask noises; and urine and stool analysis for medical monitoring. Matsushita's "Smart Toilet" checks blood pressure, temperature, and blood sugar. Some feature automatic lid operation, heated seats, deodorising fans or automated paper toilet-seat-cover replacers. Interactive urinals have been developed in several countries, allowing users to play video games as with the "Toylet", produced by Sega, that uses pressure sensors to detect the flow of urine and translates it into on-screen action (Geere, 2011).

Floating Toilets

A *floating toilet* is essentially an outhouse built on a platform built above or floating on the water. Instead of wastes going into the ground they are collected in a tank or barrel. To reduce the amount of waste that needs to hauled to shore, many use urine diversion. It was developed for residents without quick access to land or connection to a sewer systems. It is also used in areas subjected to prolonged flooding (see, Asian Development Bank website). The need for this type of toilet is high in areas like Cambodia where the World Bank cited in 2008 that nearly 10,000 people died as a result of poor sanitation (see, globalpost website).

Chamber Pots

A chamber pot is a receptacle in which one would excrete waste in a ceramic or metal pot. Among Romans and Greeks, chamber pots were brought to meals and drinking sessions. Johan J. Mattelaer said, "Plinius has described how there were large receptacles in the streets of cities such as Rome and Pompeii into which chamber pots of urine were emptied. The urine was then collected by fullers." This method was used for hundreds of years; shapes, sizes, and decorative variations changed throughout the centuries (Powell, 1996). This method is no longer used in developed countries, with the exception of hospital bedpans.

Garderobes

Garderobes were toilets used in the Middle Ages, most commonly found in upper-class dwellings. Essentially, they were flat pieces of wood or stone spanning from one wall to the other, with one or more holes to sit on. These would go into pipes that would lead outside the castle or manor (Genc, 2009). Garderobes would be placed in areas away from bedrooms to shun the smell and also near kitchens or fireplaces to keep the enclosure warm (Genc, 2009).

Toilets and Latrines in India

According to the India Human Development Report (IHDR) 2011, access to toilet facilities within the home provides privacy, dignity, and a sense of security to family members especially the female members. Similarly, the presence of toilets, safe water, and hygienic conditions at schools can reduce some of the constraints on students especially girls in attending schools (IHDR, 2011: 170). Toilets with modern or state-of-the-art technologies eliminate the need of manual handling of the human excreta. Hence modern toilets are not only good for improving sanitation practices but are also very powerful tool for eliminating the age old inhuman practice of scavenging (manual handling of human excreta). However, adoption of modern (technologically upgraded) toilets in Indian households is not a common or uniform practice.

Dr Bindeshwar Pathak, in his monumental book 'Road to Freedom: A Sociological Study on the Abolition of Scavenging in India' has traced the development of latrine system and modern toilets. In the early human civilisations, there was no specific practice of having specified places for human defecation. According to Pathak, 'People used open space, river banks and outskirts of habitas for defecation. The night-soil thus deposited on the surface of the earth got converted into soil and there was no need of disposal of human excreta. But, when the latrine system developed in civilised societies and people desired to have enclosed places for defecation, the problem of disposal of human excreta also arose. The people developed and adopted different systems of disposing of night-soil according to the level of technological knowledge as well as the circumstances and conditions prevailing in their habitas' (1991:45).

Pathak further writes: 'With the advancement of technology and scientific knowledge and rise in consciousness of the importance of sanitation, health and hygiene, improvements and modifications took place in the system of disposal of night-soil. Climate conditions, type of soil, water resources, economic conditions and social and cultural heritage also counted in developing and adopting a particular type of latrine system in a society or country. With the development of modern technology and knowledge, further modifications and improvements have been made in the toilet system. At present, different types of toilet systems are in use in different parts of the world. In India itself different designs had been developed during the British days and the post-independence era as well' (1991: 45). Some of the common toilet systems popular in India, as mentioned by Pathak are: sewerage, septic tank and two-pit systems of Sulabh Shauchalaya. Pathak gives a description of some other forms of toilets systems prevailing in different parts of India. We will include a brief description of these types as discussed by Pathak.

Trench Latrine

Trench latrine consists of a shallow pit, 2 feet to 3 feet deep and 3 feet to 4 feet wide, either circular, rectangular or square, a wooden plank having a hole in the middle and covered from three sides without roofs either by a tin or thatchet. In a trench latrine the users have to put some earth or grass-leaves after defecation. The site of the trench latrine has to be changed after every six months when it is full. Trench latrines, although better than open defecation, had some limitations. It was difficult to change the place every six months. Further, it could not eliminate fly-breeding and odour. Sometimes bacteria produced in the night-soil used to float on the surface of the latrine. Therefore, this system could not be adopted by people in general.

It is important to note here that after coming back from South Africa, Mahatma Gandhi was concerned about the sub-human practice of scavenging by a separate caste, Bhangi, and also defecation in open places. Whenever a meeting of the All India Congress Committee was organised, there was a clear instruction by Mahatma Gandhi that the disposal of night-soil would be only done by the volunteers of the Congress and not by the Bhangi. In this attempt, a trench latrine was first constructed at Sevagram, Wardha Ashram of Mahatma Gandhi.

Bore-hole Latrine

Bore-hole latrine was developed under the joint collaboration of the All India Institute of Hygiene and Public Health, Calcutta, and the Rockefeller Foundation in pre-independence days. First of all, it was installed in Singur, West Bengal. It consists of a circular hole, usually 40 cm in diameter, bored vertically into the ground by means of an earth auger to a depth of 6-8 meters. The latrine floor and its superstructure are also provided. This is used in the African countries, West-Asia, South-East Asia, Western Pacific and South America. The greatest difficulty in a bore-hole latrine is the collapse or caving-in of the pit walls particularly in alluvial soils. Fly breeding is another serious problem in this type of latrine (Bhaskaran, 1966:4). (Cited in Pathak, 1991:47)

Dug-well Latrine

The dug-well latrine was first introduced in Singur district of West Bengal in 1949-50. It is about 30 inches in diameter and 10 feet to 20 feet deep in hard soil. This well is lined to prevent caving-in of the soil and is brimmed with concrete around its entry point. The squatting plate is placed over the pit for defecation with a suitable superstructure for the privacy of the users (Bhaskaran, 1966: 5). According to Pathak, the dug-well latrine is fairly expensive and it is difficult to construct it in places where the water table is high.

Ulta Matka Privy

A large earthen-ware pot (Matka) is buried upside down in a pit, at least 0.75 meter below the ground level, which acts as a lining. The Matka is about 1.5 meter high. A hole is made to fix a pipe joining the Matka for discharging the waste. A layer of horse dung is laid at the bottom in the beginning to accelerate the process of decomposition. Salt water is also flushed once a week to help liquification of the faecal matter. The maximum leaching takes place from the open end at the bottom and a little from the porous side of the Matka. The gases produced in the pit are absorbed by the soil. When the Matka gets filled up, it is kept closed for about two years and the digested material can be used as fertiliser. During this period, an alternate Matka has to be provided (Cort, 1981: 18-19).

Gopuri

Gopuri is a form of compost latrine provided with two tanks which are constructed over the ground level, instead of being dug in the ground. A movable seat with pan is fixed on the tank in use. The filled up tank is covered with dry earth, ashes, leaves and domestic waste materials. Gopuri latrine has a permeable bottom and, like other compost latrines, the night soil filling it up is transformed into compost after a certain period of time. It has a vent-pipe which keeps it reasonably odourless (Bhaskaran, 1966:5).

Sopa Sandas Latrine

It is a type of compost latrine which was first introduced in Maharashtra. It consists of (i) RCC or stone slab with cement or mosaic W.C. pan; (ii) steep slopping pipe with a tin flap at the upper end; (iii) rectangular pit of 4 feet x 3 feet x 3 feet divided into two parts with partial honey-comb brick lining; (iv) Y-pipe to connect both pits; and (v) a vent pipe to carry away odour from the pit. The pit is covered with a sheet of tin when full and eventually the human excreta is transformed into compost (Cort, 1981: 10).

PRAI Type Latrine

After a number of trials and intensive research spread over a long period, the Planning and Research Action Institute, Lucknow has designed a hand-flush latrine with a pan and a trap. Two types were developed – a direct type in which the latrine is place over the pit and the other type in which the latrine is away from the pit and connected with a pipe. One or two jugs of water are usually sufficient to flush the faeces into the pit. When the pit is filled up with solids, the second pit is made by side of it, which is connected to the latrine. The contents of the first pit may be used as manure after it is left for a sufficient period. The one pit system is not very successful as the second pit cannot be constructed immediately after the first gets filled up (Pathak, 1991:49).

Ventilated Improved Pit (VIP) Latrine

This is based on an improved design of the latrine developed in Rhodesia. Aerobic action takes place in the pit through a cycle provided by air-suction through the toilet seat and up the vent-pipe which is warmed by the sun and thereby draws up the air. It is claimed that the odour emanating from the pit is expelled through the vent-pipe. As flies cannot enter the pit through the flue pipe, chances of fly breeding in the pit is reduced. When the pit gets filled, a new latrine has to be constructed. The VIP latrine is a considerable improvement over the traditional pit latrines.

Ventilated Improved Double Pit (VIDP) Latrine

The VIDP latrine differs from VIP in only one respect, viz., that it has two alternating pits. When one is filled up, it should rest at least for one year before it is emptied to ensure pathogen destruction. Two pits are provided by constructing a separate wall in the VIP pit or by constructing two separate pits.

Reids Odourless Earth Closet (ROEC)

An alternate design for a VIP latrine is the ROEC. In this latrine, the pit is completely offset and the excrement is introduced into the pit via chute. A vent pipe is provided as in the VIP latrine. A serious disadvantage of ROEC, however, is that the chute is easily fouled with the excrement and this may cause fly-breeding. The chute is, therefore, to be cleaned regularly.

Chemical Toilet

The chemical closet consists of a metal tank containing a solution of caustic soda. A seat with cover is placed over the tank, which is ventilated by a flue rising through the house roof. The excreta deposited in the tank is liquified and sterilised by the chemical which also destroys all pathogens. After several months of operation, this spent chemical and liquified matter are drained or removed. This system is quite satisfactory, safe and hygienic.

Service Latrines/Bucket Latrines

Services latrines developed in urban spaces historically. Such latrines are constructed in the outer side of the house in such a way that the feces is collected in some bucket placed below the place of defecation and the feces along with the water and urine stored there is removed from the bucket on daily basis. This work of removal and carrying the feces is done manually by a specific social category known as scavengers. This service or bucket latrine is completely based on in an inhuman practice of removing, cleaning and carrying the night soil by other human beings.

Technology Deficit and Sanitation

The popular types of latrines existing in India till some time back such as the trench latrines or service latrines are unhygienic and inhuman. The trench latrines created unhygienic neighbourhood. The storage of the night-soil close to the houses created several problems. The odour cannot be stopped. The germs and bacteria can easily move to other places. Often such trenches were constructed close to ponds or other water sources. The flow of the feces to the sources of water pollutes the water and such polluted water causes serious health hazards as discussed in earlier chapters. The trench latrines present their worst consequences during the rainy seasons.

The service latrine, on the hand, had several other problems. It is also based on storage of the feces in some bucket which are manually removed on daily basis. Any failure in removing the feces created similar problems. It had the added disadvantage that it promoted scavenging. Scavenging was a very inhuman practice. Kalbermatten (1980:6), on the basis of a study, concluded: 'the bucket latrine is judged to be unsuitable for replication. Problems of odour, insects, spillage and generally insanitary conditions *et al*... and transfer points were ubiquitous in all of the cases surveyed.' Pathak (1991) adds that such latrines not only pollutes the places of disposal but also the routes through which the human wastes are carried by the scavengers either in buckets or trolleys. Further, it also promoted the demeaning and inhuman conditions of carrying the night-soil on head by fellow human beings identified as scavengers. Scavenging, as a practice, prevailed within the caste system in India. Thus, both the popular types of latrines in rural and urban spaces were unable to promote sanitation at the local or collective level.

The sewerage system which developed in various cities in India in last hundred years is also not fool proof. In most of the cities, the sewerage system is devoid of sewerage treatment plants. Under such conditions, the sewage is dumped outside the city or even within the city at some open sewers. Very often, the sewage is dumped in rivers or ponds. This creates a very unhygienic environment surrounding the city. The people living in outskirts of cities are forced to live in very unhealthy conditions. Often, the untreated sewage mix up with the sources of water and create a vicious cycle of diseases and pollution. Further, even at the municipality level, the people who were employed for the cleaning work were appointed on the basis of their caste backgrounds. The association of caste with the sanitation work and especially with the cleaning work remained preserved even in the modern sewerage system giving it a traditional look and apparatus.

A sociological analysis of these conditions reflects that the creation and perpetuation of the unsanitary conditions in Indian neighbourhoods, both rural and urban, is caused by lack of use of appropriate technologies at the required level. Use of appropriate technology at various levels, in personal and social life, is a compulsory requirement in the industrialised or even industrialising societies. We have seen earlier in this chapter that different types of toilets with updated and improved technologies are used globally. The flush and the pit toilets are very scientific and hygienic. They do not pose any health or environmental challenge for the users. But the use of such toilets is very limited in India. Similarly, sewerage system has developed in many cities but there is no state-of-the-art sewage treatment plant. Very often the cleaning of sewers is conducted manually by the scavenging castes. The technology deficit caused the preservation of caste-based division of work related to sanitation and cleaning. Hence technology deficit is a very important cause of sanitation deficit in Indian society.

The reach of technology is much skewed in contemporary Indian society. The condition of Indian railways is a glaring example of how technology deficits cause sanitation deficits. Although Indian railways symbolise the modern technological innovation in the transportation system in India, the toilets made in these trains are not technologically improved. There is no provision of storing the feces and scientifically treating them at appropriate level in these toilets. The feces are dropped at the railway tracks. The toilet facility in Indian trains is nothing less than open defecation within the closed doors. Further, the cleaning work of such toilets is done manually by other human beings often the traditional scavenger class. This is, somehow, an extension of the service latrine system. Thus, the railways promote both open defecation and scavenging. Indian railways which are symbols of modernity are also carriers of insanitation and inhuman practices. This is an absolute reflection of the deep rooted prevalence of technology deficit in the sanitation environment of Indian society.

References

Asian Development Bank (no date), http://www.adb.org/Water/Photos/CAM/floating-toilets/Default.asp Sample Designs: Floating UDD Toilets, Asian Development Bank Website

Bhaskaran, T.R. (1966). Review of Work Done on Rural Latrines in India, Indian Council of Medical Research, Special Report Series No. 54, New Delhi p. 4 *cited in* Pathak 1991:47.

Cort, 1981: pp. 18-19 *cited in* Pathak 1991:47.

Geere, Duncan. (6 January 2011). Sega Installs "'Toylet' Games in Japan's Urinals". Wired UK. Retrieved 20 January 2011. Cited in Wikipedia the free encyclopedia.

Genc, M. (2009). 'The Evolution of Toilets and Its Current State', Thesis. Middle East Technical University, 2009. Harold B. Lee Library. Brigham Young University, 2009. Web. 28 Nov. 2011. as cited in Wikipedia the free encyclopedia.

Gupta, Kapil. (2007). "Strategies for Integrated Urban Drainage Management in Monsoon Rainfall areas with Special Reference to the Indian Subcontinent", *International Symposium on New Directions in Urban Water Management*, 12-14 September 2007, UNESCO Paris.

Cain, Geoffrey. (2010). "Floating toilets to clean up" http://www.globalpost.com/dispatch/asia/100416/cambodia-health-floating-toilets, Article: April 19, 2010, Global Post.

Kalbermatten, J.M. (1980), Appropriate Technology for Water Supply and Sanitation—A Sanitation Field manual, Washington, World Bank *cited in* Pathak 1991.

Kira, A. (1976). *The Bathroom*. revised edition, Harmondsworth: Penguin, pp. 115, 116.

Leeden, F.V.D., Troise, F.L. and Todd, D.K. (1990). *The Water Encyclopedia*. Lewis Publishers, Inc. Second Edition.

Ling, D. (2007). 'Squat Toilets —Where Can They Still Be Found?' Ezine Articles. Ezine Articles, 22 May 2007. Web. 28 Nov. 2011. Cited in Wikipedia the free encyclopedia.

NSS 69th Round (2013), July 2012-December 2012, Ministry of Statistics and Programme Implementation, Government of India.

Pathak, B. (1991). *Road to Freedom: A Sociological Study on the Abolition of Scavenging in India,* Delhi: Xtreme Office Aids Private Limited.

Powell, C.A. (1996). 'Port Royal Chamberpots Inroduction', Nautical Archaeology at Texas A&M University. Texas A&M University, 1 Dec. 1996. Web. 28 Nov. 2011.

Russell, J.G.B. (1969). 'Moulding of the Pelvic Outlet', BJOG: An International Journal of Obstetrics and Gynaecology, 76(9) : 817-20.

Whitaker, M. (2007). "Why Uganda Hates the Plastic Bag." *BBC News* via news.bbc.co.uk. Retrieved on 28 September 2007. Cited in Wikipedia the free encyclopedia.

Wikipedia—the free encyclopedia.

4

Sanitation and Culture

'The Employment of Manual Scavengers and Construction of Dry Latrines (Prohibition) Act' was passed by the union government of India in 1993. This Act prohibits employment of manual scavengers at household or any other level and aims to end scavenging as practice or occupation. It also prohibits construction or continuance of dry latrines as such latrines need scavenging. It is mandatory to convert dry latrines into water-seal latrines or to construct water-seal latrines in new construction. Whoever fails to comply with or contravenes any of the provisions of this Act in respect of each such failure or contravention be punishable with imprisonment for a term which may extend to one year or with fine, or may extend to two thousand rupees, or with both. Recently, the Act is modified and passed as 'The Prohibition of Employment as Manual Scavengers and their Rehabilitation Act, 2013' (see appendix). This Act prohibits the inhuman practice of scavenging which prevailed in India for thousands of years under the garb of caste system. Caste is a cultural and social reality of Indian society.

This chapter looks at the institution of caste and locates the position of people often identified as scavengers. It examines the relationship between caste and sanitation in India. It also tries to situate the issues of sanitation within the cultural constructs of 'gender' and 'religion'.

Sanitation is an integral part of human life. It is a basic and mandatory component of quality of life and wellbeing. In traditional Indian society, within the framework of *varna* and caste systems, the notion of cleanliness was more popular than sanitation. The notion of cleanliness was intermingled with the notions of ritualistic 'pollution' and 'purity'. The notion of pollution and purity created a (mythical) ritual hierarchy in which the twice born upper varnas (Brahman, Kshatriyas, and Vaishyas) were considered as 'pure' and the fourth varna (Shudra) was considered as impure or polluted. Within the caste-based division of labour, most of the jobs related to dead animals and human excreta were considered as polluting and the upper castes/varnas maintained distance from them. The human faeces were considered as polluting and physical distance was maintained between the house and place of defecation. Even in contemporary India, the traditional households maintain some kind of distance between the two. Under this historical context, although cleanliness is a value, sanitation rarely got the kind of attention it needed. As students of sociology, we have fair understanding of institutions of varna and caste and will just make an overview of our understanding here.

Caste System in India

The caste system in India is a complex system of social stratification consisting of various hierarchically arranged castes. Caste system is commonly thought of as a legacy of the ancient socio-cultural and politico-economic systems prevailing in India. A caste is considered to represent the socio-ritualistic formulations developed historically and identified often as a 'varna' and even as *jati* or *upjati*. The Brahminical texts refer to four categories of people or varnas: Brahmins, Kshatriyas, Vaishyas and Shudras. Referring to the diversity of opinion existing on issues related to caste and varna, D. D. Kosambi has noted that almost every statement of a general nature made by anyone about Indian castes might be contradicted. G. S. Ghurye has also noted that any attempt at defining caste is bound to fail because of the complexity of the phenomenon.

Ghurye did attempt to find a middle-ground between the complexity and the loose usage. He defined six characteristics of the Hindu caste system. He thought that these could be applied across the country, although he acknowledged that there were regional variations on the general theme. These characteristics are: Strict segmentation of society, with the various groups being rigidly defined and membership of them determined by birth; a hierarchical system that defines a ranking place for all of the castes; a limited choice of occupation which is enforced within a caste as well as by other castes; the general practice of endogamy, although in some situations hypergamy is acceptable; restrictions on dietary and social interactions that defines who could consume what and accept from whom; and, physical segregation in, for example, villages and this is accompanied by limitations on movement and access, including to religious and educational areas and to basic facilities such as supplies of water and further, this segregation applies at sub-caste level as well as at the higher level.

Not everyone has agreed with the definition proposed by Ghurye, which in any event was intended as an exercise to reduce the gap between lax terminological usage and the realities of an immensely complex system. The term 'caste' has no universally accepted definition. To some, it traditionally corresponds to endogamous varnas of the ancient Indian scripts. To others, endogamous *jatis* rather than *varnas* are castes, such as the 2378 occupation-classified *jatis* list created by colonial ethnographers in the early 20th century. To others, such as H.H. Risley, it means endogamous groups that resulted from interactions between what were once different races. Endogamy, the common element in these three definitions, is itself disputed. Using occupation to define castes is also confusing. While Brahmins have been defined as priests and sometimes rulers, Kshatriyas as warriors and sometimes rulers, Vaishyas as traders and sometimes agriculturists and Shudras as labourers and sometimes agriculturists, all of them have also been defined by other professions.

Ancient Hindu texts suggest caste system was not rigid. This flexibility permitted lower caste Valmiki to compose the 'Ramayana, which was widely adopted and became a major

Hindu scripture. Other ancient texts cite numerous examples of individuals moving from one caste to another within their lifetimes. Fa Xian, a Buddhist pilgrim from China, visited India around 400 AD. Only the lot of the Chandals he found unenviable; outcastes by reason of their degrading work as disposers of dead, they were universally shunned. But no other section of the population were notably disadvantaged, no other caste distinctions attracted comment from the Chinese pilgrim, and no oppressive caste 'system' drew forth his surprised censure. In this period kings of Shudra and Brahmin origin were as common as those of the Kshatriya varna and the caste system was not wholly rigid.

Caste affiliation was often loose and getting governed by principles of *jajmani* system during the medieval period but the British regime enforced caste affiliation rigorously, and constructed a much more strict hierarchy than existed previously, with some castes being criminalised and others being given preferential treatment. From a sociological point of view Ward (2006) explains that the caste system is inherently embedded in Hindu Religious practices particularly the teachings of samsara, dharma and karma. Samsara views death as a moment of transition and not an end in any person's life. Dharma encourages the belief that our destiny (caste) is fixed and it cannot be changed. Ward says that the Hindu hyper-good has provided a faithful acceptance of one's worldly fate in order to improve one's lot in the next life cycle. According to Ward, religion provides such rigorous sanctions for social life and imposes such a great fear of falling down that people through their patterned daily activity, find it impossible and abhorrent not to follow religious guidelines (Ward 2006). Karma is responsible for punishment and reward. This force is influenced by the extent they follow their dharma.

Certain groups, often known as 'outcastes', were excluded from the varna system altogether, ostracised by all other castes and treated as untouchables. Strongly identified with Hinduism, the caste system has been carried over to other religions on the Indian subcontinent, including Buddhism, Christianity, Islam, and Sikhism. Corbridge and Harriss (2000) conclude that British policies of divide and rule of India's numerous princely sovereign states, as well as enumeration of the population into rigid categories during the 10 year census, particularly with the 1901 and 1911 census, contributed towards the hardening of caste identities.

The *Jajmani* System

The *Jajmani* system conceptualises the agrarian social structure of traditional Indian society within the framework of caste system and the exchange relations inherent in it. In its classical construct, within the caste system, different caste groups specialised in specific occupations and exchanged their services through an elaborate system of division of labour. The castes living in a village were bound together by different kinds of inter-caste relations. These inter-caste relations at the village level might have economic, ritual, political and civic ties and together they were identified as jajmani system.

The Jajmani system is based on agricultural system of production and distribution of goods and services. It is the link between the landowning high caste groups and the landless occupational castes. Oscar Lewis mentions that each caste groups within a village is traditionally bound to give certain standardised services to the families of other castes. While the landowning high caste families receive services from lower castes and in return members of the low castes receive grains.

Generally peasant castes are numerically preponderant in villages and they need the carpenter, blacksmith, leather worker and other castes to perform various work. Servicing castes such as priest, barber, washerman and water carrier cater to the needs of everyone except the so called untouchables who were at the bottom of the hierarchy. Artisan castes produce goods which are wanted by everyone. Most Indian villages do not have more than a few of the essential castes and depend on neighbouring villages for certain services, skills and goods. The essential artisan and servicing castes are paid annually in grain at harvest time. In some parts of India the artisan and servicing castes are also provided with free food, clothing, fodder and residential site. On such occasions as birth, marriage and death, these castes perform extra duties for which they are paid customary money and some gifts in kind.

The landed higher castes are known as Jajman or the patron and the service castes are known as the kameen of the jajman. Jajmani System as a term was introduced into Indian social anthropology and sociology by William Wiser. In his contribution based on his study in a village in Uttar Pradesh he described how different castes interacted with one another in the production and exchange of goods and services. With variations this system existed throughout the country.

The jajmani system is characterised by the following features:

- **Unbroken relationship:** Under the jajmani system the kameen remains obliged to render the services throughout his life to a particular jajman and the jajman in turn has the responsibility of hiring services of a kameen.
- **Hereditary relationship:** Jajmani rights are enjoyed hereditarily. After the death of a man his son is entitled to work as kameen for the same jajman family or families. The son of a jajman also accepts the son of the kameen as his kameen.
- **Multidimensional relationship:** Due to the permanency of relationship both the jajman and kameen families become mutually dependent on each other. The relationship becomes very deep. They often take part in the personal and family affairs, family rituals and ceremonies.
- **Barter exchange:** Under jajmani system the payments are made mainly in terms of goods and commodities. The kameen gets his necessities from the jajman in return of his services.

Pollution/Purity

Pollution and purity have been important social and religious concepts in Hinduism from ancient times. Pollution often entails substances related to birth, death, blood, bodily processes, and leftover food. The concepts of purity and pollution are central to the notion of caste in India. People whose traditional occupations put them in contact with leather, dead animals, toilets and sewers, and sweeping (leftover substances) are usually considered outcastes or untouchables. At the other social extreme are Brahmins, who never have contact with such substances and, ideally, deal only with learning, books, or temple rituals.

They are considered pure. Other castes, which sometimes have contact with polluting substances in their traditional work, have an intermediate purity status. For example, barbers, who have contact with bodily substances as they cut people's hair, are seen as lower caste, though not untouchable. For Brahmins, purity is maintained by tradition and occupation and reinforced by vegetarianism. As new ideas of purity began to develop, Brahmins became the strictest vegetarians. When they became the measure of purity, those who did eat meat were given lower status. Because of their purity, Brahmins may offer cooked food to anyone. Conversely, Brahmins can accept food from and eat together with only a very limited group of people, their own subcaste of Brahmins. Commensality—eating food together—is a sign of an equal level of purity. People who by tradition have different levels of purity traditionally would not eat in the same place or from the same source. Furthermore, any food that has been eaten by anyone else is highly polluting, unless that person is one's infant child or husband. In villages, different castes drew water from different wells (for further details on this section, see also hinduism.enacademic.com).

Untouchability

The Constitution of India made practice of untouchability, in any form, unlawful. Untouchability was the practice of ostracising a group by segregating them from the mainstream by social custom or legal mandate. The excluded group could be one that did not accept the norms of the excluding group and historically included foreigners, nomadic tribes, law-breakers and criminals and those suffering from a contagious disease. It could also be a group that did not accept change of customs enforced by a certain group. This exclusion was a method of punishing law-breakers and also protected traditional societies against contagion from strangers and the infected. A member of the excluded group was known as an Untouchable.

The term is commonly associated with treatment of the many groups identified as Shudra (now identified as Scheduled Castes/ Depressed Castes/Dalit communities), who were considered "polluting" among the people of South Asia. Untouchability has been made illegal in post-independence India, and Dalits substantially empowered, although some prejudice against them continues, especially in rural pockets.

The Scheduled Castes

The Scheduled Castes (SCs) are not a homogenous group and are divided into many castes and sub-castes, as well as by language and geography. Traditionally they were known as "untouchables" but this term is not used in official Indian terminology after independence and the practice of untouchability has been made illegal. Politically-aware members of the Scheduled Castes are likely to use the term Dalit. Members of the Scheduled Castes are found all over India in some areas rising to over 25 per cent of the population. The Scheduled Castes comprise about 16.6 per cent of India's population (according to the 2011 census). The Constitution (Scheduled Castes) Order, 1950 lists 1,108 castes across 25 states in its First Schedule. Since independence, the Scheduled Castes were given reservation status, guaranteeing political representation. The Constitution lays down the general principles of affirmative action for SCs.

There is difference of opinions on the origin of untouchability with some accounts stating that it was a feature of ancient Indian society and others that it was introduced with the Aryan invaders in the third century BC. The philosophy of caste is contained in the Manusmriti, a sacred Hindu text related to the theory of transmigration of the soul and of karma (rebirth) and dharma (duty). "Untouchable" outcast communities were forbidden to join in the religious and social life of the community and were confined to menial "polluting" tasks such as slaughtering animals and leather working. At a later stage, the introduction of Islam led to widespread conversions by many low caste and "untouchable" groups and by the mid-nineteenth century a significant proportion of the population was Muslim. The period of British rule from the late eighteenth century brought little change. During the first half of the twentieth century the British Indian government began to take an interest in the condition of "untouchable groups" and "depressed classes" and their special position was recognised under the term "Scheduled Castes". In 1935, the British passed the Government of India Act 1935, designed to give Indian provinces greater self-rule and set up a national federal structure. The reservation of seats for the Depressed Classes was incorporated into the Act, which came into force in 1937.

Among Indian politicians two main approaches emerged, typified by two political and religious leaders who have by their ideas and actions made most impact on these castes. These two approaches were propounded by Dr B R Ambedkar and Mahatma Gandhi.

In the round table conference held on August 1932, upon the request of Ambedkar, the then Prime Minister of Britain, Ramsay Macdonald made a Communal Award which awarded a provision for separate representation for the Muslims, Sikhs, Christians, Anglo-Indians, Europeans and Dalits. These depressed classes were assigned a number of seats to be filled by election from special constituencies in which voters belonging to the depressed classes only could vote. Gandhi went on a hunger strike against this provision claiming that such an arrangement would split the Hindu community into two groups. Although Ambedkar was not convinced with the Gandhian approach in principle, he agreed with Gandhi. This agreement, which saw Gandhi end his fast and Ambedkar drop his demand for a separate electorate, was called the Poona Pact.

M.K. (Mahatma) Gandhi, whose main aim was liberation from colonial rule within a distinctive philosophical system based upon *amhinsa* (non-violence), believed in raising the status of "Untouchables" while retaining elements of the traditional caste system but removing the degrading stigma and manifestations of untouchability, and coined the term *Harijan* (Children of God) to describe them. The other approach came from Dr B. R. Ambedkar, a brilliant lawyer, who believed that only by destroying the caste system could untouchability be destroyed. Ambedkar became the chief spokesperson for Scheduled Castes who demanded recognition as a separate entity similar in status to Muslims, Sikhs and Christians. Ambedkar was forced to drop this demand after Gandhi threatened a hunger strike, but as a consequence Scheduled Castes were granted increased electoral representation and a guarantee of special protection and rights for them. Ambedkar also rejected Hindu values and in 1956 converted to Buddhism, later followed by about three million converts. Article 15 of the Constitution of India prohibits discrimination based on caste and Article 17 declared the practice of untouchability to be illegal. In 1955, India enacted the Untouchability (Offences) Act (renamed in 1976, as the Protection of Civil Rights Act). It extended the reach of law, from intent to mandatory enforcement. The Scheduled Castes and Scheduled Tribes (Prevention of Atrocities) Act was passed in India in 1989.

Most of the Scheduled Castes even after independence live in rural areas and economic exploitation remains their most acute problem. They are overwhelmingly marginal farmers or landless labourers. Large numbers migrate to cities or labour-scarce rural areas. Many among tend to do the jobs for the lowest wages. There are, however, growing numbers of Scheduled Castes in relatively secure areas such as the public service, banking and railways and sometimes in private industry. Those resident in the cities have greater access to secondary and higher education and a growing middle class has evolved within the Scheduled Caste community. Discrimination is less evident in many urban areas but residential patterns, particularly in poorer areas, are often on caste basis. As a result of the official policy of "positive discrimination" in favour of the Scheduled Castes in the civil service, there have been growing numbers of Scheduled Caste public servants. However, in some cities, many people coming from the community have continued with traditional occupations in a formal set-up such as working as sweepers in municipalities and have the advantage of regular work and wages. A pathetic development has taken place in the past few centuries is that the growth of a specific occupational category identified as 'scavenging' and the people engaged in the occupation being identified as 'scavengers'. People engaged in the inhuman work conditions of the occupation of scavenging are mostly from the Scheduled Caste (or Depressed Castes).

Scavenging

Scavenging is the practice of manual cleaning of human excreta from service/dry latrines. The scavengers crawl into the dry latrines and collect the human excreta with their bare hands, carry it as head-load in a container to dispose it off. A caste based and hereditary profession, which is handed down, as a legacy from one generation to the next; "manual scavenging" has been an age-old routine for this community, which is untouched by technological advancement in sanitary practices. Not only does the prevalence of this culture seem antediluvian, but what is worse is the fact that those born in this community are considered agents of pollution due to their background of social hierarchy, based on birth. They are the most oppressed and suppressed class of Indian society – often hated, ostracised, vilified and avoided by all other castes and classes. The appalling hardship, humiliation and exploitation they face, have no parallel in human history. The practice started in the Pauranic period continued in the Buddhist, Mauryan, Mughal and British periods.

Scavengers come in direct contact with human excreta and his/her hands are completely soiled. In a congested locality, the scavenger has to crawl through a narrow passage, pushing the basket with one hand, resting his body weight on the other to make his way up to the latrine chamber through a narrow opening. In the latrine, where the seat is deep inside, he/she has to stretch his hand to the fullest and thrust his/her head into the hole to clean the toilet. The scavenger has to bend forward into the narrow space to clean excreta from the toilet antechambers. In latrines, which have no receptacles, human excreta drops directly on the floor, which, with passage of time, wears the brickwork that becomes patchy and uneven. In most cases, the sidewalls are also without cement plaster; with the result, the excreta get stuck up everywhere on the sidewalls and also on the floor. The scavenger, while cleaning, has to scratch the floor and sidewalls to do maximum cleaning. It was a common sight to see scavengers, mostly women, moving with excreta on the head, stored in bamboo-baskets, or in leaking drums, with the muck trickling down over face and body. Passers-by avoid such persons. If a scavenger comes in close proximity, he or she is showered with a hail of abuse. In many places, latrines are so constructed that the users do not even see their own excreta. They simply squat, perform, and go away without even caring to know who cleans their toilets. No human degradation could be more cruel and inhuman than the one suffered by scavengers. The practices of pollution and purity, untouchability (in any form) and scavenging are cultural deficits.

Ritual Purification

Ritual purification is a feature of many religions. The aim of these rituals is to remove specifically defined uncleanliness prior to a particular type of activity, and especially prior to the worship of a deity. This ritual uncleanliness is not identical with ordinary physical impurity, such as dirt stains; nevertheless, body fluids are generally considered ritually unclean. Most of these rituals existed long before the germ theory of disease, and figure prominently from the earliest known religious systems of the Ancient Near East. Some writers remark that similarities between cleansing actions, engaged in by obsessive compulsive disorder sufferers and those of religious purification rites, point to an ultimate origin of the rituals in the personal grooming behaviour of the primates, but others connect the rituals to primitive taboos. Further, some others have seen benefits of these practices that as a point of health and preventing infections especially in areas where humans come in close contact with each other.

Ritual Purification in Hinduism

Various traditions within Hinduism follow different standards of ritual purity and purification; in Smartism, for example, the attitude to ritual purity is similar to that of Karaite Judaism. Within each tradition the more orthodox groups follow stricter rules, but the strictest rules are generally prescribed for Brahmins, especially those engaged in the temple worship.

An important part of ritual purification in Hinduism is the bathing of the entire body, particularly in rivers considered holy such as the Ganges; it is considered auspicious to perform this form of purification before any festival, and it is also practised after the death of someone, in order to maintain purity. Although water pollution means that in modern times there is a need for care during bathing in such rivers, the physical impurities within the river do not diminish the attributed power they have to bring ritual purity. Lesser aspects of Hindu purification ritual include *achamana* —the touching and sipping of pure water while reciting specific mantras —and the application of a *tilaka* on the forehead. Punyahavachanam is a ritual performed before any ceremony such as Marriage, Homa etc. Mantras are chanted and then water is sprinkled over all the people participating and the items used. There are various kinds of purificatory rituals associated with death ceremonies. After visiting a house where a death has recently occurred, Hindus are expected to take bath. Women take a head bath after completing their menstrual period.

Women and Menstrual Cycle

Menstruation is the shedding of the lining of the uterus (endometrium) accompanied by bleeding. It occurs in approximately monthly cycles throughout a woman's reproductive life, except during pregnancy. Menstruation starts during puberty (at menarche) and stops permanently at menopause. By definition, the menstrual cycle begins with the first day of bleeding, which is counted as day one. The cycle ends just before the next menstrual period. Menstrual cycles normally range from about 25 to 36 days. Only 10 to 15 per cent of women have cycles that are exactly 28 days. Also, in at least 20 per cent of women, cycles are irregular. That is, they are longer or shorter than the normal range. Usually, the cycles vary the most and the intervals between periods are longest in the years immediately after menarche and before menopause.

Menstrual bleeding lasts three to seven days, averaging five days. Blood loss during a cycle usually ranges from half to two and half ounces. A sanitary pad or tampon, depending on the type, can hold up to an ounce of blood. Menstrual blood, unlike blood resulting from an injury, usually does not clot unless the bleeding is very heavy. The menstrual cycle is regulated by hormones. Luteinising hormone and follicle-stimulating hormone, which are produced by the pituitary gland, promote ovulation and stimulate the ovaries to produce estrogen and progesterone. Estrogen and progesterone stimulate the uterus and breasts to prepare for possible fertilisation. The cycle has three phases: follicular (before release of the egg), ovulatory (egg release), and luteal (after egg release) (for details see www.merckmanuals.com)

Menstrual Taboo

A menstrual taboo is any social taboo concerned with menstruation. In some societies it involves menstruation being perceived as unclean or embarrassing, extending even to the mention of menstruation both in public (in the media and advertising) and in private (amongst the friends, in the household, and with men). Different cultures view menstruation differently. Many traditional religions consider menstruation ritually unclean. Wikipedia, the free encyclopedia has mentioned the religious views related to menstrual cycle of women.

These views are very important as they determine the overall status of women in relevant cultures also.

Judaism: In the Torah (Leviticus 15:19-30), a menstruating woman is considered ritually unclean —"anyone who touches her will be unclean until evening" (New International Version). Touching her and touching an object she had sat or lain on makes a person ritually unclean. The extent to which these rules are observed in modern Judaism varies depending on the degree of conservatism/orthodoxy.

Christianity: Christians throughout history have disagreed about whether menstruation makes a woman unclean. In spite of the restrictions in Leviticus, Jesus allowed himself to be touched by a hemorrhaging woman and cured her (Mark 5:25-24). Some Church fathers defended the exclusion of women from ministry based on a notion of uncleanness. Others held that purity laws should be discarded as part of the Old Covenant. There has never been any official teaching that menstruation makes women unclean in any major Christian denomination.

Bahá'í Faith: Bahá'u'lláh, the founder of the Bahá'í Faith, in the Kitáb-i-Aqdas abolished all forms of ritual impurity of people and things and stressed the importance of cleanliness and spiritual purity. Menstruating women are encouraged to pray and are not required to fast, they have the (voluntary) alternative of reciting a verse instead.

Islam: In Islam, a woman is not expected to offer prayer or to perform other religious activities such as fasting, etc., during her menstruating cycles. However, she can perform all other acts of social life as normal. There is no restriction to her physical movement. She needs a bath after completion of the menstruating cycles.

Hinduism: In the Hindu faith, women were prohibited from participating in normal life while menstruating. She must be "purified" before she was allowed to return to her normal family life, and this had been considered as a negative view of menstruation. Menstruating woman were forbidden from performing any rituals. Contact with menstruating woman was also forbidden (with exception of small children). However, in some regions menstruation, especially first menstruation or menarche, is seen as a positive aspect of a girl's life. In South India and also in the Assamese community, girls who experience their menstrual period for the first time are given presents and celebrations to mark this special occasion, though women who are menstruating are not allowed in the household for a period of three nights. This certainly does not mean that they are driven away from the house during the cycle of their menstruation: according to Indian architecture, in a house with four blocks, 'dakkini' the south block, is for women and during the menstrual cycle women would confine themselves within this block, and would not even enter the kitchen or go to the north and east sides of the house, nor would they go near a temple.

Sikhism: In Sikhism, a woman is given equal status to man and is regarded as pure as man is. The Gurus teach that one cannot be pure by washing his body but purity of mind is the real pureness. They are not called pure, who sit down after merely washing their bodies. Guru Nanak, the founder of Sikhism, condemned the practice of treating women as impure while menstruating. In Sikhism, the menstrual cycle is not considered a pollutant. Certainly, it can have a physical and physiological effect on the woman. Nonetheless, this is not considered a hindrance to her wanting to pray or accomplish her religious duties fully. The Guru makes it very clear that the menstrual cycle is a God-given process. Meditating on God's name is of importance. Whether your clothes are blood-stained or not (including clothes stained from menstrual blood) is not of spiritual importance. Thus, there are no restrictions placed on a woman during her menstruation. She is free to visit a gurdwara, take part in prayers and do Seva.

Sanitation and Other Religions

Christianity

Baptism, as a form of ritual purification, occurs in several religions related to Judaism, and most prominently in Christianity; Christianity also has other forms of ritual purification. In older churches, and modern Roman Catholic churches, there are a number of lavers around the building for the laity to use as ritual symbolism of cleansing themselves, usually by dipping the fingertips in the holy water, and then making the sign of the cross. In traditional liturgical churches a laver, often embedded in the wall, exists for the priest and deacon to wash their hands before celebrating the Eucharist.

Many ancient churches were built with a large fountain in the courtyard. It was the tradition for Christians to wash before entering the church for worship. Traditionally, Christianity adhered to the biblical regulation requiring the purification of women after childbirth; this practice, was adapted into a special ritual known as the churching of women, for which there exists liturgy in the Church of England's Book of Common Prayer, but its use is now rare in Western Christianity. The churching of women is still performed in a number of Eastern Orthodox, Oriental Orthodox and Eastern Catholic churches. In Reformed Christianity, ritual purity is achieved though the Confession of Sins, and Assurance of Forgiveness, and Sanctification. Through the power of the Holy Spirit, believers offer their whole being and labour as a 'living sacrifice'; and cleanliness becomes a way of life.

Islam

Islamic ritual purification is particularly centred on the preparation for ritual prayer; theoretically ritual purification would remain valid throughout the day, but is treated as invalid on the occurrence of certain acts, flatulence, sleep, contact with the opposite gender (depending on which school of thought), unconsciousness, and the emission of blood, semen, or vomit. Some schools of thought mandate that ritual purity is necessary for holding the Holy Qur'an.

Ritual purification takes the form of ablution, in a lesser form (wudu), and greater form (ghusl), depending on the circumstance; the greater form is obligatory by a woman after she ceases menstruation, on a corpse that didn't die during battle and after sexual activity, and is optionally used on other occasions, for example just prior to Friday prayers or entering *ihram*. An alternative "dry ablution" (tayammum), involving clean sand or earth, is used if clean water is not available or if suffering from an illness which would be worsened by the use of water; this form is invalidated in the same circumstances as the other forms, and also whenever water becomes available and safe to use. And it is also necessary to be repeated (renewed) before every obligatory prayer.

The obligatory activities of the lesser form include beginning with the intention to purify oneself, washing of the face, arms, head, and feet. While some optional acts also exist such as recitation of the Bismillah, Oral hygiene/the brushing of the teeth, the washing of the mouth, nose at the beginning, washing of arms to the elbows and washing of the ears at the end; additionally recitation of the Shahadah. The greater form (ghusl) is completed by first performing wudu and then ensuring that the entire body is washed. Some minor details of Islamic ritual purification may vary between different schools of thought as well as scholarly opinions and between the different sects of Islam.

References

Corbridge, S. and Harriss, J. (2000). *Reinventing India: Liberalisation, Hindu Nationalism and Popular Democracy*. Polity press.

Ward, M . (2006). 'Philosophising Religion: Why so much Debate about Exploitation in the Hindu Caste System', *Journal of Human Values*, Vol. 12, No. 2 195–201, (October 2006)].

www.merckmanuals.com

Wikipedia—the free encyclopedia at en.m.wikipedia.org

5

Sanitation and Planned Development

Any effort to understand the sanitation situation cannot escape a discussion on social planning and development perspectives in contemporary scenario as the state apparatus has attained a very important role in regulating and often controlling changes in most of the societies. Sanitation, as we have seen in earlier chapters, is a desirable and conscious social action attained at the level of collectivity. Sanitation, even if attained at the individual level, cannot get translated into public life naturally if the public domains are surrounded by cumulative deficits and especially the cultural deficits. A social desire and agreement is necessary for attending sanitation at the level of collectivity. Public sanitation is a great measure of social welfare and needs to be seen from social planning perspective. Social planning, as a tool of bringing planned change, is socially responsible process of attaining social welfare or welfare of the masses. Till the 1960s and 70s, the term planning was generally used to mean "economic planning". "Social planning" is advancement over the notion of "economic planning" and intends to address the deprivations and deficits created by the earlier notions of planning or trajectories of development.

The courses and discourses of planned development, in themselves, are not necessarily very even or smooth. The first and the second world countries have significant differences in developing the trajectories of social planning. The third world countries have been witnessing the involvement of several internal and external forces in deciding the courses and directions of these changes. The experience of colonial past, in many of these countries, also creates a unique situation. The significance of understanding the mechanisms of planned development is relevant in the contemporary situation as sanitation, as a socio-economic and politico-cultural issue, finds its relative importance within the context of larger paradigms of planning and perceptions on development.

The experience of technological deficits or perpetuation of cultural deficits figures out the prevalence of a larger lacuna in the planning process in India—the existence of planning deficit. The planning deficit is multi-faceted and multi-fold in India. The widespread economic and regional disparities also reflect the planning deficit. The lack of developing proper sanitation culture or adopting some sanitation standard in the developmental processes related to industrialisation and urbanisation or a perpetual ignorance about the situation of open defecation are nothing but reflections of planning deficit prevailing in India. These unique situations are seen as reflections of planning deficits as the processes of social planning and models of social development, in principle, claim to widen the social bases of development trajectories and incorporate the diverse social needs of various sections of the societies within their agenda. When seen from this perspective, the lack of specific concern for the public health facilities in the overall development agenda is also a reflection of planning deficit.

Our main objective, in the present chapter, is to argue that the poor sanitation infrastructure in the various states and union territories of India is not only a result of poor technological or cultural factors but also a result of poor approach towards planned development. The figures provided by the NSSO (69th round) reflect that there is huge deficit in sanitation infrastructure in urban and rural spaces of India. Further, there is also huge gap among various states in attaining the sanitation goals.

Table 1 and 2 reflects the shortage or deficit of sanitation infrastructure prevailing in various states of India. Table 3 reflects the concentration of population below poverty line in few major states. The states having the highest proportion of people below poverty line are also the states with the poorest sanitation infrastructure. On the other hand, barring few exceptions, states having better sanitation infrastructure are the states having least proportion and number of people below poverty line.

Table 1: Indicators on households with sanitation facilities during 2012

State/UT	*Proportion (per 1000) of households*					
	Without bathroom facility		*Without latrine facility*		*Having access to improved source of latrine*	
	Rural	*Urban*	*Rural*	*Urban*	*Rural*	*Urban*
1	2	3	4	5	6	7
Andhra Pradesh	454	68	543	81	445	910
Arunachal Pradesh	525	14	126	0	465	979
Assam	456	92	137	3	754	971
Bihar	819	390	728	208	258	784
Chhattisgarh	849	345	767	249	200	749
Delhi	67	68	0	0	1000	987
Goa	77	2	97	40	858	960
Gujarat	539	157	587	62	407	936
Haryana	144	46	254	14	742	982
Himachal Pradesh	317	126	257	43	737	957
Jammu & Kashmir	405	71	443	60	441	794
Jharkhand	894	299	905	177	89	801
Karnataka	481	112	708	90	284	877
Kerala	97	53	28	12	969	988
Madhya Pradesh	756	149	790	140	207	849
Maharashtra	542	179	540	69	443	927
Manipur	502	299	12	0	796	912
Meghalaya	449	79	45	2	860	994
Mizoram	128	9	7	0	934	999
Nagaland	130	22	0	0	981	994
Odisha	882	259	813	182	173	805

contd...

State/UT	Proportion (per 1000) of households					
	Without bathroom facility		Without latrine facility		Having access to improved source of latrine	
	Rural	Urban	Rural	Urban	Rural	Urban
1	2	3	4	5	6	7
Puducherry	256	54	474	63	526	936
Punjab	226	181	222	62	776	933
Rajasthan	586	158	730	142	261	783
Sikkim	63	22	2	0	991	1000
Tamil Nadu	577	155	664	122	330	866
Tripura	897	488	14	1	886	981
Uttar Pradesh	796	242	753	107	224	867
Uttarakhand	205	24	197	16	802	976
West Bengal	730	266	397	54	580	932
A & Nicobar Is	358	92	288	50	712	950
Chandigarh	179	217	3	16	997	984
D & Nagar Have	841	676	493	322	507	678
Daman & Diu	520	683	268	1	732	999
Lakshadweep	0	1	0	23	1000	977
all-India (2012)	623	167	594	88	388	896
all-India (2008-09)	644	215	652	113	-----	----

Source: Compiled from various table of NSS 69th round (2013)

Table 2: Number per 1000 households with improved drainage facility and Garbage disposal arrangement

State/UT	Number per 1000 households with			
	Improved drainage facility		Garbage disposal arrangement	
	Rural	Urban	Rural	Urban
Andhra Pradesh	422	903	502	903
Arunachal Pradesh	112	685	353	646
Assam	41	519	275	631
Bihar	206	644	128	335
Chhattisgarh	182	613	639	551
Delhi	913	964	775	926
Goa	550	663	295	438
Gujarat	261	873	496	834
Haryana	817	949	760	862

contd...

State/UT	Number per 1000 households with			
	Improved drainage facility		Garbage disposal arrangement	
	Rural	Urban	Rural	Urban
Himachal Pradesh	240	708	227	661
Jammu & Kashmir	342	815	185	664
Jharkhand	110	623	141	402
Karnataka	433	896	569	862
Kerala	413	644	123	243
Madhya Pradesh	197	818	215	683
Maharashtra	430	892	549	908
Manipur	100	288	661	826
Meghalaya	179	704	206	834
Mizoram	48	485	439	775
Nagaland	288	689	767	948
Odisha	91	682	163	630
Punjab	793	890	289	694
Rajasthan	222	796	285	615
Sikkim	374	936	119	856
Tamil Nadu	290	796	363	834
Tripura	12	353	71	311
Uttarakhand	425	890	262	912
Uttar Pradesh	495	899	276	681
West Bengal	87	648	112	681
all-India (2012)	317	825	320	758
all-India (2008-09)	245	794	243	786

Source: Compiled from various table of NSS 69th round (2013).

Table 3: Number and percentage of population below poverty line by States, 2009-10

State/UT	Number and percentage of population below poverty line					
	Rural		Urban		Total	
	% of persons	No. of persons (in lakh)	% of pers-ons	No. of persons (in lakh)	% of pers-ons	No. of persons (in lakh)
1	2	3	4	5	6	7
Andhra Pradesh	22.8	127.9	17.7	48.7	21.1	176.6
Arunachal Pradesh	26.2	2.7	24.9	0.8	25.9	3.5

contd...

State/UT	Number and percentage of population below poverty line					
	Rural		Urban		Total	
	% of persons	No. of persons (in lakh)	% of pers-ons	No. of persons (in lakh)	% of pers-ons	No. of persons (in lakh)
1	2	3	4	5	6	7
Assam	39.9	105.3	26.1	11.2	37.9	116.4
Bihar	55.3	498.7	39.4	44.8	53.5	543.5
Chhattisgarh	56.1	108.3	23.8	13.6	48.7	121.9
Delhi	7.7	0.3	14.4	22.9	14.2	23.3
Goa	11.5	0.6	6.9	0.6	8.7	1.3
Gujarat	26.7	91.6	17.9	44.6	23.0	136.2
Haryana	18.6	30.4	23.0	19.6	20.1	50.0
Himachal Pradesh	9.1	5.6	12.6	0.9	9.5	6.4
Jammu & Kashmir	8.1	7.3	12.8	4.2	9.4	11.5
Jharkhand	41.6	102.2	31.1	24.0	39.1	126.2
Karnataka	26.1	97.4	19.6	44.9	23.6	142.3
Kerala	12.0	21.6	12.1	18.0	12.0	39.6
Madhya Pradesh	42.0	216.9	22.9	44.9	36.7	261.8
Maharashtra	29.5	179.8	18.3	90.9	24.5	270.8
Manipur	47.4	8.8	46.4	3.7	47.1	12.5
Meghalaya	15.3	3.5	24.1	1.4	17.1	4.9
Mizoram	31.1	1.6	11.5	0.6	21.1	2.3
Nagaland	19.3	2.8	25.0	1.4	20.9	4.1
Odisha	39.2	135.5	25.9	17.7	37.0	153.2
Puducherry	0.2	0.0	1.6	0.1	1.2	0.1
Punjab	14.6	25.1	18.1	18.4	15.9	43.5
Rajasthan	26.4	133.8	19.9	33.2	24.8	167.0
Sikkim	15.5	0.7	5.0	0.1	13.1	0.8
Tamil Nadu	21.2	78.3	12.8	43.5	17.1	121.8
Tripura	19.8	5.4	10.0	0.9	17.4	6.3
Uttar Pradesh	39.4	600.6	31.7	137.3	37.7	737.9
Uttarakhand	14.9	10.3	25.2	7.5	18.0	17.9
West Bengal	28.8	177.8	22.0	62.5	26.7	240.3
all-India	33.8	2782.1	20.9	764.7	29.8	3546.8

Source: Government of India (2012) Press note on Poverty Estimates, 2009-10, March, New Delhi.

A sociological understanding of the wide spread disparities prevailing in India makes it necessary to revisit not only the processes and outcomes of social planning but also to understand at length the goals and assumptions of it. The founding fathers of this nation-state had shown great trust in the instrument of planned development in India. Unfortunately, over a period of time, the whole mechanism of planned development missed its shine and created planning and development deficits. In next few pages, we will try to understand the basic assumptions and principles of social planning, the various approaches opted to attend such planning and the various models of development we have experienced. It will help us to identify the core deficiencies existing in the entire process and will help us to find out the corrective mechanisms. We will also include a brief discussion on the Five Year Plans (FYPs) as they play a very important role in deciding the direction, pace and magnitude of planned development. An overview of the FYPs will reflect that sanitation could not attract the kind of attraction it needed in past few decades. Lastly, we will try to situate the sanitation issues within the various models of development we follow.

Social Planning and Sanitation

According to G.R. Madan (1973), economic planning generally refers to the rational allocation of limited resources determined by a public authority. In the economic context, planning was generally understood as opposite of *laissez faire*. As against planning, in a *laissez faire* state, the production and distribution of economic goods is governed by market prices and individual decisions, and there is no coordination between various sectors of the economy. Looking at sanitation from the perspective of the a laissez faire state would mean that those who needed the sanitation facilities should have opted for them on their own motivation paying the cost and the state would have nothing to do with it. Economic planning, on the other hand, saw the economic returns of the sanitation infrastructure and promoted sanitation for enhancement of economic gains at the collective level. Social planning is an effort to widen the horizon of planning and include not only the production processes but also the distribution processes in such ways that it can become a tool of achieving equity and social justice. Hence, from the perspective of social planning, sanitation is itself a value and attainment of sanitation facilities, at the collective level, is a goal in itself.

According to William P. Scott (1988), social planning is any conscious and relatively large-scale, coordinated effort to recognise old or anticipate new problems or opportunities and to propose solutions for the benefit of a society, community, or organisation. Social planning is a specialist area of planning concerned specifically with creating better social outcomes for communities, including assessing the social impacts of development. Social planning focuses on social externalities, redistribution, and the equitable distribution of social benefits. This is not an activity limited to government, but includes activities of the private sector, social movements, professions and other organisations focused specifically on social objectives. According to David Hulchanski (1999), social planning is the process by which a group or community decides its goals and strategies relating to social issues, such as aspects of the quality of life and the circumstances of living in society.

Sanitation is definitely a social issue related to quality of life and circumstances of living. Hence, sanitation is a thrust area of the social planning processes globally. Sanitation, along with other important social issues like availability of drinking water, education, food and nutrition, employment, healthcare etc., have changed the quality of life of people in most of the developed and even developing countries in past few decades. However, the realities in India are quite different. Sanitation here could not attract the focus of social planning processes. It remains unfocussed not only in the initiative taken by the government but also in the initiatives taken by the private sectors. We do not witness any large scale initiative taken even in the form of corporate social initiatives. Sulabh International, as an NGO, has promoted the cause of sanitation in several states in last four decades. But it could not attract the support of other agencies which could have jointly promoted the cause. The failure of the social planning approach to absorb the sanitation goals is visible in India. We will briefly discuss the purposes and principles of social planning approach for closely observing the genesis of failure of social planning approach to absorb the sanitation goals in India.

Purpose of Social Planning

The commonly agreed purposes of the social planning are mentioned here:

- investigate, understand and respond to the social needs and aspirations of various groups and communities;
- provide a framework and set of principles that will underpin the social policy direction of the various agencies responsible for development;
- plan for the educational, health, employment, housing, and other development needs of various demographic groups within the state; build the capacity of the state/ government/society/community to become more viable and sustainable;
- assist all agencies functioning at national, international or even regional and local level to direct resources towards addressing social issues of importance to the community, and to particular groups through community development strategies;
- mobilise the not for profit organisations and even the profit making organisations for their social concern and corporate responsibility towards ameliorating the social conditions of the vulnerable and marginalised groups;
- check the recurrence of social problems and to bring about a harmonious adjustment of relationship between different parts of the society; and
- develop integrity and minimise discrimination and disparity of any kind between individuals and especially social groups.

Even a cursory look on these agreed purposes of social planning reflects that social planning takes into consideration the social needs of all sections of societies. Sanitation is a very important need of the masses in general and the economically poor and socially marginalised sections of the Indian society. But, till recently, this important need was ignored. Even the public health needs of the population in general was not addressed properly. The important social players like the industrial houses, the various agencies responsible for planned change, the elites and very often, even the government agencies have not played socially sensible role in attaining the socially desirable purposes of social planning. Hence, the purposes of social planning have not been attained in true spirit of the designs.

Principles of Social Planning

Social planning is based on certain principles. These principles help them to attend the purposes of social planning in heterogeneous societies. In a society like India which is very heterogeneous and even stratified, these principles are very important. An adherence to these principles, in letter and spirit, will ensure an all round development of any society and a departure from these principles will cause a dismantling of the goals of social planning. Some of these principles of social planning are discussed here so that we can identify their presence or otherwise in the trajectories of growth and development. An assessment of the planning processes followed in India, when seen from the perspectives of these principles, reveal that many of these principles were compromised during the actual courses of planning. Hence, a planning deficit was caused because of omission of the basic principles in the followed trajectories of social planning.

Social Equity: Equity is about fairness. Social equity implies fair access to public goods like education, livelihood, resources and full participation in the political and cultural life of the community. Many people consider social equity as synonymous with social equality. Jim Falk and his colleagues put it this way: "Equity derives from a concept of social justice. It represents a belief that there are some things which people should have, that there are basic needs that should be fulfilled, that burdens and rewards should not be spread too divergently across the community, and that policy should be directed with impartiality, fairness and justice towards these ends (Falk *et al.* 1993, p. 2). In the narrowest terms it means that there should be a minimum level of income and environmental quality below which nobody falls. It also means that everyone should have equal access to community resources and opportunities.

Social Equality: Social equality is a state of affairs in which all people within a specific society or isolated group have the same status in certain respects. At the very least, social equality includes equal rights under the law, such as security, voting rights, freedom of speech and assembly, property rights, and equal access to social goods and services. However, it also includes concepts of economic equity, i.e., access to education, healthcare and other social securities. It also includes equal opportunities and obligations, and so involves the whole of society. Social equality requires the absence of legally enforced social class or caste boundaries and the absence of discrimination motivated by an inalienable part of a person's identity. For example, sex, gender, race, age, sexual orientation, origin, caste or class, income or property, language, religion, convictions, opinions, health or disability must not result in unequal treatment under the law and should not reduce opportunities unjustifiably.

Community Involvement and Participation: Community involvement refers to engaging and partnering with communities in meaningful and appropriate ways, ensuring they are involved in local government planning and decision-making. It aims at developing partnerships with key stakeholders, including state and federal governments and non-government agencies to advocate for improved services and infrastructure within the region. It aims at ensuring open communication and transparent decision-making processes.

Access: Access means the opportunity to reach to available choices and services. Inequalities prevalent in societies cause restrict accessibility of various groups to the entitlements. Access refers to fair and equal reach to range of quality services essential to achieving and maintaining a reasonable quality of life.

Choice: Choice is an important indicator of freedom and empowerment. People should be choosing from a range of options and alternatives in housing, education, and employment opportunities as well as community support services.

Advocacy: Advocacy refers to mobilisation and lobbying for the needs and aspirations of the people and community. It includes advocating for the provision of and access to community services and facilities, cultural facilities, healthy environments, and economic opportunities for all groups in the community to increase their wellbeing. It also includes Advocacy for services, resources, facilities, spaces and opportunities that are physically and psychologically accessible to all community members.

Communication and Consultation: Implicit in any definition of social planning is an understanding that decisions which relate to quality of life issues must be informed by community involvement and the views of those people who will in some way be affected by the decisions must be included. Communication and consultation not only helps in including the views of the stake holder in the decision making but also enhances opportunities for all community members to participate in community life and economic outcomes of the region.

Community Cohesion and Cooperation: It refers to building community identity and connecting people to place within local communities to build a strong sense of community. An even and balanced growth in the social, economic and environmental domains ensures long term cohesion in the community. Applying the principle of intergenerational equity has impacts on the long term wellbeing of communities. Social cohesion can be created through community capacity building projects.

Timeliness: Welfare measures have their relevance when seen in the context of timeliness. A small help at the time of trouble and destitute can be of great importance than any major provision when that is not much required. Availability of resources and services, when they are needed the most, is very important component of social planning.

Adaptability and Flexibility: Rigidity is a typical authoritarian feature. Flexibility reflects sensitivity to the changing and dynamic discourses. Adaptability refers to capacity to include new modules and opportunities as and when required. Thus, adaptability and flexibility are important principles of social planning.

Approaches of Social Planning in India

Social planning finds central place in development economics and became very popular in the newly developed states which became independent in the post-second world war era. The classical and neo classical economics have promoted free market economies which were not very functional in the less developed countries because of severe resource crunches there. The Marxist economics talked about socialist patterns of development but even this approach has limited applicability in developing countries as they had not witnessed proper industrialisation. The new developments of the early twentieth century emphasised on the need of internal expansion as well as foreign aid and direct role of the government in promoting the less developed sectors/domains within the development framework. Growth of several schools of thought in economics like structural, neo-structural, Marxist, neo-Marxist, dualistic, dependency and the neo-liberal economies talked about varying role of the state in regulating the economic and social affairs for the welfare of the populations and especially the vulnerable and poor population. Social planning developed as a strategy to ensure the welfare and social measures like education, health, employment, better service conditions etc., to various segments of the population especially women, children, indigenous people, poor, racial and ethnic minorities in various contexts. A very strong advocacy for the promotion of social planning is the viewpoint that economic production should be a means to social ends and not the end in itself. In this approach, social planning becomes the first concern and economic planning has only instrumental value. According to G.L. Shukla (1998), an economic project is not only evaluated for its capacity to bring in economic returns today and tomorrow but also in terms of its social contribution. However, sanitation in India could not get the much needed impetus because sanitation could not become a desirable state of attainment in our early approaches.

Planning process followed in India, after independence, is generally known as the sectoral planning. It divides the various goals to be achieved in specific sectors. The individual sectors like education, health, housing, rural development, urban development, employment, social security etc., have their own specific targets and specific budget is allocated for the attainment of the specific time bound goals. The sectoral approach of planning has its own advantages and disadvantages. Although the sectoral planning has helped in achieving some of the goals in specific sectors but it has failed to attain those goals which need cross-sectoral planning. Health, sanitation, environment and educations are some of those goals which have cross-sectoral social bases and definitely needed cross-sectoral planning. The issues related to sanitation are overlapping as they related to housing, health, rural and urban development, environment and pollution, education and poverty alleviation etc. Health and sanitation in India are the worst victims of the sectoral planning and grossly reflect the prevailing planning deficit.

The decentralisation of the planning processes, as initiated in the last few decades of the past century, are yielding good results in fields needing regional or local level planning. Decentralisation is a movement which permits the wider involvement of people in the process of planning and implementation, and reduces the discrepancies between the national and sub-national plans which arise from regional or area characteristics that differ from national assumptions. The faith expressed in panchayti raj institutions or urban local bodies is a part of the decentralisation of the planning mechanisms. The sanitation programmes adopted in 1980s and 1990s were based on the decentralised principles. However, the decentralised sanitation programme missed the national zeal and vision. The national standards could not develop. The states having poor performance in other economic and social indicators could not focus much on sanitation programmes. This is also a reflection of the larger planning deficit.

Social Planning, Sanitation and Five Year Plans

Independent India gave herself a constitution informed by the ideals of liberty, equality and social justice. Fundamental rights relating to the freedom of speech, association, and vocation have been built into it and the directive principles of state policy invest it with forward looking dynamics. In sum, the constitution aims at the establishment of a welfare state. It accepts the parliamentary form of government with a federal set-up. Benefiting from its own history and from the experiences of other countries, it created a strong central government. The division of powers between the centre and states is embodied in the union, state and concurrent lists but all the residuary powers have been vested in the centre (G.L. Shukla, 1998).

The government of India established the Planning Commission on 15th March, 1950. In December 1954, Parliament adopted the resolution which declared a socialist pattern of society as the objective of economic policy laid down that the accent of the socialist pattern of the society is on the attainment of positive goals, the raising of living standards, the enlargement of opportunities for all, the promotion of enterprise among the disadvantaged classes, and the creation of sense of partnership among all sections of the community. The Second Five Year Plan elaborated the socialist pattern stating that essentially this means the basic criteria for determining lines of advance must not be private profit but social gain and that the pattern of development and the structure of socio-economic relations should be so planned that they result not only in appreciable increases in national income and employment but also in greater equality in incomes and wealth.

India launched its First FYP in 1951, immediately after independence under socialist influence of first Prime Minister Jawaharlal Nehru. The total planned budget of Rs 20.69 billion was allocated to seven broad areas: irrigation and energy (27.2 per cent), agriculture and community development (17.4 per cent), transport and communications (24 per cent), industry (8.4 per cent), social services (16.64 per cent), land rehabilitation (4.1 per cent), and for other sectors and services (2.5 per cent). The most important feature of this phase was active role of state in all economic sectors. Many irrigation projects were initiated during this period, including the Bhakra Dam and Hirakud Dam. The Indian government also made considerable effort in improving posts and telegraphs, railway services, road tracks, civil aviation. Sufficient fund was also allocated for the industrial sector. In addition, measures were taken for the growth of the small scale industries.

Unlike the First Plan, which focused mainly on agriculture, domestic production of industrial products was encouraged in the Second Plan (1951-56), particularly in the development of the public sector. The plan followed the Mahalanobis model, an economic development model developed by the Indian statistician Prasanta Chandra Mahalanobis in 1953. The plan attempted to determine the optimal allocation of investment between productive sectors in order to maximise long-run economic growth. Hydroelectric power projects and five steel mills at Bhilai, Durgapur, and Rourkela were established. Coal production was increased. More railway lines were added in the north-east.

The Third Five Year Plan stressed agriculture and improvement in the production of wheat, but the brief Sino-Indian War of 1962 exposed weaknesses in the economy and shifted the focus towards the defence industry and the Indian Army. The war led to inflation and the priority was shifted to price stabilisation. The construction of dams continued. Many cement and fertiliser plants were also built. Punjab began producing an abundance of wheat. Besides these, Panchayat elections were started and the states were given more development responsibilities. State road transportation corporations were formed and local road building became a state responsibility.

During the Fourth FYP (1969–1974), the government nationalised 14 major Indian banks and the Green Revolution in India advanced agriculture. In addition, the situation in East Pakistan (now Bangladesh) was becoming dire as the Indo-Pakistan War of 1971 and Bangladesh Liberation War took funds earmarked for industrial development had to be diverted for the war effort. The Fifth Five Year Plan (1974–1979) laid stress on employment, poverty alleviation (Garibi Hatao), and justice. The plan also focused on self-reliance in agricultural production and defence. But in 1978 the newly elected Morarji Desai government rejected the plan.

The Sixth Five Year Plan (1980–1985) marked the beginning of economic liberalisation. Price controls were eliminated and ration shops were closed. This led to an increase in food prices and an increase in the cost of living. This was the end of Nehruvian socialism. Family planning was also expanded in order to prevent overpopulation. The Seventh Five Year Plan (1985–1990) laid stress on improving the productivity level of industries by upgrading of technology. The main objectives of the Seventh Five Year Plan were to establish growth in areas of increasing economic productivity, production of food grains, and generating employment. The thrust areas of the Seventh Plan were: Social Justice; Removal of oppression of the weak; Using modern technology; Agricultural development; Anti-poverty programmes; Full supply of food, clothing, and shelter; Increasing productivity of small—and large-scale farmers; Making India an Independent Economy.

Modernisation of industries was a major highlight of the Eighth Plan (1992–1997). Under this Plan, the gradual opening of the Indian economy was undertaken to correct the burgeoning economic deficit and foreign debt. Meanwhile India became a member of the World Trade Organisation on 1st January 1995. The major objectives included: controlling population growth; poverty reduction; employment generation; strengthening the infrastructure; institutional building; tourism management; human resource development; involvement of Panchayat Raj, Nagar Palikas, and NGOs; decentralisation; and, people's participation.

The Ninth Five Year Plan (1998–2002) came after 50 years of completion of Indian Independence. The Plan tried primarily to use the latent and unexplored economic potential of the country to promote economic and social growth. It offered strong support to the social spheres of the country in an effort to achieve complete elimination of poverty. It also saw joint efforts from the public and the private sectors in ensuring economic development of the country. It focused the relationship between the rapid economic growth and the quality of life for the people of the country. The main objective of the plan was to correct historical inequalities and increase the economic growth in the country. The other objectives included: population control; generating employment by giving priority to agriculture and rural development; reduction of poverty; ensuring proper availability of food and water for the poor; availability of primary healthcare facilities and other basic necessities; primary education to all children in the country; empowering the socially disadvantaged classes like Scheduled Castes, Scheduled Tribes and other Bbackward Classes; developing self reliance in terms of agriculture; acceleration in the growth rate of the economy with the help of stable prices.

The Tenth Five Year Plan (2002-2007) targeted to renovate the nation extensively, making it competent enough with some of the fastest growing economies across the globe. It also intended to initiate an economic growth of 10 per cent on an annual basis. Chief objectives of the plan included: schooling to be compulsory for children by the year 2003; the mortality rate of children must be reduced to 45 per 1000 livings births and

28 per 1000 livings births by 2007 and 2012 respectively; there should be a decrease in gender discriminations in the spheres of wage rate and literacy by a minimum of 50 per cent; ensuring persistent availability of pure drinking water in the rural areas of India; the rate of literacy must be increased by at least 75 per cent within the tenure of the Plan; there should be a decrease in the Maternal Mortality Ratio (MMR) to two per 1000 live births by 2007.

The Eleventh FYP (2007–2012) had the following objectives: economic growth by creating 70 million new work opportunities and reducing unemployment to below five per cent; reducing dropout rates of children from elementary school from 52.2 per cent in 2003–04 to 20 per cent by 2011–12; increasing literacy rate for persons of age seven years or above to 85 per cent; reducing infant mortality rate to 28 and maternal mortality ratio to one per 1000 live births; reducing Total Fertility Rate to 2.1; providing clean drinking water for all by 2009; reducing malnutrition among children of age group 0–3 to half its present level; ensuring that all children enjoy a safe childhood, without any compulsion to work; attaining WHO standards of air quality in all major cities by 2011–12; and, treating all urban waste water by 2011–12 to clean river waters.

The theme of the Twelfth FYP (2012-2017) Approach Paper is "faster, sustainable and more inclusive growth". The Approach Paper laid down the major targets of the Twelfth Plan, the key challenges in meeting them and the broad approach to be followed to achieve the stated objectives. It proposes a growth target of eight per cent. The document proposes to bring down poverty by 10 percentage points by the end of the 12th Plan and generate five crore new jobs in non-farm sector. For Infrastructure sector, it talks about the positive efforts which should be made to increase investment in this sector to nine per cent of the GDP by the end of the Plan period. Some other major targets are: increasing green cover by one million hectare every year and adding 30,000 MW of renewable energy generation capacity in the Plan period; reducing emission intensity of the GDP in line with the target of 20-25 reduction by 2020 over 2005 levels; raising agriculture output to four per cent for the full Plan; manufacturing sector growth to 10 per cent for the full Plan.

Besides these, the plan has made specific provisions related to urbanisation and sanitation. We will discuss this aspect of the Twelfth Plan in the succeeding chapter separately.

A review of the five year plans reflects that the major thrust of almost all the plans were economic growth and infrastructure development. Some of the plans did talk about the advancement in the social sectors through better education and literacy, employment generation, health and nutrition, removal of poverty and other similar measures. But there is no major focus on improvement in housing conditions, urban living patterns, pollution and waste disposal, environmental protection, construction of toilets etc., in most of the plans. Thus, there is a visible absence of adopting the goals of social planning in the planning process in India. There is hardly any committed move to improve the sanitation situation prevailing at the national level. Government of India started few sanitation programmes in last few decades. An assessment of these programmes is made in a separate chapter. The evidences suggest that the success of these programmes is also very limited. Hence, we can conclude this section by stating that India is lacking in adopting the social planning approach and this is a clear evidence of prevalence of planning deficit in India.

Sanitation and Planned Development

Sanitation is not only an important indicator of development; it is also an important determinant of development; and it is, above all, an important goal of development. According to Mahbubul Haq, 'the basic purpose of development is to enlarge people's choice' (2011: 32). For Haq, these choices can be infinite and can change over time. According to Amartya Sen, 'the central issue in economic development is to expand the social opportunities open to the people' (2011: 22). Sanitation is one such choice; it is a social opportunity that needs to be open to the people. Sanitation is important not only for the elites; it is important for the masses, and above all, it is important for the social categories that remained absorbed in the occupations which were considered as unclean. The objective of development is to create an enabling environment for people to enjoy long, healthy and creative lives. Sanitation is an integral component of all the models of development, viz. economic, social, human, or sustainable development. In India, sanitation initiatives could not become integral components of these models of development. This chapter looks at the functioning of various development models and the causation of development deficit in India with special reference to sanitation.

Economic Development and Sanitation

Economic progress is an essential component of development. The classical and neo-classical theorists of the nineteenth and early twentieth century viewed the process of development as series of successive stages of economic growth through which all countries must pass. Such theorist primarily focused on right quantity and mixture of saving, investment, and economic expansion to enable an economic growth path. Development, thus, became synonymous with rapid and aggregate economic growth. This model of development is generally identified as the economic development model. However, plurality of viewpoints exists even within paradigm of development.

Classical or neo-classical economics is concerned primarily with the efficient and cost-effective allocation of scarce resources and with the optimal growth of those resources over time. They hold that countries develop economically via the market. In a market economy, economic benefits flow to participants, be they individuals or countries, from self-interested and voluntary acts. Marxist political economy provides a broader view of economic development. Like classical and neo-classical economists, political economists are concerned with the efficient and cost-effective allocation of scarce resources. They, however, bring a new coefficient politics into the development equation. When addressing why some groups or countries are better off than others, political economists do not look solely at market forces for an explanation. They focus on the social and political mechanisms that economic groups have created to control the allocation of scarce resources.

Development economics goes beyond the scope of either classical/neo-classical economics or Marxist economics. It, too, is concerned with the efficient allocation of scarce resources. Its main concern, however, is sustained economic growth over time that improves the standard of living for the masses who live in poverty in developing countries. To that end, one of the main goals of development economics is the formulation of public policies designed to bring about rapid economic growth. The structuralists focus on the mechanism by which "underdeveloped" economies transform their domestic economies from a traditional subsistence agricultural base into a modern economy. A modern economy is defined as one in which most of the population is urban and the bulk of the country's output is in the form of manufactured products or services. Under this model, the object of development is the structural transformation of underdeveloped economies so as to permit a process of self-sustained economic growth.

To neoclassical economists, economic stagnation in developing countries was a by-product of poorly designed economic policies and excessive state interference in the economy. They argued that to stimulate the domestic economy and promote the creation of an efficient market, developing country governments had to eliminate market restrictions and limit government intervention. This was to be accomplished through the privatisation of state-owned enterprises, promotion of free trade, reduction or elimination of restrictions on foreign investment, and a reduction or elimination of government regulations affecting the market.

Sanitation, under this economic model of development was largely considered as an investment to enhance productivity and combat spread of diseases. The developing countries, in the Post Second World War era, came under the direct influence of economic growth model of developed countries but ignored the investment in widening the civic amenities and public health structures. India, in the first three decades after achieving independence, mainly followed the economic development model. But, it failed to realise the productive utility of sanitation infrastructure. No systematic effort has been made to take care of the sanitation needs of people, especially the rural and urban poor. Sanitation deficit is very visible during these three decades not only at the household or community level but there is a complete absence of sanitation standards in the industrial developments. Industrial pollutant, urban wastes and sewerage systems never got the attention that they needed in many states of India.

Social Development and Sanitation

James Midgley (1995) conceives social development as a process of planned social change designed to promote the well-being of the population as a whole in conjunction with a dynamic process of economic development. The goal of social development in the context of modern welfare is to produce a social well-being that makes people capable of acting and making their own decisions in the broadest sense. According to this perspective, equal access to society's goods (such as health, education, or civic amenities like sanitation) should be available for all. Equal participation should provide everybody with opportunities for fulfillment. This model of development believes in extension of civic amenities and facilities to all. The need of sanitation facilities can't be ignored in this framework. Further, it believes in social planning for ensuring social justice. Thus, those who lagged behind in the trajectory of development must be guarded to come forward.

This model is very relevant in Indian context because the historically prevailing structural inequality has caused exploitation and seclusion of the several social categories like lower castes, poor, women and workers. Social development gives an inclusive trajectory of development. It not only talks about the fair share in the fruits of development for all social categories, it also assures preferential treatment for those who lagged behind. However, the social development model, which became popular in 1980s and 1990s, could not think beyond the protective discrimination in government services and little specific welfare measure for the specific categories. Availability of public goods, the core of the social development model, could not become the thrust of the social planning. The absence of public goods and especially the public health and sanitation facilities made the social development model a policy deficit model. Social justice could not get translated into social empowerment exhibiting implementation deficits and just remained a political instrument to mobilise voters.

Human Development and Sanitation

Human development is about expanding the choices people have, to lead lives that they value, and improving the human condition so that people have the chance to lead full lives. Fundamental to enlarging these choices is building human capabilities—the range of things that people can do or be in life. Human development disperses the concentration of the distribution of goods and services that underprivileged people need. Investment in people can enable growth and empower people to pursue many different life paths developing human capabilities. The most basic capabilities for human development are: to lead long and healthy lives; to be educated; to have access to the resources and social services needed for a decent standard of living; and, to be able to participate in the life of the community. Without these, many choices are simply not available, and many opportunities in life remain inaccessible. Healthy life needs fulfilment of several choices and removal of all those handicaps which may adversely affect it. Ensuring proper hygiene and sanitation is an integral component of a healthy life.

Human Development Index (HDI) became an important indicator of human development in last two decades reflecting upon the combined achievements in health, education and economic fields of the communities. Quantified and comparative measurement of HDI at the global level exposed India's poor performance in such capacity and capability building measures. The disparity between and among the various states of India also became very visible. The HDI also reflected on the relative positioning of the various indicators of development. Many countries are doing much better in HDI even when their per capita income is not very high because of their better performance in health and education. The government at the Union level was forced to make dedicated planning to improve literacy level and health facilities. The macro level changes taking place at economic spheres because of the beginning of the LPG (Liberalisation, Privatisation, and Globalisation) era and the changed political equations (because of beginning of the coalition government) at the central and federal levels witness the launch of National Literacy Mission, National Rural Health Mission and National Mission on Skill Development, Right to Education, Employment Guarantee Programmes etc. Amidst these changed circumstance, there is beginning of programmes like

Total Sanitation Campaign and National Urban Sanitation Policy which promise to contribute in enhancing sanitation and combating the premature mortalities caused by large scale prevailing communicable diseases and ever increasing non-communicable diseases.

Sustainable Development and Sanitation

The last two decades also witness a new development approach in the form of sustainable development because of compulsions related to environmental degradation and sustainability needs. Sustainable development advocates policies that allow for economic growth while at the same time minimising damage to the environment. A holistic view of sustainable development basically opts for the doctrine of inter-generational equity. From this view point, sustainable development is the integration of environmental, economic and social concerns of society so as to arrive at development paths which meet the needs of present generation without compromising the ability of future generations to meet their own needs. In other words, sustainable development allows a long term utilisation of environmental resources for social and economic development while at the same time, attempts to maintain the quality of the environment. Environmental sanitation is an integral element of sustainable development approach. And further, the sustainable development perspective gives the viable alternatives for the sanitation models in various contexts.

The sustainable development perspective has a long term vision for development planning. It does not believe in excessive exploitation of resources for short term gains. It believes in sustaining utilities. It has redesigned the goals and strategies of economic development. Globally, sustainable development talks about maintaining ecological and environmental equilibrium. It has redefined the technologies also. It believes in minimising pollution and wastages. It believes in recycling of material resources. It talks about protecting natural resources like water. Technologically, it is the most sanitation friendly model of development. However, in India, the model has not been adopted at larger level. Sustainable development strategies, if implemented effectively, will pave the path of achieving sanitation goals naturally.

References

Dash, L. N. (2000). *World Bank and Economic Development of India*, New Delhi: APH Publishing.

Falk, Jim. *et.al.*, (1993), *Social Equity and the Urban Environment, Report to the Commonwealth Environment Protection Agency*, AGPS, Canberra.

Government of India (2012). Press note on Poverty Estimates, 2009-10, March, New Delhi.

Hulchanski, David. (1999). "Social Planning Approaches and Issues", SWK 4663, University of Toronto, 246 Bloor St. West, Room 538.

NSS (National Sample Survey) 69th Round (2013). Ministry of Statistics and Programme Implementation, Government of India.

Scott, William P. (1988). Dictionary of Sociology, (Special Indian edition), New Delhi: Goyl Saab.

Shukla, G.L. (1998). "Social Planning and Social Policy" in K.K. Jacob (ed.) *Social Policy in India*, Udaipur: Himanshu Publications, (Rajasthan), pp. 33-44.

Singh, Katar (2009). *Rural Development Principles, Policies and Management*, 3rd edition, Sage Publications, New Delhi.

Weiss, Edith Brown (1990). 'In fairness to future generations', *Environment*, Vol. 32, No. 3, Apr., pp. 7-11, 30-1.

www.buckleyvann.com.au

6

Sanitation Programmes in India

We have seen in earlier chapters that the Five Year Plans and the other processes of social planning have not focussed much on the sanitation needs of the Indian population. Few initiatives have been taken in past three decades in this regard. The first sanitation programme of independent India—the 'Central Rural Sanitation Programme' (CRSP) was started in 1986. It was followed by the 'Total Sanitation Campaign' (TSC) started in 1999. The sanitation needs of the urban spaces were addressed by National Urban Sanitation Policy in 2008. The responsibility for providing sanitation facilities in India is decentralised and primarily rests with the local government bodies: Gram Panchayats (GPs) in rural areas and Municipalities or Corporations in urban areas. The state and central governments have a facilitating role that takes the form of framing enabling policies/guidelines, providing financial and capacity-building support and monitoring progress. This chapter makes an assessment of the sanitation programmes in India.

Sanitation Programmes in India (CRSP and TSC)

Sanitation could hardly attract the sustainable attention of government policy-makers of India till the last decade of the last century. The 'Central Rural Sanitation Programme' (CRSP) was started in 1986 by the 'Rural Development Department', Government of India as India's first national programme on rural sanitation. The CRSP interpreted sanitation as construction of household toilets, and focused on the promotion of a single technology model (double pit pour-flush toilets) through hardware subsidies to generate demand. To overcome the lapses of the earlier programme (the CRSP) and to widen the horizons of sanitation interventions, the Government of India launched the 'Total Sanitation Campaign' (TSC) in 1999 with the goal of achieving universal rural sanitation coverage by 2012. The specific advancement of this programme was the fact that it engaged the local governments (Panchayati Raj Institutions — PRIs) with significant involvement of communities. Further, the CRSP was a supply driven, infrastructure oriented programme that relied heavily on high levels of subsidy for latrine construction but the TSC was based on demand driven and awareness generating approach. The state and central governments had a facilitating role in the TSC that took the form of framing enabling policies, providing financial and capacity-building support, and monitoring progress.

The main objectives of the TSC included: bringing about an improvement in the general quality of life in the rural areas; accelerating sanitation coverage in rural areas to provide access to toilets to all by 2012; motivating communities and Panchayati Raj Institutions promoting sustainable sanitation facilities through awareness creation and health education; providing sanitation facilities and promoting hygiene education/sanitary habits in rural schools and Anganwadis by March 2013; encouraging cost-effective and appropriate technologies for ecologically safe and sustainable sanitation; and, developing community-managed environmental sanitation systems focusing on solid and liquid waste management.

The TSP began with start up activities related to conducting preliminary survey to assess the status of sanitation and hygiene practices and Information, Education and Communication (IEC) Activities which intend to create demand for sanitary facilities in the rural areas for households, schools, Anganwadis, Balwadies and Community Sanitary Complexes. It intended to develop Rural Sanitary Marts and Production Centres which are outlet dealing with the materials, hardware and designs required for the construction of not only sanitary latrines but also other sanitary facilities, such as soakage and compost pits, vermi-composting, washing platforms, certified domestic water filters and other sanitation and hygiene accessories. Production Centres are the means to improve production of cost-effective affordable sanitary materials. The Production Centres/Rural Sanitary Marts could be opened and operated by NGOs/SHGs/Women Organisations/Panchayats etc.

There was a sum of upto Rs 50 Lakhs, subject to the restriction of 5 per cent earmarked for alternate delivery mechanism (which included the cost for setting up RSMs and PCs) might be given to each TSC project as revolving fund. Further, the programme aimed to cover all the rural families. Incentive, as provided under the scheme, may be extended to Below Poverty Line (BPL) families, if the same is considered necessary for full involvement of the community. The construction of household toilets should be undertaken by the BPL household itself and on completion and use of the toilet by the BPL household, the cash incentive can be given to the BPL household in recognition of its achievement. All houses constructed for BPL families under Indira Awas Yojana shall invariably be provided with a toilet under TSC for that district. It is assumed that APL families, through motivation, will take up construction of the household latrines on their own. Further, the existing bucket latrines, if any, should be converted to sanitary latrines and the unit cost and sharing pattern shall be identical to that of construction of individual house hold latrines.

The Community Sanitary Complex, comprising an appropriate number of toilet seats, bathing cubicles, washing platforms, wash basins etc., can be set up in a place in the village. Construction of community complexes will be restricted only to places where individual household latrines cannot be constructed, for whatever reason. It also aimed at construction of institutional toilets including etc. (i) School Toilets and (ii) Anganwadi Toilets. Further, Panchayati Raj Institutions (PRIs) are required to put in place mechanisms for garbage collection and disposal and for preventing water-logging.

Further, to give a fillip to the TSC, the government introduced an innovative incentive programme known as

Nirmal Gram Puraskar (NGP) in 2003. The NGP offers a cash prize to motivate Gram Panchayats (GPs) to achieve total sanitation. In addition, the NGP is an attractive incentive as winners are felicitated by the President of India at the national level and by high-ranking dignitaries at the state level. The TSC has recently completed a decade of implementation (1999-2009) and the NGP has completed five years of operation (2005-10). Since its launch, the programme framework of the TSC and NGP has been based on a common national guideline whereas implementation has been decentralised to the state and district levels. The government launched National Urban Sanitation Policy in 2008 and identified 100 per cent sanitation as a goal during the 11th Five Year Plan.

Sanitation Programmes under NRHM

The National Rural Health Mission (NRHM) brought a strategic shift in the health structure and arrangements in India. It has made provisions of several new initiatives. It has new strategies, goals, plans of actions and institutional arrangements. The goals, core strategies and the plan of action of NRHM promise converging sanitation and hygiene programmes (mainly TSC) under NRHM. The convergence incorporates Information, Education and Communication (IEC) activities, rural sanitary marts, individual household toilets, women sanitary complex, and School Sanitation Programme. Under NRHM, Village Health and Sanitation Committee (VHSC) need to be formed in all the 6.38 revenue villages of India for promoting sanitation, hygiene and nutrition. In 2011, the mandate of the pre-existing Village Health and Sanitation Committee was expanded and the component of nutrition was added. They were renamed as Village Health, Sanitation and Nutrition Committee. Untied grants of Rs 10,000 are provided annually to VHSNC under NRHM, which are utilised through involvement of Panchayati Raj Representatives and other community members in many states. The number of VHSNCs constituted has increased to 4.95 lakhs in 2011 (as on June 2011). The District Health Mission guide activities of sanitation at district level, and promote joint IEC for public health, sanitation and hygiene, through the Committee, and promote household toilets and School Sanitation Programme. ASHAs are incentivised for promoting household toilets by the Mission. The guidelines for the functioning of the VHSC/VHSNC under the NRHM are also discussed here.

Goals: The VHSC/VHSNC is responsible for the overall health and development of the village. It will take into consideration of the problems of the community and the health and nutrition care providers and suggest mechanism to solve it. It will create public awareness about the essentials of health programmes, inform the community about all the government schemes and monitor all the health activities that are conducted in the village such as Village Health and Nutrition Day, mothers meeting etc. It will also play vital role for selecting and supporting the ASHA from the community.

Mechanisms: It will discuss and develop a village health plan based on an assessment of the village situation and priorities identified by the village community. It will analyse key issues and problems related to village level health and nutrition activities, give feedback on these to the Medical Officer of the PHC, and shall ensure that Public Dialogue is organised at regular intervals (once in six month) in the presence of Medical Officer of the Primary Health Care Centre.

Responsibilities: It will maintain village health register and the health information board. The health register and board will be put up at the most frequented section of the village and will have information about the mandated services in the Sub Centre/PHC. Along with the ANM, it will be responsible to conduct household survey in the village. It will ensure that the ANM visit the village on the fixed days and perform the stipulated activity as per the Sub Centre work plan; discuss the report submitted by ANM in the village level meeting and take appropriate action. Besides these, it will discuss every maternal or neonatal death that occurs in their village, analyse it, suggest necessary action to prevent such deaths and get these deaths registered in the Panchayat.

Utilisation of the Untied Grant: The untied grant of Rs 10,000 is a resource for community action at the local level and shall only be utilised for community activities after taking resolution in the VHSC monthly meeting. The VHSC will be responsible for arranging all the essential instruments such as BP instruments, weighing machine, examination table, screen for maintenance of privacy during health check up and other support required in organising Village Health and Nutrition Day in the village by the ANM. The committee from its untied fund will arrange for the tea/snacks for the gathered women, children and other beneficiaries during the Village Health and Nutrition Day; will contribute on behalf of 10 poor BPL families in a year @ Rs 300 for allotment of sanitary latrine under Total Sanitation Campaign; and provide Rs 100 to ASHA for organising monthly Village Health and Nutrition Day. Further, the fund can be utilised for village level activities such as cleanliness and sanitation drive, school health activities, building transport communication link for transferring the patient to health facilities, improving the facilities of the Anganwadi Centre and any other developmental activities for the village/community. During emergency like flood or any epidemic the committee will utilise the fund for the relief camps or supplies such as in case of flood it can supply Halogen tablet for purification of water, ORS, Bleaching powder etc.

An Assessment of Sanitation Programmes

The CRSP launched in 1986 could not succeed because of several policy and implementation limitations. The thrust of the programme was construction of latrines in households. However, soon it was realised that the constructed latrines were not being utilised by people. There were other limitations related to supportive infrastructure, designs and technology of the toilets also. However, the reasons for the failure of the CRSP were not assessed properly. A simplistic lack of motivation and behaviour change theory was proposed and the entire government machinery rested on that. And hence proper design, supportive infrastructure, institutional care, and awareness generation for motivation, behaviour change became the main thrust of the TSC programme. The CRSP metamorphosed into the TSC in 1999 and the later had broader designs, support base and supportive structures as discussed earlier.

An assessment of the TSC was carried out by the 'Department of Drinking Water and Sanitation', Ministry of Rural Development, Government of India after completion of one decade of the programme. The report (A Decade of the Total Sanitation Campaign: Rapid Assessment of Processes and

Outcomes, year not mentioned) finds that the TSC has achieved significant success in one decade. The sanitation coverage has increased significantly from 21 per cent in 2001 (Census, 2001) to more than 65 per cent. The number of Gram Panchayats which have won the Nirmal Gram Puraskar for achieving total sanitation has also increased to more than 22,000. The report finds that there is an undeniable upward trend in scaling up rural sanitation coverage. But the national performance aggregates conceal significant disparities among states and districts when it comes to the achievement of TSC goals. It also acknowledges that open defecation is a traditional behaviour in India and in most of the states, changing this practice is the biggest challenge.

A recent 'Evaluation Study on Total Sanitation Campaign' carried out by Programme Evaluation Organisation, Planning Commission (2013) has evaluated the sanitation programmes {including the pre-NRHM phase (1999-2005) and the NRHM phase (2005 onwards)} says that if we consider a household as a household practicing open defecation if at least one member of the family practices open defecation, the estimated percentage of open defecation in rural India comes to 72.63 per cent. It adds that during the first six years of its implementation (i.e., 1999-2005), TSC programme did not focus on Solid and Liquid Waste Management and it was included as separate component only in 2006. The study found that only 14 per cent of the Gram Panchayats have adopted any kind of waste management system. Though, individual cases of success have been observed but collective institutional effort in this direction still remains a distant dream.

In terms of states, except in the state of Karnataka, Kerala, Sikkim, Tamil Nadu, Haryana and Gujarat, households in most of the other states reported that there exist issues relating to toilet structures like roof, walls, doors as well as depth of the pit. Only 59 per cent households have toilets that are both covered on all sides and have a roof. The percentage ranges from only 12.3 per cent in West Bengal to 99 per cent in Sikkim. Non-availability of adequate water is also a problem. Only about 46 per cent households are reported to have adequate water for flushing and tap water is available in the latrines in only 3.61 per cent households.

Under TSC there is a provision for conversion of existing bucket latrines to sanitary latrines since bucket latrines are not permitted. The study found that 4.4 per cent households are still using bucket toilets. Bucket type toilets are still prominently used by the households of Manipur. Although interpersonal communication has been the most effective communication tool within the IEC framework, the report finds that, most projects have not used this tool in the prescribed manner. Only 46 per cent Gram Panchayats have appointed motivators and most of the motivators have been assigned the role to persuade people to construct the latrines. The outcome of the IEC activities may be the construction of a number of household latrines, but it has been unable to create demand for sanitation by way of making people aware of public health impact of this.

The important thrust of the TSC was to develop the start up activities and supportive infrastructure for sanitation. Community Sanitary Complexes were to be constructed where individual household latrines cannot be constructed or at the public places, markets etc, where large scale congregation of people takes place. The study found that 83 per cent of the selected Gram Panchayats have no community sanitary complexes. Till March 2009 only about 50 per cent target of the construction of community sanitary complex/women sanitary complex could be achieved. Maintenance of these complexes appeared to be the biggest problem. The idea of using community toilets as an effective alternative for the poorest section has not really caught up in most of the states. About 25 per cent selected households in Maharashtra are using community toilets. Besides this, a small percentage of households in Gujarat, Tamil Nadu and Haryana are using community toilets as an alternative. Though it was expected that by the year 2009 all government schools and anganwadi centres would be provided with the toilet facilities, the study found that many government schools in Manipur, Assam, Bihar, Meghalaya, Madhya Pradesh and Jharkhand are still without any sanitary facilities. Many anganwadis are still without toilets even in NGP awarded Gram Panchayats. The scheme of "enhanced rent" for anganwadis situated in the private buildings has not delivered the desired result. Hence, sanitary facilities could not be provided to the most of the anganwadis in private buildings.

One of the purposes of launching of Nirmal Gram Puraskar was to recognise the efforts made by PRIs and institutions towards ensuring full sanitation. About 80 per cent Gram Panchayats who have been awarded with NGP have said that there has been remarkable decrease in open defecation. It was also found that more people in NGP villages are adopting better hygienic practices and hence less affected by the water borne diseases. The evaluation study has found that the people in the Nirmal Grams Panchayats are enjoying better quality of life by way of fewer incidences of diseases caused by improper hygiene and unsafe water supply, reduced medical expenses and increased time for earning. Nearly 90 per cent of the selected households who are having toilets feel that their "general well being" have been improved and 96 per cent of the households in this category feel that with the availability of the toilet women feel more secured. But the veracity of ODF (Open Defecation Free) status is a matter of concern. About 15 per cent households of the Gram Panchayats awarded with Nirmal Gram Puraskar have reported that some of their family members still resort to open defecation. Though only 0.65 per cent NGP awarded Gram Panchayats reported non-availability of toilets in the schools, for anganwadis, this percentage comes to 17 per cent.

Further, the success achieved in the NGP villages is also not very sustainable. Overall, Kerala is the best performer with 87 per cent of its GPs having won NGP awards. By contrast, only two per cent GPs in Bihar have won this award, reflecting the state of sanitation in the region (India Human Development Report, 2011: 172-73). In a study conducted by UNICEF and TARU in 2008, of 162 GPs which had received NGPs in six states (Andhra Pradesh, Chhattisgarh, Maharashtra, Tamil Nadu, Uttar Pradesh, and West Bengal), it was found that 81 per cent households had individual household toilets. Of these only 64 per cent were reported to be using them and six per cent were using community toilets. The remaining households (30 per cent) were going for open defecation. Further, many toilets were not used for the purpose of defecating but for storing, bathing, and washing purposes. Of the 162 GPs which had received NGPs, only four per cent (mostly from Maharashtra) had sustained the Open Defecation Free (ODF) status. In the remaining GPs, there were households who had gone back to defecating in the open (*ibid*: 173-74).

The Sixth Common Review Mission Report on NRHM (Common Review Mission, 2012) finds effective functioning of VHSNCs in several states. Support for water and sanitation activities through ASHA and VHSNCs in states correlates with a strong, well constituted and functional VHSNCs. This was evident in Odisha, Chhattisgarh and Tamil Nadu. Odisha has vibrant Gaon Kalyan Samitis that meet regularly and effectively use untied funds for water and sanitation activities and awareness programmes on Water, Sanitation and Hygiene (WASH). ASHA plays an important role in mobilising communities for promotion of individual household toilets. In Tamil Nadu vigilant VHSNCs ensure adequate coverage of water and sanitation programmes. However, in Chhattisgarh in spite of good village level convergence through the medium of VHSNCs, a prominent involvement of VHSNC and/or Mitanins in water and sanitation activities could not be established.

In Uttar Pradesh VHSNCs are active in water purification, prevention of water logging, vector control etc., but challenges such as, low utilisation of allocated funds on account of lack of co-ordination with PRI, or delayed fund transfer remain. They are yet to adopt the new nomenclature of 'VHSNC'. Inclusion of nutrition component is limiting their efficiency on this aspect (Common Review Mission, 2012: 56-57). Further, in Assam, ASHAs are member secretary of VHSNCs. VHSNC fund is largely being used for water and sanitation activities (*ibid*: 114). In Kerala, all 19291 wards have VHSNC equivalent ward health sanitation and nutrition committee. Participation of PRIs is high in Ward Health Sanitation and Nutrition Committees (WHSNCs) and Rogi Kalyan Samitis (RKS) equivalent Hospital Development Committees (*ibid*: 116).

The fifth Common Review Mission Report on NRHM (Common Review Mission, 2011) gives the details of the VHSNCs formed in revenue villages in various states as given in Table 2. The figures reflect that in three states, namely—Bihar, Himachal Pradesh and Uttar Pradesh, the number of VHSNCs formed is much lesser than the revenue villages. The NRHM has assigned most of the tasks of TSC to the VHSNCs.

However, such committees are not formed in all the villages of all the states. Further, the infrastructure development activities can't be performed by such committees. The untied funds sanctioned to such VHSNCs are too little to take up any infrastructure development work. The district health committees also can't help the VHSNCs in such assignments.

Table 1: Number of VHSNCs and Revenue Villages in Various States

States	*VHSNCs formed*	*Revenue Villages*	*States*	*VHSNCs formed*	*Revenue Villages*
Andhra Pradesh	21916	26613	Jharkhand	32643	30012
Assam	26312	26312	Karnataka	24208	27481
Bihar	7978	45098	Odisha	45471	47529
Chhattisgarh	18706	19642	Rajasthan	43437	44672
Goa	308	359	Sikkim	641	452
Gujarat	17954	17330	Uttarakhand	15431	16826
Haryana	6280	6955	Uttar Pradesh	51914	106000
Himachal Pradesh	3243	17595			

(5th Common Review Mission Report, 2011 p. 114)

The VHSCs/VHSNCs have been primarily assigned the responsibility to motivate rural people to have latrines in their houses. If we look up the VHSNCs from the perspective of the priorities and targets of the TSCs, we find that many of the targets of the TSCs go unattained under the NRHM. This is a major departure from the goals of the TSC. The findings of another study carried out in seven states to assess the functioning of NRHM regarding promoting adequate sanitation with special reference to the functioning of VHSNCs reveal that although the VHSNCs report some success in performing various tasks assigned to them, their performance on motivating people to construct toilets in their houses are almost marginal. The specific findings of the study in relation to the seven states are given in brief. The findings of 'Evaluation Study of National Rural Health Mission (NRHM) in seven States' (2011) suggest the following:

Uttar Pradesh: In Uttar Pradesh about 41 Gram Panchayat (GP) members were interviewed in the selected districts. All of these respondents told about existence of VHSC in their village. However, the VHSC is not playing its roles properly and even among these, only 44 per cent VHSCs are involved in preparing any Village Health Plan (VHP) and get consulted over the issues/ problems related to village level health and nutrition. Regarding availability of sanitation facilities in village, only 15 per cent have reported availability of community toilets in the village. In 63 per cent village sanitation is good. Seventy-one per cent VHSCs have received untied funds and 27 per cent have reported about facing problems in the implementation.

Madhya Pradesh: In Madhya Pradesh, 39 GP members have been interviewed in the selected districts for evaluation. Their opinion and perception about existing facilities and services reveal that 95 per cent reported about the existence of VHSC in their village. VHSC is not playing its roles properly and nearly 70 per cent VHSCs are involved in preparing any VHP and analysis of issues/problems related to village level health and nutrition. Seventy per cent GP members have reported that they are maintaining village health calendar. Regarding availability of common health and sanitation facilities in village, only eight per cent have reported availability of community toilets in their villages. In only 50 per cent village sanitation is in good condition and 51 per cent VHSCs have received untied funds.

Jharkhand: In Jharkhand state, 26 GP members have been interviewed in the selected districts for evaluation. Only eight per cent of them reported existence of VHSC in the village. Further, only 31 per cent VHSCs are involved in preparing any VHP and analysis of the issues/problems related to village level health and nutrition and only four per cent GP members have reported maintenance of any village health calendar. No community toilet is available in the villages. As reported, only 27 per cent villages' sanitation is in good condition.

Odisha: In Odisha state, 39 GP members have been interviewed in the selected districts for functioning of VHSCs. No one has told about existence of VHSC in the village. Further, only 31 per cent VHSCs are involved in preparing VHP and analysis of the issues/problems related to village level health and nutrition and only four per cent GP members reported that they are maintaining any village health calendar. There are no community toilets in the village. In only 27 per cent village, sanitation is in good condition.

Assam: In Assam state, 40 GP members have been interviewed in the selected districts for evaluation of functioning of VHSCs. In the case of Assam about 85 per cent GPs has reported about preparing any VHP and analyse the issues/problems related to village level health and nutrition and only 67 per cent GP has told that they are maintaining any village health calendar. There are no community toilets in the village and no one has reported about sanitation is in good condition. Almost 95 per cent VHSC has received untied funds.

Jammu and Kashmir: In Jammu and Kashmir state, 38 GP members have been interviewed in the selected districts. No one has reported about existence of VHSC in the village. Only 26 per cent GPs has reported about preparing any VHP and 13 per cent analyse the issues/problems related to village level health and nutrition. No community toilets is there in the village and only 13 per cent has reported about sanitation is in good condition. Thirty seven per cent VHSC has received untied funds.

Tamil Nadu: In Tamil Nadu state, 37 GP members have been interviewed in the selected districts for evaluation of functioning of VHSCs. Interestingly, 87 per cent VHSCs are involved in preparation of their VHPs and 56 per cent had reported about analysing the issues/problems related to village level health and nutrition. The results show active involvement of VHSCs in controlling the healthcare services in the villages. Regarding availability of common health and sanitation facilities in village, 70 per cent village have community toilets. In 81 per cent village sanitation is in good condition. Further, 97 per cent VHSC has received untied funds.

A critical inquiry of the findings of the various evaluation report, as discussed above, suggest that the assessments report are primarily programme evaluations and hence simplistic (mostly bureaucratic) and missing the basic ground realities of causation of poor sanitation. Broadly, the report finds that lack of toilets (individual as well community) and lack of motivation cum awareness are the main reasons of non-adoption of latrines/ toilets and continuation of the open defecation behaviour. The assessment report blames the IEC and the GPs for their underperformance. However, the report fails in identifying the 'strategic wrongs' inherent in the whole approach and design of the government run programmes.

Urban Sanitation Policy

The government launched National Urban Sanitation Policy in 2008 and identified 100 per cent sanitation as a goal during the 11th Five Year Plan. According to NUSP, 7.87 per cent of urban households defecate in the open, 8.13 per cent use community latrines, 19.49 per cent share latrines, 18.5 per cent have no access to drainage, and 39.8 per cent are connected to open drains. The ultimate objective was that all urban dwellers get access to and be able to use safe and hygienic sanitation facilities and arrangements so that no one defecates in the open. The states were expected to prepare their own strategies and the cities were to prepare model city sanitation plans. The overall goal of this policy is to transform urban India into community-driven, totally sanitised, healthy and livable cities and towns.

Urbanisation and Sanitation

According to the 12th Five Year Plan document, about 377 million Indians comprising of about 31 per cent of the country's population live in urban areas (as per Census 2011). The urban population in India is relatively smaller than several other countries in the world for example, 45 per cent in China, 54 per cent in Indonesia, 78 per cent in Mexico and 87 per cent in Brazil (12th Five Year Plan, Vol. II, 2013). With the more rapid growth of the Indian economy in recent years, the rate of urbanisation will increase. Projections are that by 2031, about 600 million Indians will reside in urban areas, an increase of over 200 million in just 20 years.

The 12th Plan document reveals that there is a concentration of the urban population in large cities and existing urban agglomerations in India. As per census 2011, there are 53 million plus cities accounting for about 43 per cent of India's urban population. Class-I cities with population over three lakh accounted for about 56 per cent of the urban population and with a population ranging from one lakh to three lakh accounted for another 14 per cent. This pattern of population concentration in large cities reflects spatial polarisation of the employment opportunities. While it is expected that gains from an agglomeration economy would lead to some polarisation of economic activities, there is a need for developing an optimal portfolio of cities by drawing regional development plans and promoting growth centres that are employment intensive and consistent with the economic potential including the natural endowment of cities and regions. The availability of water to provide for the needs of a large urban population must be a critical factor in plans for urban development.

Census 2011 notes that the number of towns in India increased from 5,161 in 2001 to as many as 7,935 in 2011. It points out that almost all of this increase was in the growth of 'census' towns (which increased by 2,532) rather than 'statutory' towns (which increased by only 242). 'Statutory' towns are towns with municipalities or corporations. Whereas, census' towns are agglomerations that grow in rural and peri-urban areas, with densification of population that do not have an effective urban governance structure or requisite urban infrastructure, for example, sanitation, roads and so on in place.

These patterns of urbanisation often increase the load in urban spaces and manifest in multiple types of problems. According to the Twelfth Plan, broadly, the urban sector in India faces two distinct but mutually linked sets of challenges. Based on NSS Report No. 508 (2004–05) it is estimated that the number of urban poor had increased by 34.4 per cent from 1973 to 2004. The NSS (66th round) has estimated that during the period 2004–05 and 2009–10, the unemployment rate in terms of the usual status decrease by one percentage point for both, urban male and females notwithstanding an impressive growth registered by the economy in this period. Hence, the first challenge is to significantly step up the rate of creation of jobs in the urban sector. The second set of challenges before the Government is to guide the process of urbanisation and ensure that basic services, for example, sanitation, water supply, and basic housing are provided to urban citizens expected to be around 600 million within 20 years. Sanitation and water supply are very basic problems in urban spaces in India. In a city sanitation study, conducted by the MoUD (2010) none of the 423 cities where the study was conducted were found to be 'healthy and clean'. The Water and Sanitation Programme of the World Bank, using data for 2006, suggested that per capita economic cost of inadequate sanitation in India is Rs 2,180. The cost in terms of Disability Adjusted Life Years (DALY) of diarrhoeal disease for children from poor sanitation is estimated at Rs 500 crore (HPEC, 2011).

The 12th Plan document specifically talks about the sanitation conditions prevailing in many of the urban spaces. Even a partial sewerage network is absent in 4,861 cities and towns in India. Almost 50 per cent of households in cities like Bangalore and Hyderabad do not have sewerage connections. As per 2011 census, about 13 per cent of urban households do not have access to any form of latrine facility and defecate in the open. Census 2011 also revealed that about 37 per cent of urban households are connected with open drainage and another 18 per cent are not connected at all. Less than 20 per cent of the road network is covered by storm water drains. As per the report of the Central Pollution Control Board (CPCB) 2009, only about 20 per cent sewage generated was treated before disposal in Class I cities and Class II towns (as per 2001 census). As per CPCB report brought out in 2005, about 1,15,000 MT of Municipal Solid Waste is generated daily in the country. However, scientific disposal of the waste generated is almost non-existent.

The Jawaharlal Nehru National Urban Renewal Mission (JNNURM) was launched in December 2005 for a period of seven years with an outlay of Rs 66,085 crore. The objectives of the scheme included empowerment of Urban Local Bodies (ULBs), planned and holistic development of cities and making them inclusive. The scheme mandated preparation of City Development Plans (CDP) and a set of urban reforms at State and Municipal levels. JNNURM renewed the focus on urban renewal and gave impetus to many urban reforms. Central allocation of Rs 66,085 crore led to overall commitment of investment of Rs 1,23,711 crore under the scheme.

The JNNURM integrates urban drainage within the overall

urban development plans in 63 of the largest cities in India.

This initiative is part of the Government of India's commitment to meet the Millennium Development Goals and is targeted to be achieved by 2011. The JNNURM covers integrated infrastructural development with provision of planned roads, environmental upgradation and adequate urban infrastructure, particularly provision of drinking water in each house, rain water harvesting, planned sewage and modern drainage systems and water recycling. The Ministry of Urban Development (MUD) has been designated as the Executing Agency (EA) for the infrastructure and governance component of the JNNURM and the total budget outlay is 9000 million Euros over a seven year period (Gupta, Kapil, 2007).

Some of the key inadequacies noted during implementation of the programme included failure to mainstream urban planning, incomplete reforms and slow progress in project implementation. Delay in securing land for projects and obtaining approval from various regulatory authorities also led to delay in implementation of some of the projects. Despite the stress on urban planning, in many cities the planning process is yet to be strengthened and made participatory. Invariably peri–urban areas around cities' limits have grown haphazardly. Lack of participatory planning has resulted in programmes suffering from 'lack of ownership'.

Lapses in Sanitation Programmes in India

The sanitation promoting programmes in India (CRSP, TSP and initiative taken under NRHM) fail to develop strategies to develop sanitation standards in India at large. There is visible 'sanitation deficits' in policy formulation, implementation and technology appropriation within not only these sanitation promoting programmes but in the larger development strategy followed in India. The important sanitations lapses are given here:

- Sanitation standards are undefined in India. 'Open defecation free environment' is not the only measurable standard or indicator. Many other standards need to be defined.
- Sanitation is yet to become a core thrust of the public health facilities and primary healthcare.

- There is no defined sanitation standard for industries, factories, urban spaces, Municipalities, housing colonies or even neighbourhoods.
- Associating sanitation only with open defecation of the households is giving a very narrow meaning to sanitation.
- Sanitation infrastructure and its technological base is highly inadequate in India.
- Sanitation is neither seen as a right nor a duty. There is no punishment for violators.
- There is no binding sanitation policy at national or even state level.
- The religiously, culturally or even socially approved insanitary works are not banned.
- No effort has been made to understand the 'open defecation' behaviour of people. It has been assumed that provision or availability of toilets/latrines will change the behaviour automatically or awareness generation will help in changing the behaviour. This is the biggest strategic lapse. A sociological explanation will help in understanding the behaviour more appropriately and will suggest measures to control it also (for further details, see Akram, 2014).

India is yet to witness the sanitation phase or a public health movement. Even the primary healthcare is not much grounded in many of the states of India in the true spirit of the concept. The Health Survey and Development Committee, also known as the Bhore committee, had submitted its report way back in 1946. This report is considered as the backbone of India's health planning and programmes. It laid emphasis on integration of curative and preventive medicine at all levels. It suggested development of one primary health centre (PHC), manned by two doctors, one nurse, four public health nurses, four midwives, four trained dhais and two sanitary inspectors and few other staff. The sanitary inspectors were expected to take care of the sanitations needs of people. The primary health centres are yet to appoint the sanitary inspectors.

Till the launch of NRHM, health policies and programmes in India didn't treat sanitation as a component of health or public health. Although NRHM promises some efforts in ensuring sanitation at village level through promoting construction of individual household toilets, the construction of community toilets, sanitary complexes and supportive infrastructure, as designed by the TSC, are almost missing in various states. The household or public toilets cannot work without continuous availability of water. Further, the toilets cannot be used unless hygienic conditions are maintained through proper cleaning and maintenance. But such facilities are poorly funded in India. And further, such facilities are poorly designed and even more poorly implemented (through bureaucratic targetism). The under achievements of various development plans and programmes and the wastage and pilferage of the resources are 'bureaucratically managed' by blaming the people for their cultural poverty and illiteracy (povertism). In a society which is culturally distanced from the notion of scientific sanitation, massive public health intervention for sanitation could have helped in achieving the goals. Unfortunately, it is missing.

The cultural taboos still work as barriers in constructing toilets in many households. On the other, population living below poverty line find it difficult to construct and maintain toilets. The lack of sanitation values and uniform standards create other hurdles in promoting sanitation for all. Both the incentive based and the demand driven programmes fail to address the sanitation needs because of the lack of sanitation socialisation at individual and family level. The urban as well as rural local bodies, responsible for ensuring public sanitation, somehow miss in mobilising comprehensive engagement of masses in sanitation programmes. Hence, the myopic programmes, cannot help in achieving sanitation goals for India. India needs a massive drive for achieving universal sanitation.

References

A Decade of the Total Sanitation Campaign: Rapid Assessment of Processes and Outcomes (year not mentioned) Vol. 1: Main Report, WSP, DDWS, Ministry of Rural Development, Government of India, New Delhi.

Akram, M. (2014). 'Sanitation Needs of India and NRHM: A Strategic Assessment' in *National Rural Health Mission: An Unfinished Agenda*, edited by Sharma, S. and Joe, W., New Delhi: Bookwell Publications.

Annual Report to the People on Health (2010), Ministry of Health and Family Welfare, Government of India, September 2010.

Common Review Mission Report, Fifth (2011), Ministry of Health and Family Welfare, Government of India, Nirman Bhawan, New Delhi.

Common Review Mission Report, Sixth (2012), Ministry of Health and Family Welfare, Government of India, Nirman Bhawan, New Delhi.

Evaluation Study of National Rural Health Mission (NRHM) in 7 States (Feb 2011), Programme Evaluation Organisation, Planning Commission, Government of India, New Delhi.

Evaluation Study on Total Sanitation Campaign (2013), Programme Evaluation Organisation, Planning Commission, Government of India, New Delhi.

Gupta, K. (2007), 'Strategies for integrated urban drainage management in monsoon rainfall areas with special reference to the Indian subcontinent', *International Symposium on New Directions in Urban Water Management,* 12-14 September 2007, UNESCO Paris.

India Human Development Report: Towards Social Inclusion (2011), Institute of Applied Manpower Research, Planning Commission, Government of India, New Delhi: Oxford University Press.

Wikipedia—the free encyclopedia at en.m.wikipedia.org

7

Sanitation Reforms and Social Movement

Sanitation is a way of life. Sanitation deficits prevailing in India questions the rationale of Indian ways of living on many accounts. Public sanitation cannot be ensured only through personal hygiene or private cleanliness; it can be attained through public and community hygiene and healthy life styles. The western or industrial societies attained it through massive sanitation reforms in 19th and 20th centuries. Improved technology and awakened public conscience played very important role in actualising sanitation reforms. The need of engaging the masses in attaining public sanitation is still the biggest challenge in India. The government initiative to achieve the goals of various sanitation programmes could yield little rewards. Public sanitation cannot be attained in India without engaging the citizens at the mass level.

Sanitation problems in India are centred on the realities of caste, class, religion, ethnicity and region. Governance, administration and management of sanitation initiatives have their effectiveness or otherwise depending upon the activism, passivism, neutrality or apathy of social groups/communities around which these initiatives operate. The negative impacts of sanitation deficits also depend upon the socio-administrative variables.

A cursory looks on availability of sanitation infrastructure in general and improved toilets in particular across the states of India reveal that states of India do not present a uniform sanitation pattern. There are inequalities and inequities in terms of availabilities of such infrastructure. What does cause such differentials? We have discussed in earlier chapters that several factors work together in causing sanitation deficit. Sanitation deficit is a cumulative manifestation of technological deficit, public health deficit, cultural deficit, development deficit, policy deficit and implementation deficit. In the first chapter, we have argued that contestation deficit is also an important factor for causation and perpetuation of insanitation in India as social arrangements producing insanitation need to be contested and corrected. In a society where cultural factors play an important role in preservation of insanitation, social contestation is very important. The present chapter looks at sanitation from this perspective.

Sanitation, as a hygienic and scientific social action, is yet to become a part of socialisation goal of individuals at a larger level in India. Socialisation is a process of internalisation of the norms, values and cultural patterns by the individuals. Socialisation is a lifelong process and engages several agencies at different levels. Socialisation begins just after birth and continues till death. It takes place both at formal and informal levels. According to sociologists, a very important goal of socialisation, during early childhood, is toilet training. An infant starts to develop an independent identity only after proper toilet training. In a country like India, where toilets themselves are not available, toilet training is far away cry. A country having huge population who are never getting any toilet training cannot attain public sanitation as such. The family is the first agency of socialisation and the parents and kins are the most important role models for the infants. An environment in which the role models fail to impart any hygienic and scientific training related to toilets manners, the process of even early socialisation is never complete. There are several factors responsible for this situation. We will see them one by one:

1. Lack of technological support and absence of improved infrastructure has created a gap; the masses in general are not

exposed to a hygienic way of life. Socialisation agencies failed to impart the necessary techniques and tools for adopting sanitation in the personal life of individuals or families. The first formal agency of socialisation-schools, failed to inculcate the sanitation values among the children because of lack of proper infrastructure. Majority of government schools, almost in all states of India, till very late were deprived of toilet or proper bathrooms/drinking water facilities. The situation has not improved even these days as large percentage of primary and secondary level schools (both government and private) are not having toilets.

The situation is even worse for those who do not go to schools as most of the cities in India do not have hygienic public toilets. In rural areas, the exposure to public toilets is a rare thing. We have seen in earlier chapters that almost fifty per cent of the households in India still do not have proper toilet facilities. Hence, the sanitation socialisation never take place for at least half of the Indian population and majority of this population come from socio-economically deprived categories like SCs, STs, BCs and poor cutting across the caste, religious and regional identities.

Public health institutions are also major agency for popularising healthy and hygienic life styles. The lack of proper public health facilities fail to create a health friendly environment. Sanitation is a healthy behaviour and public health institutions play very important role in popularising the sanitation goals. Differential access to public health institutions also causes differential sanitation socialisation.

2. Social control as a process, play very important role in regulating the public behaviour of the members of human societies. Social control adopts different mechanisms and agencies at different levels. Social sanctions related to unhygienic or insanitary behaviour are conspicuous because of their absence at the level of mass culture in India. The massive prevalence of open defecation in Indian states categorically reflects that there are no sanctions against such behaviour and open defecation is a socially approved behaviour.

3. The prevalence of notion of pollution and purity is a very important cultural practice responsible for the prevalence of

insanitary practices. Human faeces are culturally (also religiously) considered as 'polluted' and people maintain a physical distance from their own faeces after defecation. Hence, cleaning of the faeces is a culturally disapproved behaviour as any direct / indirect contact with them will pollute the person. This convention of maintaining a physical distance from the faeces has caused the growth of a mindset (worldview) which results into not having toilets inside the house or even close to dwelling places. People consequently prefer not to have a toilet at all.

4. The caste-based division of labour has created and preserved a social practice in which the cleaning of toilets or human faeces are the occupational duty of a specific caste popularly identified as scavengers. Scavenging caste is a historical-cultural creation. It frees the twice-born upper castes from the responsibility of cleaning both at the household and the public sphere levels. The scavengers are culturally (and religiously) bound to clean all pollutants from the households of others and also from the public places. Thus, one specific caste is bounded with the entire responsibility of maintaining cleanliness and rest of the communities have no responsibility related to it. This is the creation of sanitation unfriendly social environment.

5. The scavenging castes were considered as polluted and needed no hygienic way for performing the caste assigned roles. Members of these communities cleaned all pollutants including human faeces without using any hand gloves or sanitary tools. The lack of any sanitary protection not only demeaned the job but also the 'person' of those engaged in such works. They were also considered as polluted and physical distance from them was maintained by the pure castes.

6. The sewer system in modern cities adopted the scientific tools but continued the cultural practices of caste-based division of work and insanitary practices. The sewer systems, controlled and developed by urban local bodies, also suffer from technology deficit. They are not supported by proper sewage treatment plants. Hence the sewage is not treated properly and is simply dumped outside the cities. This is very unhygienic and insanitary. Further, the workers employed at the lower level are mostly the persons coming from lower castes (often the ex-scavengers).

Thus, it did not break the caste-based division of work rather reinforce it. Besides, the number of such workers is much lesser than their required number (as per the work load). Hence the excessive workload on few people leave lots of backlog and the work is never completed as per the required schedule.

7. The availability of even well-equipped sewer system is not very common in many states of India. The newly developing census towns and cities often do not have the sewer systems in many states. The drainage system is also not functioning well. Water logging is a very common problem in such cities. The blocked drainage system creates several types of problems.

8. The sanitation culture is not prevailing because of absence of participation of masses in the sanitation work. The public spheres present dirty and filthy looks. Littering is very common in all public places. The public toilets are very unhygienic and dirty. The individual houses are without proper sanitation infrastructure. Society, as such, does not disapprove the insanitary behaviour. At a larger level, we can say, the culture of insanitation prevails. The polluting industries and factories play role of catalysts in adding on the insanitary environment. We have also discussed earlier how Indian railways platforms, railway tracks, bus stands, river banks etc., present the ugly picture of insanitation.

9. The lack of proper employment conditions (largely contractual labour) for the sweeper, cleaner and other staff engaged in cleanliness and sanitation related work also create hindrance in smooth functioning of the local bodies. Strike, *dharna*, rallies are very common. All these activities adversely affect their work. The pollutants, dirt, filth and other such things, if not removed on daily basis, create a very unhygienic surrounding and neighbourhood. The lackadaisical approach of the government and the local level bodies are quite visible from their ad hoc approaches.

10. The lack of sanitation standard is a major cause of prevailing sanitation deficit in India. A defined sanitation standard, at the macro level, helps in making the sanitation goals clear and visible. The factories and industrial houses including the public sector units fail to provide the necessary sanitation infrastructure. The industrial pollution is a major cause

of insanitation. The cities, tourist places and other public spheres do not follow any specific sanitation standard.

11. The sectoral planning mechanism in India is also responsible for causation of insanitation. Sanitation and environmental concerns were not declared objectives of any of the ministries till very late. India has no sanitation policy. There is hardly any public law related to sanitation guidelines.

12. Contestation deficit is also an important factor for perpetuation of insanitation. Social arrangements producing insanitation needs to be contested and corrected. In a society where cultural factors play an important role in preservation of insanitation, social contestation is very important. Lack of social reforms addressing the sanitation issues is a major cause of prevailing insanitation culture in India.

These problems together create a culture of insanitation. The situation gets worst when collaborated by culture of poverty and governmental apathy. The bureaucratic managerialism is responsible for failure in incorporating any sincere innovation for improving sanitation. The lack of corporate sensitivity is also responsible for compounding of the problem.

Sanitation Reforms

Sanitation, as we have defined it in the first chapter, is a conscious and deliberate behaviour. It is a rational social act. It is learnt through training and socialisation. It needs some form of formal and informal social control also. It needs a sense of duty and responsibility; it needs a sense of responsible citizenship. Looking at it from the perspective of socialisation and voluntarism, it finds close association with notions of civil liberty and civil societism. Looking at it from the perspective of social control and dutifulness, it finds close association with systems of governance. India, being the largest democracy of the world, provides enough opportunity for both. However, even after six decades of attaining independence from the imperialist forces, India has failed to attain the sanitation goals at the larger level. The democratic planning and the socialist goals could not help to attain the sanitation goals. Both the cultural deficits and technological deficit operate simultaneously to cause sanitation deficit in India. Sanitation reforms need to challenge the barriers created by cultural ethos as well as the technological gaps.

When not supported by the prevailing cultural patterns, sanitation reforms need a kind of protest against the cultural patterns and even ethos. It needs a social reform and even a social transformation. The biggest hurdle in the path of adopting a sanitised way of life is the cultural practice of pollution and purity. Sanitation in India needs to challenge the age old practices of pollution and purity. Sanitation needs a mass mobilisation against the practice of pollution and purity. Sanitation needs a social movement to transform the caste-based division of labour with special reference to the caste bases of scavenging and sweeping occupations. At the same time, sanitation reforms need a technological upgradation at every possible level. The reforms need realistic and sustainable planning and sincere implementation. It needs committed governance.

The issue of sanitation reform is not merely related to availability of sanitation infrastructure. Sanitation reform needs reforms at the level of governance, citizenship, dutifulness, planning, implementation and above all the worldviews of the people. Sanitation reforms need the much awaited democratic and civil reforms in India. The problems related to insanitation victimise those who are at the bottom of social and economic hierarchy. Sanitation needs are the needs of the deprived, marginalised and excluded social categories. The perpetuation of the insanitary situation in India is a reflection of the continued marginalisation of the socially and economically deprived categories. The problem is structured in the structured inequalities of India. The structural reforms cannot be attained merely through cosmetic efforts; they need massive mobilisation. They need social contestation and social movements.

Thinking of a mass mobilisation supporting sanitation reforms in India poses several questions: Will that be a spontaneous mobilisation or a deliberate? If spontaneous then why it did not occur so long in India? If deliberate then how it can be achieved? Who will take the initiative? Who will get benefitted by such reforms? Who will oppose such mobilisation? What will be the impact of such mobilisation in the structural and cultural patterns? Will this influence the electoral politics? What will be the economic consequence of such moves? For answering such questions, we need to sociologically examine various types of social mobilisations and especially the social movements.

The recently launched *Swachh Bharat Abhiyan* (SBA) by the union government is definitely a positive step. The initiative has drawn the attention of the urban masses towards the need of cleanliness in public sphere. Participation of the politicians, bureaucrats, academicians, social activists, celebrities, sports persons and above all the common people in such drives at collective level will have lasting impact. It has brought the cleanliness issue to the forefront. A clean neighbourhood is the first step towards sanitation. It has reduced the distance between the broom and the masses. This symbolic effort has made people conscious about the dirty and filthy micro environment we live in. But, there are simple questions: Can this cleanliness drive be sustained? Can it be converted into a mission or a movement? Are we ready to initiate a social movement for achieving sanitation for all? These are some of the questions coming to our mind at this moment.

When we look at the initiatives made through SBA from sanitation perspective, we are left with a simple question: Can we equate cleanliness with sanitation? The answer is no. Cleanliness is one step towards sanitation; but sanitation includes several other things. We have seen in earlier chapters that sanitation is a multi-dimensional phenomenon and can be addressed only through multi-dimensional and multi-layered efforts. Sanitation is a healthy way of life adopted at the collective level; it is promoting hygiene in public life; it is related to technological improvement; it is associated with public health facilities and public health culture; it is related with improving the infrastructure facilities; it is associated with public services; it is related with dutifulness and social responsibility; it is attached with better governance and administration; it is integrated with resource management and better planning and many more such things.

Sanitation, as a healthy and hygienic way of life, cannot be seen without public health culture. Any effort for promoting sanitation in India cannot overlook the public health facilities and above all the public health structure. The shortcoming related to sanitation, very often are shortcoming related to the public health culture of our nation. The states performing well in sanitation are the states having better public health facilities.

Other social determinants, like poverty and education also play very important role in this regard.

Hence, sanitation requires a larger social movement in India; a social movement which will address all the possible dimensions related to causation of insanitation. We have summarised the important factors causing insanitation in India, earlier, in this chapter. A social movement should address to all these factors. But again, an important question is arising: Can any single social movement bring the desirable changes in all the causative factors of insanitation? Before answering this question, we need to briefly see, what we mean by social movement. We also need to understand how a social movement comes into existence.

Understanding Social Movement

Social movements are closely connected with the general problems of society. Different social movements came into existence in different contexts at different periods of time globally. Social movements have been seen from different perspectives. We have several theories related to social movements. The theories of social movements are based on general approaches to the principles of society's development. The question of classification of the theories of social movements is complicated, as there are many points of view on this question. However, according to Sergey Mamay, four main approaches for understanding social movements can be distinguished. Mamay has also provided a brief description of these four approaches.

1. Collective Behaviour Theory/Structural Strain Theory

Collective behaviour accounts are recognised as an orthodoxy in studies of social movements. The supporters of this approach consider social movements as semi-rational responses to abnormal conditions of structural strain between the major societal institutions; that strain causes malfunctioning of the whole social system. Ralph Turner, Lewis Killian, Talcott Parsons and Neil Smelser and others are some of the supporters of this approach. Smelser explained the mechanism of the emergence of social movements. This mechanism includes as the steps of movement articulation:

structural conduciveness ⟶ generalised belief ⟶ structural strain ⟶ precipitating factors ⟶ mobilisation of participants ⟶ mechanisms of social control.

In general, according to the collective behaviour approach, social movements are the symptom and manifestation of a sick society. A healthy society does not have social movements; it has a conditional form of political and social participation. 'Mass society accounts' and 'mass deprivation' accounts are close to the approach of 'collective behaviour' but there are some differences. Arendt and Kornhauser elaborated the mechanism of the emergence of social movement. According to their position, the normal or healthy society is characterised by strong class and group solidarities, which play the controlling function and prevent the manipulation of the people. But when this class or group solidarity becomes weak under the conditions of industrialisation and urbanisation, the processes of 'massification' ('anomie', 'atomisation', 'rootlessness') begin. These uprooted and atomised masses become vulnerable to direct mobilising appeals by powerful elites and charismatic leaders. Totalitarian movements emerge as a result. The 'mass deprivation' accounts (Gurr and others) add to the 'collective behaviour' approach that a social movement is a 'mild' (aborted, weak, undeveloped) form of revolutionary outbreak or an aspect of revolution.

2. Resource Mobilisation Theory

The second main approach to the problems of social movements is the 'resource mobilisation' approach. Among its exponents are Tilly, Zald, Ash, and Kitschelt. The 'resource mobilisation' theorists point out that social movements are rational and novel responses to new situations and new opportunities in society. Movements are seen as innovative forms of political participation which create and tap new political resources available in modern democratic societies. They are treated as emerging pressure groups or as embryonic parties. Social movements are no longer seen as symptomatic of social malfunction or pathology. They appear as a part of the political process.

3. New Social Movements' Interpretations

The third main approach is the 'new social movements' approach (Habermas, Offe and others), which is similar, to the 'new values' approach (Cotgrove, Inglehart, and others). The 'new social movements' interpretations treat social movements as both symptoms of, and solutions to, the contradictions inherent in the modern super-bureaucratic society. Social movements articulate the tension between the expanding spheres of human autonomy and growing regulation inherent in the logic of post-industrial development. This contradiction is reflected in new conflicts which, according to Habermas, no longer arise in the areas of material reproduction; they are no longer channeled through parties and organisations. Rather, the new conflicts arise in areas of cultural reproduction, social integration and socialisation.

The main feature of social movements, according to 'new social movements' theorists is their anti-state, anti-apparent turn of mind and action. New social movements, in contrast to old social movements, are produced by new contradictions of society, contradictions between individual and state. 'New values' theorists also stress that the condition of economic prosperity and political stability experienced by the post-1945 cohorts in the West, allow them to de-emphasise material values and lead them to embrace post-materialist values, reflecting 'higher' aesthetic, self-realisation, and creative needs. Inglehart's new values are essentially the anti-state contradictions identified by Habermas. These approaches change class interests (or transform them) into non-class but 'universal human' interests.

4. The Action-identity Approach

The fourth and last approach is the 'action-identity' paradigm (the main representatives are Touraine, Castells). Touraine considers that social movements are far from abnormal or pathological. Social movements not only prevent social stagnation, but also promise social emancipation. The established institutional forms and the underlying norms of knowledge (cognitive rules) and investment against which movements erupt are seen as impositions of the ruling classes, that is, of groups that dominate the processes of socio-economic reproduction and shape social norms. All these class-related social forms of domination are challenged by social movements, which are the principal class counter-actors.

The old form of industrial capitalism, according to Touraine, is gradually replaced by a new post-industrial, 'programmed' society with a fundamentally different pattern of class relations and class conflicts. In a programmed society the dominant class is the technocracy, and workers cease to be the main challengers of the status quo. The key class conflict is socio-cultural rather than socio-economic; it revolves around the control of knowledge and investment. A social movement is, according to Touraine, is the organised collective behaviour of a class actor struggling against its class adversary for the social control of its historicity.

The many approaches to the explanation of the phenomenon of social movements suggest that no one of them is able to explain everything. All the approaches may be correct in their local sphere, but they either stress attention to specific types of social movements and consider them as universal or put all the attention on a single aspect of the phenomenon of social movements and ignore others. Different accents give diverse outcomes.

Social Movement and Change

The 'collective behaviour' approach stresses the structural function of society and ignores its developing function. The normal state of society, according to Smelser, is the state where civil society completely correlates to social order. In practice, Smelser considers the situation when civil society does not develop. That is why the proponents of the 'collective behaviour' approach assess the situation of society's development as abnormal. That is why the 'collective behaviour' approach considers social movements irrational and psychopathological. This approach cannot answer the question: 'Why do dysfunctions emerge in the society?' But this approach is very successful in describing the mechanism of emergence and functioning of social movements during relatively stable stages of society's development. It is also very successful in describing the different biases in the process of emergence of social movements.

The 'resource mobilisation' approach, by contrast, explains the causes of the emergence of a social movement as a reaction of society to new changes. It also explains in a successful way the nature of social movements as an attempt to renew the social order in correspondence with the new changes in society. But the explanation of the causes of the emergence of social movements has only a general character and does not touch the contents of this process. The 'resource mobilisation' approach cannot answer the question, why and how do pathological social movements like fascism emerge and why do they lead society to self-destruction. This approach cannot explain the mechanism of emergence of social movements and ignores the principal differences between diverse types of social movements. Lastly, this approach cannot explain the existence of contradictions between social movements and the political system, which can lead to social explosions like revolution, harmful radical social change and the elimination of principal social actors and the old political system.

'New social movements', 'new values' and 'action-identity' approaches have one mutual foundation: the consideration that types of social movements depend on the stage of society's development. 'New social movement' supporters define 'old' social movements, which exist in industrial society, and 'new' social movements, which exist in post-industrial society. The mechanisms of emergence of social movements according to this approach are:

definite type of society ⟶ definite type of social contradictions ⟶ definite type of social movements

Industrial society produces contradictions between classes (with material group interests). The social order in this society cannot satisfy all the class interests in an adequate way and this is a base for the emergence of social movements. These movements have a class character; that is why the activity of movements became part of class struggle. The main contradiction of post-industrial society is the contradiction between the broadening autonomy of the individual and increasening regulation by the state. This is not a contradiction between groups of people, between classes; this is a contradiction between the individual as a person and the state as an institution. The contradiction is connected not with the material interests of people, but with non-material interests.

The position of the 'new values' approach does not touch class interests and deals with values. Industrial society has 'old' values and post-industrial society has 'new' values. When describing post-industrial societies and their social movements this is almost the same position as the 'new social movements' approach.

The point of view of the 'action-identity' approach is different. It also stresses differences between industrial and post-industrial societies, but does not abandon the framework of the class approach. It considers that classes in post-industrial society are different from those in industrial society, but they remain classes with material interests.

In order to explain the differences in these positions and demonstrate what they mean we must take into consideration that the transition from industrial to post-industrial society takes place over a long period of time, and any actually-existing western society has elements from both industrial and post-industrial societies. If the 'action-identity' paradigm exaggerates the elements from industrial society and underestimates the elements of post-industrial society, then the position of the 'new social movements' and 'new values' approaches is reversed. So it is senseless to judge any approach to social movements as wrong or right in general. Each of these approaches can be appropriate to a definite social (and political) situation, to definite social and historical circumstances of society.

Authors have also established that social order normally corresponds with civil society. Civil society and social order mutually affect each other, but the main role civil society plays is as a foundation to this connection. If there is full correlation between civil society and social order then society realises its interests through conventional forms and there is no need of social movements. But full correlation between civil society and social order is a rare event. As a rule, there is always a small or large degree of discrepancy between civil society and social order. This discrepancy produces new social interests which are not incorporated by social order. And, on such bases, social movements emerge. Social movements emerge, then, as a reaction of society to the discrepancy between civil society and social order. Social movements are not only a reaction, but are also an attempt to change social order in correspondence with civil society.

Thus the nature of social movements and their main cause —the discrepancy between civil society and social order — produces new, unsatisfied social interests. As the social movements are the consequences of new elements of civil society which are not incorporated into the social order, they are always unconventional. Civil society is normally in a state of change, but social structures are stable by their nature or at least have a tendency to stability. That is why social movements almost always exist. If the discrepancy between civil society and social order is large, then social movements are strong and numerous. If the discrepancy is small, then social movements are weak and more conventional.

Thus, the main notion for understanding social movements is that of social interests which are not adequately incorporated into the social order. Different types of interests produce different types of social movements. In principle, one society can produce several different types of social movements, but usually there is one main type of movements corresponding to each type of society.

What are the main social interests in a particular society? It depends on the characteristics of civil society and on the stage of its development. For example, industrial society produces one type of interests, post-industrial another. The hierarchy of interests at different stages of society's development is also different. So, post-industrial society lowers the importance of class interests (as material interests lose their centrality) and increases the importance of other interests.

Social Movement and *status quo* in India

Social movements play very important in bringing long lasting and radical changes. The theories discussed above reflect that social movements are relevant in almost all contexts and situations. Every society, in some or the other form, is in need of some social movement. If we look at the basics of social movement, we find that social movement has several basic components which are: ideology, identity, organisation, leadership, collective mobilisation, change orientation, mass interest etc. Out of these components, which ones are more important is a matter of debate and specific context.

A social movement is generally defined as an organised, sustained and collective effort that focuses on some aspect of collective benefit. However, for many scholars, a social movement need not be very organised in a structural sense.

Some scholars define it as unstable and transitory phenomenon as it may not have a clear beginning and a clear point of termination. Very often, smaller initiative may take the form of mass movement depending upon the enlargement of the goals and mass bases. On the other hand, some large scale and well organised initiative do not turn into social movement because of lack of mass support or ideological inconsistency.

The role of state is very important in any analysis of contemporary social movements. The attitude of the state towards a social movement generally depends on the nature, scope and leadership involved in the movement. Shah talks about four types of social movements which are; revolt, rebellion, revolution and reform. M S A Rao classifies movements into reformatory, transformative and revolutionary. T K Oomen talks about three types of social movements: ideological, charismatic and organisational. All these types of movements intend to change some structural or cultural patterns which become socially harmful. The state generally opposes the politically revolutionary or rebellious forms of movements as they challenge the legitimacy or the agency of the state. Social revolutions are also discouraged by the state because that may disturb the established social patterns on which the political legitimacy is attained. Further, social movements are discouraged or opposed by other influential sections of the society also.

Ideological movements are discouraged by the power elites as it may disturb status quo for their disadvantage. Religious and cultural reforms are discouraged and even opposed by the clergy. Administrative reforms are discouraged by the bureaucratic elites (unofficially) for fear of marginalisation in the new setups. Similarly, economic reforms are discouraged by other vested interests. Hence, any large scale change in the form of a social movement is not appreciated by the status quo. Moderate or incremental reforms are the only form of permissible reforms which may take place without facing irk of the establishment. A social movement for sanitation, located within the cultural patterns and administrative mechanisms, needs to be several challenges and even oppositions.

Social Movement for Sanitation

Sanitation reforms in India need to be seen at multiple levels. The role of the state is very important in achieving the sanitation goals. However, as an agency, the state alone cannot achieve the goals of sanitation for all. The other important agency is people or the masses. A collaborative effort between the 'state' and 'people' can only attain the sanitation goals. While talking about state, we need to note that, state does not refer only to the union or state level governments; it refers to all legitimate bodies constitutionally defined as the organs of the governments. It includes the political institutions, legal institutions, economic and industrial organisation, bureaucratic setups, local self-government bodies and all other institutions representing the government. On the other hand, people include the entire civil society including all private and community setups. There are several established ways for developing such collaborations. Sanitation deficit prevailing in India is a reflection of deficits prevailing in these established ways or mechanisms. The reforms or the transformations are required within these established ways because they are unable to address the sanitation needs of the society. Government initiatives, through various programmes, intend to make corrections in these mechanisms. But the perpetual failure of such initiatives reflects that the problems are deep rooted or structural.

The established mechanisms for ensuring sanitation is under the shadow of multiple deficits like cultural deficits, policy deficits, planning deficits, development deficit etc., as we have explained in earlier chapters. These multiple deficits are structured within the status quo. Hence the structural patterns need improvement so that the deficits can be removed. The improvements in the structural patterns are generally missing at a larger level because of lack of contestation or contestation deficit. Hence, the contestation deficit is the major hindrance in achieving the goals of public sanitations in India.

Any large scale and multi-faceted effort to bring sanitation reforms cannot take place without challenging those established patterns which create hindrances in achieving the sanitation goals. Such established patterns may be cultural, structural or administrative. At this stage, we can identify the reforms which are required to achieve the goals of sanitation for all. Some of these are politico-administrative, some are socio-economic and some are ideological. The common thread that connects all of them are their common socio-cultural base—the notions of pollution and purity; a factor which cannot be changed without some large scale mass mobilisation and social movement. If the stigma of 'polluting' or 'impure' is removed from the works and tools related to achieving sanitation goals, all the other stipulated goals can be achieved through better governance; if the sanitary works are continued to be perceived as 'stigmatised', the reforms attained will only be cosmetic and statistical.

The suggested measures which can be attained through better governance or politico-administrative reforms are the following:

I. Availability of Toilets

(i) Construction of improved sanitation infrastructure mainly toilets at the household level through incentive as well as creating demands.

(ii) Availability of toilets in hundred per cent schools and all educational institutions.

(iii) Availability and maintenance of sanitation facilities at public places.

(iv) Technological up gradation of all public toilets including those in trains, platforms, bus stands, tourist places, markets, religious places etc.

II. Sewer System and Sewage Treatment Plants

(v) Proper sewer systems in all urban areas.

(vi) Sewage treatment plants in every city as per the population and density of population.

III. Local Self-government

(vii) Proper staffing of all the municipal and local self government bodies.

(viii) Proper employment conditions for the sanitation related staff.

(ix) Overcoming the caste base of sanitation related occupations.

(x) Community participation through community organisation and village level sanitation committees.

IV. Socialisation and Social Control

(xi) Sanitation training to school going children and engagement of parents /families in sanitation promoting programmes.

(xii) Making sanitation a part of the curriculum at different levels.

(xiii) Sanitation rules and laws at all public places.

(xiv) Sanitation standards for industries and entrepreneurs.

(xv) Promotion of sanitation values.

(xvi) Strict regulation against the industries and corporate houses spreading insanitary practices/processes.

(xvii) Promotion of public sanitation should be made a fundamental duty.

(xviii) Strong social disapproval and formal punishment for the rule breaker.

V. Public Health Facilities and Infrastructure

(xix) Focusing on Primary healthcare.

(xx) Proper staffing of PHC, SCs and CHCs and removing the shortfall.

(xxi) Promotion of sanitary and hygienic ways through health and paramedical staff.

(xxii) Emphasis on social determinants along with bio-medical factors.

(xxiii) Preservation of water resources and availability of water.

(xxiv) Developing public health and sanitation standards.

(xxv) Increasing public health expenditure.

VI. Social Development, Welfare, Justice, Liberty and Equity

(xxvi) Social and human development instead of economic development alone.

(xxvii) Social equity to minimise the disparities.

(xxviii) Promoting civil society groups.

(xxix) Political initiatives.

(xxx) Corporate social responsibility for promotion of sanitation.

(xxxi) Welfare of the marginalised groups through social inclusion.

(xxxii) Social recognition and awards for those promoting sanitation.

The above mentioned initiatives are very important for ensuring a sanitation friendly environment in any society. These initiatives are closely interrelated and embedded in each other. One initiative without the other cannot be functional or productive. If we look at the government programmes launched for achieving sanitation goals, we find that many of the above mentioned initiatives are not included in them resulting into failure of such programmes. Government programmes mainly focus on construction of toilets at the household level but such initiatives, in isolation, fail to produce sanitation friendly habitas. The government hardly focuses on the socialisation and social control aspects and removing the social taboos associated with them. Further, the sanitation values need to change. Our sociological understanding tells us that it is very difficult to change the cultural practices. For changing the cultural practices, large scale reforms are required. Hence, we make an advocacy for a large scale social mission or social movement for achieving the sanitation reforms in India.

The required social movement for sanitation may not appropriately find fit in any of the established trajectories of social movement as explained earlier because of the diverse courses involved in the path of attaining full sanitation. However, out of the above stated various measures for attaining full sanitation, few measures need structural and cultural transformation within the society. Improvement in notions related to impurity/pollution of human excreta at ritual level or the caste base of sanitation related occupations cannot be attained without social movements. Similarly, improvement in the sanitation related public health structure cannot be attained without some radical transformation in the health structure. Further, the sanitation values cannot get established at grass root level without some massive efforts for sanitation socialisation. And finally, the goals of social justices, freedom, liberty and equality cannot be attained without some civic transformation. These core reforms are very important for sanitation reforms in India. Along with these structural and cultural reforms, the various other initiatives are also equally necessary for achieving the goal of sanitation for all.

References

Castells, M. (1976). Theoretical Proposition for an Experimental Study of Urban Social Movements. In C.Pickvance (ed.) Urban Sociology: Critical Esasays. London: Tavistock.

Habermas, J. (1981). New social movements. Telos. 49 (Fall): 33-37.

Sergey Mamay, Theories of social movements and their current development in Soviet society, online available at http://damienlanfrey. net/web/index.php?option=com_content&view=article&id=51per cent3Atheories-of-social-movements&catid=15 per cent3Aadvocacy-activism&Itemid=26

Smelser, N. (1962). Theory of Collective Behaviour. London: Routledge and Kegan Paul.

Touraine, A. (1981). The Voice and the Eye. Cambridge: CUP.

Turner, R. and Killian, L. (1972). Collective Behaviour. New York: Prentice Hall.

8

Sanitation and Sulabh Initiatives*

Sulabh International Social Service Organisation, a non-profit voluntary social organisation founded in 1970 by Dr Bindeshwar Pathak, is dedicated to Gandhian ideology of emancipation of scavengers. Sulabh has been working for the removal of untouchability and social discrimination against scavengers, a section of Indian society condemned to clean and carry human excreta manually. Sulabh is noted for achieving success in the field of cost-effective sanitation, liberation of scavengers, social transformation of society, prevention of environmental pollution and development of non-conventional sources of energy.

Sulabh Shauchalaya is the most important contribution of Dr Bindeshwar Pathak. Sulabh Shauchalaya is environmental friendly two-pit, pour-flush compost toilet. It is socially acceptable, economically affordable, technologically appropriate and does not require scavengers to clean the pits and implemented in more than 1.2 million houses all over India that has helped liberate over a million scavengers.

Construction and maintenance of public toilets at public places and in slums on 'pay & use basis' is a landmark of Sulabh in the field of sanitation. So far it has constructed and is maintaining over 8000 such public toilets in India and has constructed 200

*The source of the information and the images presented in this chapter is Sulabh International. The author acknowledges the support of the organisation and Dr B. Pathak for this.

biogas plants all over the country. Production of biogas from public toilets and recycling and reuse of effluent through simple and convenient method is the major breakthrough in the field of sanitation and community health.

Advantages of Sulabh Toilets

Key advantages of Sulabh flush composting toilets are :

- Hygienically and technically appropriate, and socio-culturally acceptable.
- Affordable and easy to construct with locally available materials.
- Design and specifications can be modified to suit householder's needs and affordability.
- Eliminates mosquito, insect and fly breeding.
- Can be constructed in different physical, geological and hydrogeological conditions.
- Free from health hazards and does not pollute surface or ground water, if proper precautions and safeguards are taken during construction.

- Can be located within the premises as it is free from foul smell and fly/mosquito nuisance etc.
- Can be constructed on upper floors of houses.
- Pits are generally designed for three -year desludging interval, but if desired, it can be designed for longer periods or it can be reduced even to two years.
- Maintenance is easy, simple and costs very little.
- Needs only 1.5 to two litres of water for flushing, while conventional flush toilet needs 12 to 14 litres of water.
- Needs less space than a septic tank toilet system.
- Does not need scavengers for cleaning the pits or disposal of sludge. This can be done by the householder.
- Makes available rich fertiliser and soil conditioner.
- Can be easily connected to sewers when introduced in the area.
- A low volume flushing cistern could be attached to avoid pour flushing.

Specific Features of Sulabh Technology

No Need of Vent Pipe

Sulabh flush compost toilets do not need vent pipes as gases are dispersed into the soil.

Two Pits are Better Than One Pit

Single leach pit is appropriate only if they can be desludged mechanically by a vacuum tanker, since its contents are not pathogen-free. In the two-pit system, since one pit is used at a time, the filled up pit can be cleaned manually even by the householder himself because of the long period of digestion which makes it free of foul smell and safe for handling. In the single pit system, desludging has to be done almost immediately after the pit has been filled to enable its reuse; this involves handling of fresh and undigested excreta which is hazardous for health. If a deeper and larger single pit is provided, desludging operation will be difficult and chances of pollution would be more especially where the ground water table is high.

Fixing of Pan and Trap

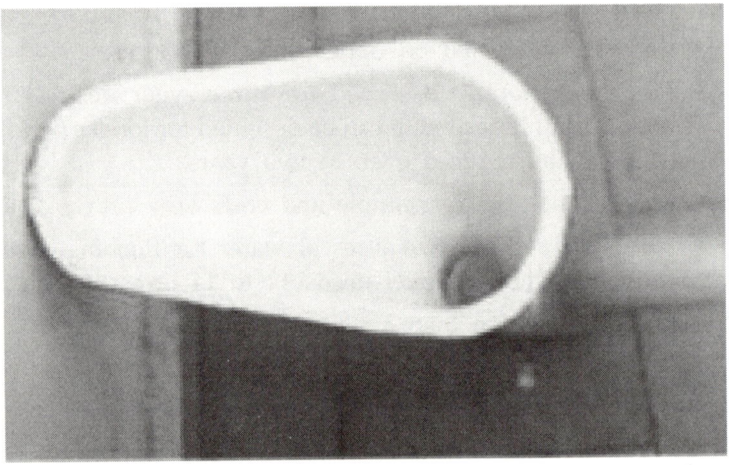

Squatting pan of design specified for pour flush and trap with 20 mm water seal are used in Sulabh toilets. The pan can be of ceramic, fibre glass, PVC, mosaic or cement concrete. With fibre glass pan, traps of HDPE are used. With ceramic and PVC pans, traps of the same material are used. For mosaic and cement concrete pans, traps are of cement concrete.

Shape of Two Pits

As far as possible, separate circular pits should be constructed as these are structurally more stable and the sludge is dry and safe to handle. Where separate circular pits of standard sizes can not be constructed due to space constraint, pits of smaller diameter (not less than 750 mm) be provided, but the depth should be increased suitably to provide required storage volume and infiltration surface area. If it is not possible to construct small diameter pits, combined oval, square or rectangular pits divided into two equal compartments by a partition wall can be provided. The partition wall should be taken 300 mm below the bottom of the pit and be plastered on both sides with cement mortar of 1 : 6 ratio. The partition wall and pit lining in 300 mm width adjoining the partition wall should not have holes. However, the possibility of water from one pit finding its way to the other pit is very much there. Therefore the desludging of the filled up pit has to be done with care to avoid health hazards.

Spacing Between Two Pits

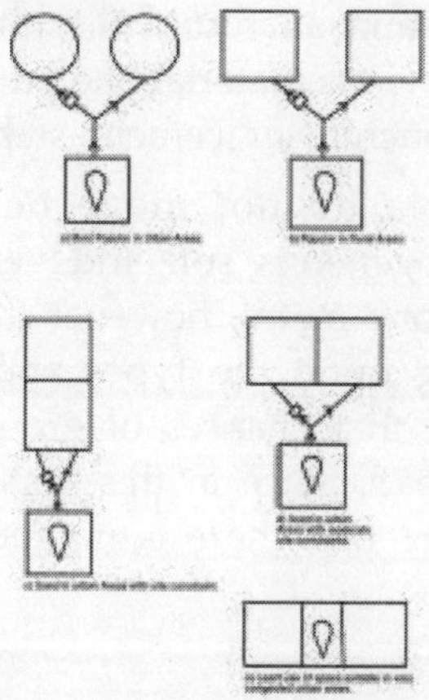

The minimum space between the two pits should be one metre or equal to the depth of pits below the level of incoming pipe or drain, whichever is more. Where it is not possible to maintain this space, an impervious barrier like cut off screen or a mud wall may be provided between the two pits.

Lining of Pits

The pits should be lined to avoid collapsing. Lining could be in brick work, stones, laterite bricks, burnt clay or cement concrete rings. Lining could be done with treated bamboos, wooden logs, tar drums depending upon availability etc. 50 mm wide holes should be provided in alternate brick courses by laying bricks 50 mm apart. Above the invert of incoming pipes or drains, no holes should be provided. Where the soil is sandy, sand envelope is provided or where there are chances of damage by field rats, the width of the holes should be reduced to 12-15 mm.

Prevention of Pollution

To check pollution of drinking water sources, the pits in fine soils (effective size 0.2 mm or less) should be located at a minimum distance of three metres from open wells and shallow hand pumps provided ground water table throughout the year is two metre or more below the bottom of the pit; if water table is higher, the distance should be increased to 10 metres. In coarser soils (effective size more than 0.2 mm), the same safe distances can be maintained by providing 500 mm thick sand envelope of 0.2 mm sand all round the pit and sealing the pit bottom by some impervious material like puddled clay, polythene sheet, lean cement-concrete or cement stabilised soil.

Normally bacteria do not move beyond three metres horizontally in homogeneous soil and vertically they do not permeate more than one metre, however there can be marginal deviations depending upon the types and compaction of the soil. It may be noted that chances of ground water occur due to higher hydraulic load. Since in this system hydraulic load is only 1.5 to 2 litres per use, there is no such chance of ground water pollution.

Sizes of Pits

The sizes of pits where ground water level is always below the bottom of the pit and infiltration rate of soil is 30 1/m2/ day, for three years sludge storage volume works out as follows:

No. of Users per day	*Diameter mm*	*Depth mm*	*Length mm*	*Breadth mm*	*Depth mm*
5	1050	1000	850	850	850
10	1200	1520	1100	1100	1050
15	1460	1530	1400	1400	1200

The above depths are from the invert of incoming pipes or drains to the bottom of the pit. These depths are to be increased by 225 mm to provide free space above the invert of the pipes/ drains.

Pits in High Subsoil

In waterlogged, flood prone and high subsoil water areas, the pits should be raised so that the invert of pipe or drain is just above the likely water level. The raising of pits will necessitate raising of toilet floor also. Earth should be filled and well compacted all round the pit. The trap should be connected to leach pits through 'U' shape covered brick drains of 75 mm dia PVC non-pressure pipes. Keeping the basic design unchanged, Sulabh has a number of such toilet models for demonstration.

Uses of Pit Cover for Household Purposes

Since the pits are covered air tightly with RCC slabs, they can be used for different household purposes or even for running a small shop and so forth.

Cost of Sulabh Flush Compost Toilet

The cost of Sulabh flush composting toilets varies widely to suit people of every economic stratum. The cost ranges from US$ 10 to US$ 1000 per unit. It depends upon materials of construction of pits and seat as well as of the superstructure. The pits can be constructed with bricks or any locally available materials like stones, woodlogs, burnt clay rings, concrete rings or even used coaltar drums. Similarly, the quality of superstructure ranges from simple gunny bag sheets, or thatch to well finished tiles with R.C.C. roof, doors, wash basin, etc. Cost varies also due to size and capacity of the pits, varying from two years to twenty years capacity for each pit. Keeping the basic design unchanged, Sulabh has a number of such toilet models for demonstration.

Manure from Human Excreta

One of the major difficulties for the use of human excreta as manure is the presence of bacterial and other pathogens. Human excreta contains a full spectrum of pathogens causing various infections. It should be free from pathogens before being used as manure. Another problem is psychological/religious taboos associated with it. The studies carried out by the Sulabh have revealed that the content of a Sulabh toilet pit is almost free from pathogens when taken out after two years of resting period. To make it completely pathogen free, digested sludge is sun dried for two to three weeks. During drying of sludge big lumps are formed making it difficult to mix in soil homogeneously. Sulabh developed a technology to granulate such dried lumps into small size graded granules which look like processed tea leaves. Before granulating, it is processed in a ball mill to break it into small pieces. Then it is passed through the mass mixer where the moisture content of manure is regulated by adding water. Such manure has a good percentage of plant nutrients. Besides, it increases humus and water holding capacity of the soil. The Institute has carried out experiments to monitor its manurial effects on different vegetables and flowering plants. In all the cases tested, the effect of manure on the growth of plants was very encouraging.

Operation and Maintenance

Operation and maintenance of a Sulabh flush compost toilet is very easy and simple:

- Before use, wet the pan by pouring only a little quantity of water.
- After defecation, pour 1.5 to 2 litres of water in the pan for flushing.
- Pour about half litre of water in the pan after urination.
- The pan should be cleaned once a day with a brush or a broom and with soap powder periodically.
- One of the pits is to be used at a time by plugging the drain for the other pit.
- Kitchen, bathroom waste water or rain water should not be allowed to enter the pits.
- Other solid wastes like kitchen waste, rags, cotton, sweepings etc. should not be thrown in the pan, this could block the toilet.
- When the first pit in use is full, the flow should be diverted to the second pit and the filled up pit should be desludged after 1.5 to 2-year rest period. The first pit can then be put to reuse, when the second pit fills up.

Sulabh-movement-India

Social Aspect

Considering the role played by soil in the spread of infectious diseases, proper sanitary practices need to be evolved to protect it from pollution. There is an urgent need for sanitation facilities in our cities and towns in view of rapid urbanisation and increasing population. Sanitation, drainage and maintenance of these services are important functions of municipal bodies. In villages where people defecate in fields, the natural biological degradation processes take place. But here too, the soil can get overloaded with faecal microbes. Contaminated top soil can be rich in different pathogenic bacteria (Salmonella and Shigella) known to cause typhoid, dysentery and several other infectious diseases. People are also known to use the top soil to clean their hands and utensils. These practices need to be discouraged. Sanitation should not be dismissed in a casual manner by any community. Disposal of excreta and household wastes, combined with aspects of personal hygiene, especially washing of hands, are directly related to an individual's health status.

The Sulabh Movement launched in the country by Dr Bindeshwar Pathak in recent years needs special mention. A rough analogy can be drawn between it and the Great Sanitation Movement in the 1860s in the West. History reveals that standards of public hygiene deteriorated considerably in the early nineteenth century, especially in England. This was the time when the Industrial Revolution was at its peak and increasing numbers of people were daily crowding into towns and cities for jobs. Entrances of houses and any odd corners were used as lavatories, garbage was found all around, and people rarely bathed. Diseases such as cholera, tuberculosis, and typhoid took many lives.

By the 1840s, the scene started to change as several public-spirited men which included writers, lawyers and other professionals, examined the living conditions of the poor. Edwin Chadwick, a lawyer, studied this situation in a systematic manner, and ingeniously grasped the strong correlation between a dirty environment and the spread of infectious diseases. (This correlation was apparently known to Indians also and perhaps can account for many of our strict norms of personal hygiene). Chadwick became convinced that cities and towns needed to be cleaned up and in 1842 submitted a Report, 'Sanitary Conditions of the Labouring People of Great Britain' to the Council of London. Among other recommendations, he urged the public construction of simple family houses with a garden and a toilet block away from residential quarters. Public parks were also a prominent feature of his city-plans. But his most radical recommendation was his emphasis on an underground sewage system which would collect liquid household wastes and discharge it far from residential quarters onto an open municipal ground. This report ushered in the Great Sanitation Revolution in the western world. The Public Health Acts of 1845 and 1875 and The Royal Commission of 1989 initiated civic action in sewage collection and treatment.

Unwittingly, Chadwick's report led to the elimination or cleaning up of the many places —reservoirs —where disease-causing agents used to breed and thrive, which among other included mosquitoes, rats flies, animals and, of course, a whole world of microorganisms. Today we have come a long way from Chadwick's time in the treatment of sewage and other wastes, with these processes becoming highly automated and specialised.

The situation is quite dismal on the sanitation front in India. Flush-toilets and underground sewerage systems are taken for granted by many in urban areas. In cities too, sanitation and waste water disposal are often the last facilities to be laid out in the process of city planning. Even today, several suburbs of the city of Bombay do not have an underground sewerage system! Sewage treatment is often a tardy and incomplete process. In villages and small towns, the situation is worse. Recent attempts of the government to introduce *'shauchalaya'* in different districts is making rather slow progress where sanitation is viewed as a convenience, and not as a measure which promotes good health.

According to the UNICEF, 'sanitation should not be treated just as an annex to water supply, nor should it be considered only in relation to water supply programmes...the disposal of excreta and household wastes and aspects of personal hygiene such as hand washing, are even more directly related to health status than is water supply'.

Sulabh Movement —Towards a Social Revolution

In 1970, Dr Bindeshwar Pathak founded the *Sulabh Shauchalaya Sansthan*, later named Sulabh International. The primary objective of this organisation is to prevent environmental pollution by promoting low-cost sanitation facilities. Equally important, this movement has freed lakhs of people from the humiliating scavenging job imposed on them by a cruel societal order. *Sulabh* is a complete movement, radical in its approach. While trying to solve the problem of sanitation in the country, it also seeks to rehabilitate scavengers and their family members into the mainstream. This is done by providing them with education and training for several types of jobs. Dr Pathak has given a fresh impetus to the work initiated by Mahatma Gandhi and Babasaheb Ambedkar.

Provision of clean drinking water and sanitation facilities are important for any society in India these are available to a very small fraction of our population. Absence of sanitary facilities forces people to defecate and urinate in the open and thus pollute the soil and air with harmful microorganisms. However, to provide water-borne sewerage or even septic tanks, as is done in some cities, is an expensive and a difficult proposition. The untreated or partially treated sewage is often dumped in the seas and rivers making them highly polluted.

In 1970, Dr Pathak came up with his simple design of *Sulabh Shauchalaya* (latrines-pour-flush toilet with twin leach pit). The advantages of *Sulabh Shauchalaya* are many: they are hygienically and technologically appropriate, low cost and easy to construct with locally available materials; the design and specifications can be modified to suit the needs and the paying capacity of the users; there is no different physical, geological and hydrogeological conditions and do not pollute surface or ground water, if proper precautions are taken in construction; their maintenance is simple and does not require the services of a scavenger or large volumes of water; fertiliser is made available; there is high potential for upgradation as it can even be connected to sewers when sewerage is introduced in the area; a low-volume flushing cistern can also be attached and the whole set-up needs very little space.

Dr Pathak has an impressive list of achievements to his credit. Some of these are: evolving a system of rehabilitating, educating and training of scavengers and their adoption by elite members of the society; entry of scavengers into temples; and setting up of public toilets and baths, and biogas plants for generating energy from human excreta. Recognising his yeoman services, he has been awarded several national and international awards, including the Padma Bhushan, K.P. Goenka Award and the International Saint Francis Prize.

Liberation of Scavengers

The problems arising from casteism and untouchability are complicated, old and deeprooted. Even the scavengers, considered unclean and untouchable by society, accept their lowly position in society.

The problem of Balmikis is as much economic as it is socio-cultural. In fact, it is woven into the fabric of India's culture. Traditions take time to change and require the will and support from all sections of society. Sulabh has evolved the concept of 'social adoption' with this end in view. It is purely voluntary. All it costs is the willingness to shed social prejudice and show some compassion for fellow humans.

A committed citizen publicly 'adopts' a Balmiki family. Subsequently, the two closely interact and visit each other's home. Occasionally help is rendered towards social adjustment. As the adopters are usually persons of social standing and prestige, their action becomes a role model for others. Social adoption has helped significantly in the integration of the Balmikis in the mainstream of society.

So far 10,000 scavenger families have been adopted by well-known personalities including the former Prime Minister of India, Mr I. K. Gujral. Dr Pathak also led 100 Balmik caste people to the Nathdwara temple in Udaipur, Rajasthan, in 1988 to promote religious and social cohesion. This courageous act defied human orthodoxy and helped evolve cultural integration.

Rural Sanitation

Sulabh has taken up a programme of rural sanitation in 350 districts of the country, where volunteers have been trained in the technology, methodology implementation and follow-up work. Masons have been trained. Pans and water seals have been made available at various centres so that people of the area can have the facility to construct toilets to suit their income and choice. The cost ranges from US$ 10 to US$ 600.

A campaign has been launched to make the people in rural areas aware of the fact that they should not go barefoot for open defecation; should put soil on human excreta after defecation so that flies do not sit on excreta and, carry the pathogens to the food, which is the main cause of diarrhoea, dysentery, cholera etc. Literature has been published in 18 languages of the country and social workers distribute them to the beneficiaries. The mass communication workers perform dramas, mono acts, hold painting competitions in schools, to promote awareness. A full-fledged two-hour feature film has been made to make the people aware of the importance of sanitation. The film will also provide entertainment. In rural areas, most children suffer from worm infestation viz. hookworm, roundworm, tapeworm etc. Apart from other medicines available, people are advised to take Anjir (fig.); to take it themselves and also give to children – one in the morning after putting it for the whole night in water. This kills bacteria responsible for growth of worms – a cost effective device.

Most schools in rural areas do not have toilets for children. Consequently, boys and girls face a lot of difficulty. This increases drop-out rates particularly of girl students. Apart from the Government programmes, Sulabh has initiated a programme to get toilets constructed in schools by taking donations from private people as well as NRIs. Within 10 years, every school in India will be provided with Sulabh toilet facilities in this way. Teachers and students are also taught how to keep the toilets clean. Children are given responsibility by turns to maintain the toilets and teachers also inspect and supervise by turns. The number of toilets is as per the strength of the students. As already mentioned various programmes such as health check-up camps, rural sanitation etc. have been taken up in villages in

Maharashtra, Uttaranchal and Haryana. For the speedy implementation of sanitation programme in rural areas Sulabh has made the following proposals:

1. A nation-wide campaign is necessary to make people aware of the adverse effects of open air defecation which is responsible for infections and a number of diseases. The people should be motivated not to be bare-footed while going for open defecation as this will save them from parasitic diseases. This type of education will be necessary until adequate toilet facilities are available in the villages.
2. People in rural areas going for open defecation should be educated to put soil on human excreta after defecation so that flies may not sit on the night soil and become carriers of diseases like diarrhoea, dysentery, dehydration and cholera etc. which are responsible for the death of about half a million children every year in the country.
3. Experience shows that it is not practicable to impose any uniform design of a toilet on users. There should be several designs of pour flush toilets meant for families below poverty line or those belonging to middle income group or higher income groups. (Sulabh has prepared 46 designs which form part of its Project Report). The choice of designs should be left to beneficiaries who will take a decision, keeping in view their resources.
4. The possible help either in the form of subsidy or loan or both should be extended to all beneficiaries who want to have toilets in their homes irrespective of income groups. The criteria for the selection should be first-come first-served.
5. The programme of construction of toilets in rural areas is linked to making people aware of sanitation standards and the adverse health impact of insanitary conditions which require house-to-house contacts and follow-up. This can only be done effectively by NGOs. The role of NGOs is, thus, very crucial in the implementation of the sanitation programme throughout the country.
6. The NGOs should be identified either by the State Governments or the District Administration. The selection

of NGOs should be based on their experience, expertise and infrastructure.

7. The NGOs identified for implementation of the programme should be given proper training in various aspects of the programme. A comprehensive programme of giving them training at various levels has been prepared which forms part of the Project Report.
8. The entire range of training starting with information, education, communication implementation and follow-up should be given to the same NGO. It has been experienced that if the work is divided among various organisations, it becomes a case of divided responsibilities that hamper progress of the work.
9. The NGOs selected for sanitation work should be allowed 15 per cent of the estimated cost of the IEC activities, including implementation and follow up services. In addition, 10 per cent of the project cost should be allowed for training and support services, like publicity which would include printing of booklets, literatures, posters, organising dramas and nukkad plays etc. For setting up sanitary marts and production centres, subsidy as admissible under Government of India Sanitation Programme should also be paid to the NGOs.
10. Interest-free bank loans should be provided to all beneficiaries who want to have toilets in their houses.
11. A nation-wide campaign should be launched through media for generating demand for safe hygienic toilets. The people would, thus, be saved from diseases which occur on account of open air defecation and insanitary toilets. The women will also be saved from the agony and humiliation of open air defecation. Apart from a door-to-door campaign, it will be the responsibility of NGOs to publish literature in local languages and make them available to the people. For a wide publicity of the sanitation programme among the beneficiaries through pamphlets, booklets, calendars, etc. Ten per cent should be given to the same NGO which will be identified for implementation of the sanitation programme.

12. The implementation of the programme will require social mobilisation on a large scale which will include people belonging to various groups. Politicians and policy-makers will have to be involved in a big way so that they can take interest in policy decisions in favour of sanitation programmes. The social mobilisation would also include village elders, doctors, lawyers and school teachers. Print media, radio and television will have to be fully involved in the implementation of the programmes.
13. School sanitation will form an important component of the programme as it is through school teachers and students that the message of sanitary toilets will reach the villages. The NGOs which have been identified by the State Governments or district administration, in a particular area for construction of toilets, should also be allowed to do construction and maintenance work of toilets in schools in that area, as also to impart training about construction and maintenance to teachers and students.
14. Public toilets in rural areas are generally not favoured. Public toilets, however, should be constructed near Panchayat Bhawans, village markets, health centres, bus-stands and other public places where people congregate in large numbers. Such public toilets shall be constructed by NGOs and maintained by them on a 'pay & use basis.'
15. The following recommendations of the Planning Commission in the 10th Five Year Plan should be accepted in implementation of the rural sanitation programme successfully:
    - Under the existing arrangement subsidy is available only for substructure. The Planning Commission has recommended that the subsidy should be inclusive of sub and superstructure for the basic twin-pit pour-flush system.
    - The subsidy for low-cost household toilets should be given to rural families below poverty line and it should be at par with subsidy in the urban households. The Planning Commission has recommended that the present subsidy level should be increased to 50 per cent.

Social Reform

Dr Pathak clearly realised that the liberation and rehabilitation of scavengers or Balmikis was not an easy task. It was indeed difficult, for the worst victims of institutionalised discrimination over the centuries, to break out of the vicious circle and join the mainstream of society. Hence, he devised a well thought-out and multi-pronged strategy to rehabilitate the Balmikis by providing them alternative employment and integrating them into the mainstream. His strategy for liberation of Balmikis through the Sulabh movement consists of a mixed package of technology, rehabilitation, with alternative employment and social reform. This holistic approach is radically different from other social reform movements in that it combines technology with social idealism. His scientific and humane approach towards abolishing scavenging is inspired by a commitment to basic human rights and based on years of research and study of the problem.

The Sulabh approach to restore human dignity to Balmikis has five distinct stages:

(a) Liberation;

(b) Rehabilitation;

(c) Vocational training;

(d) Proper education of next generation; and

(e) Social elevation.

Sulabh's determined and principled intervention has yielded good results. It has been able to liberate and rehabilitate more than a million Balmikis during its four-decade old struggle.

Traditionally, no attention was paid to occupational hazards of hygiene and health, associated with scavenging. On the one hand, society required scavengers to remove night soil by hand and carry the buckets on their hip or head. On the other side, they were socially looked down upon, and boycotted for their unclean work. Moreover, people don't realise how cruel and callous they have been towards this community and that Balmikis' civic disabilities are largely a result of the open and prolonged exploitation. There is need to sensitise people, particularly the new generation, about the nightmarish plight of this community.

Committed to stave off the historical and prolonged injustice against Balmikis, he strove hard and finally came up with a suitable technology to convert lakhs of bucket latrines into flush toilets. The two-pit pour-flush toilets developed by Sulabh caught the imagination of the nation and as a result Sulabh public and individual toilets came up all over India. At the same time, Sulabh took care to provide alternative jobs to the Balmikis, rendered jobless by large-scale conversion of privy latrines into Sulabh toilets.

Skill development is important for all but it is crucial for the less educated. To the members of depressed classes, particularly Balmikis, it has a pointed relevance. Not only are they low in literacy and education, but also possess few skills that merit market demand. Sulabh has paid special attention to skill-development and vocational training of the children from the Balmiki community. It has set up many centres and institutions across the country to equip wards from this community with vocational training in many market-friendly trades.

The problem of Balmikis is as much economical as it is socio-cultural. Traditions take time to change and require the will and initiative from all sections of society. Sulabh has evolved the modality of 'social adoption' with this in view. It is purely voluntary. All it costs is a will to shed social prejudices and compassion for fellow humans.

Education

The Sulabh Sanitation Movement started with the objective to liberate and elevate the status of scavengers. Towards this, it adopted a two-pronged strategy; a state-of-the-art technology to reach sanitation facilities even to the poorest, and to bring scavengers in the mainstream of Indian society. The Sulabh International, under the inspiring leadership of its Founder, Dr Bindeshwar Pathak, branched into several inter-related activities meant not only to rehabilitate, socially and economically, those weaned away from scavenging, but also to restore their self-esteem and self-respect. Towards this, the Sulabh International Centre for Action Sociology (SICAS) was established in 1993. The main objectives were to develop a systematic understanding of the social, economic and psychological problems of scavengers or Balmikis and to evolve and implement a range of innovative, sustainable and replicable activities which would bring the Balmikis into the national mainstream.

Education holds the key to any major change and development. Literacy and education in India are woefully low, particularly among Dalits and Balmikis. In recent years, the educational infrastructure has expanded considerably and schools have been set up on commercial lines. These schools offer physical and instructional facilities comparable to those in developed countries. But very few children coming from low-income households, particularly Balmikis have access to these centres of quality education. Moreover, since most of them are first generation learners, they are hardly inclined towards the education of their children, especially of girls. With this objective of imparting quality education, Sulabh Public School was set up in Delhi in 1992. The school aims to prepare children from the weaker sections of society for a better life.

The school brings quality education within the reach of boys and girls from Balmiki families. Apart from English and Hindi, Sanskrit is also included in the curricula, not only to provide modern, but also the traditional learning, so that the children do not forget the roots of Indian culture. Previously Balmikis were not permitted to learn Sanskrit! The school also offers a wide range of support facilities. In addition, it regularly organises co-curricular activities with a view to promote social integration. This serves as a role-model to be replicated throughout India towards providing quality education to poor students.

The Sulabh Public School has marked features that distinguish it from others. The ratio of the students is 60 per cent Balmikis and 40 per cent from the general category. Balmiki students are provided free tuition fee, uniform, books and stationary. The School is recognised by the Directorate of Education, Govt. of Delhi. It provides education up to tenth standard. The present strength of the School is nearly 400 students.

Sources

http://www.sulabhinternational.org/content/meet-sulabh

http://www.sulabhinternational.org/content/advantages-sulabh-toilets

http://www.sulabhinternational.org/content/chadwick-movement-uk-and-

http://www.sulabhinternational.org/content/rural-sanitation-0

http://www.sulabhinternational.org/content/environmental-sustainability

http://www.sulabhinternational.org/content/social-reform

http://www.sulabhinternational.org/content/education

Appendix

The Prohibition of Employment as Manual Scavengers and their Rehabilitation Act, 2013

रजिस्ट्री सं॰ डी॰ एल॰—(एन)04/0007/2003—13 REGISTERED NO. DL—(N)04/0007/2003—13

भारत का राजपत्र
The Gazette of India

असाधारण
EXTRAORDINARY
भाग II — खण्ड 1
PART II — Section 1
प्राधिकार से प्रकाशित
PUBLISHED BY AUTHORITY

सं॰ 35] नई दिल्ली, बृहस्पतिवार, सितम्बर 19, 2013/ भाद्र 28, 1935 (शक)
No. 35] NEW DELHI, THURSDAY, SEPTEMBER 19, 2013/ BHADRA 28, 1935 (SAKA)

इस भाग में भिन्न पृष्ठ संख्या दी जाती है जिससे कि यह अलग संकलन के रूप में रखा जा सके।
Separate paging is given to this Part in order that it may be filed as a separate compilation.

MINISTRY OF LAW AND JUSTICE

(Legislative Department)

New Delhi, the 19th September, 2013/Bhadra 28, 1935 (Saka)

The following Act of Parliament received the assent of the President on the 18th September, 2013, and is hereby published for general information:—

THE PROHIBITION OF EMPLOYMENT AS MANUAL SCAVENGERS AND THEIR REHABILITATION ACT, 2013

NO. 25 OF 2013

[18th September, 2013.]

An Act to provide for the prohibition of employment as manual scavengers, rehabilitation of manual scavengers and their families, and for matters connected therewith or incidental thereto.

WHEREAS promoting among the citizens fraternity assuring the dignity of the individual is enshrined as one of the goals in the Preamble to the Constitution;

AND WHEREAS the right to live with dignity is also implicit in the Fundamental Rights guaranteed in Part III of the Constitution;

AND WHEREAS article 46 of the Constitution, inter alia, provides that the State shall protect the weaker sections, and, particularly, the Scheduled Castes and the Scheduled Tribes from social injustice and all forms of exploitation;

AND WHEREAS the dehumanising practice of manual scavenging, arising from the continuing existence of insanitary latrines and a highly iniquitous caste system, still persists in various parts of the country, and the existing laws have not proved adequate in eliminating the twin evils of insanitary latrines and manual scavenging;

AND WHEREAS it is necessary to correct the historical injustice and indignity suffered by the manual scavengers, and to rehabilitate them to a life of dignity.

BE it enacted by Parliament in the Sixty-fourthYear of the Republic of India as follows:—

CHAPTER I

PRELIMINARY

Short title, extent and commencement.

1. (1) This Act may be called the Prohibition of Employment as Manual Scavengers and their Rehabilitation Act, 2013.

(2) It extends to the whole of India except the State of Jammu and Kashmir.

(3) It shall come into force on such date as the Central Government may, by notification in the Official Gazette, appoint:

Provided that the date so notified shall not be earlier than sixty days after the date of publication of the notification in the Official Gazette.

Definitions.

2. (1) In this Act, unless the context otherwise requires,—

(a) "agency" means any agency, other than a local authority, which may undertake sanitation facilities in an area and includes a contractor or a firm or a company which engages in development and maintenance of real estate;

(b) "appropriate government", in relation to Cantonment Boards, railway lands, and lands and buildings owned by the Central Government, a Central Public Sector Undertaking or an autonomous body wholly or substantially funded by the Central Government, means the Central Government and in all other cases, the State Government;

(c) "Chief Executive Officer", in relation to a Municipality or Panchayat, means, its senior-most executive officer, by whatever name called;

(d) "hazardous cleaning" by an employee, in relation to a sewer or septic tank, means its manual cleaning by such employee without the employer fulfilling his obligations to provide protective gear and other cleaning devices and ensuring observance of safety precautions, as may be prescribed or provided in any other law, for the time being in force or rules made thereunder;

(e) "insanitary latrine" means a latrine which requires human excreta to be cleaned or otherwise handled manually, either in situ, or in an open drain or pit into which the excreta is discharged or flushed out, before the excreta fully decomposes in such manner as may be prescribed:

Provided that a water flush latrine in a railway passenger coach, when cleaned by an employee with the help of such devices and using such protective gear, as the Central Government may notify in this behalf, shall not be deemed to be an insanitary latrine.

(f) "local authority" means,—

(i) a Municipality or a Panchayat, as defined in clause (e) and clause (f) of article 243P of the Constitution, which is responsible for sanitation in its area of jurisdiction;

(ii) a Cantonment Board constituted under section 10 of the Cantonments Act, 2006; and

(iii) a railway authority;

(g) "manual scavenger" means a person engaged or employed, at the commencement of this Act or at any time thereafter, by an individual or a local authority or an agency or a contractor, for manually cleaning, carrying, disposing of, or otherwise handling in any manner, human excreta in an insanitary latrine or in an open drain or pit into which the human excreta from the insanitary latrines is disposed of, or on a railway track or in such other spaces or premises, as the Central Government or a State Government may notify, before the excreta fully decomposes in such manner as may be prescribed, and the expression "manual scavenging" shall be construed accordingly.

Explanation.—For the purpose of this clause,—

(a) "engaged or employed" means being engaged or employed on a regular or contract basis;

(b) a person engaged or employed to clean excreta with the help of such devices and using such protective gear, as the Central Government may notify in this behalf, shall not be deemed to be a 'manual scavenger';

(h) "National Commission for Safai Karmacharis" means the National Commission for Safai Karamcharis constituted under section 3 of the National Commission for Safai Karmacharis Act, 1993 and continued by Resolution of the Government of India in the Ministry of Social Justice and Empowerment vide No.17015/18/2003-SCD-VI, dated 24th February, 2004 and as amended from time to time;

(i) "notification" means a notification published in the Official Gazette and the expression "notify" shall be construed accordingly;

(j) "occupier", in relation to the premises where an insanitary latrine exists, or someone is employed as a manual scavenger, means the person who, for the time being, is in occupation of such premises;

(k) "owner", in relation to the premises where an insanitary latrine exists or someone is employed as a manual scavenger, means, the person who, for the time being has legal title to such premises;

(l) "prescribed" means prescribed by the rules made under this Act;

(m) "railway authority" means an authority administering railway land, as may be notified by the Central Government in this behalf;

(n) "railway land" shall have the meaning assigned to it in clause (32A) of section 2 of the Railways Act, 1989;

(o) "sanitary latrine" means a latrine which is not an 'insanitary latrine';

(p) "septic tank" means a water-tight settling tank or chamber, normally located underground, which is used to receive and hold human excreta, allowing it to decompose through bacterial activity;

(q) "sewer" means an underground conduit or pipe for carrying off human excreta, besides other waste matter and drainage wastes;

(r) "State Government", in relation to a Union territory, means the Administrator thereof appointed under article 239 of the Constitution;

(s) "survey" means a survey of manual scavengers undertaken in pursuance of section 11 or section 14.

(2) Words and expressions used and not defined in this Act, but defined in the Cantonments Act, 2006, shall have the same meanings respectively assigned to them in that Act.

(3) The reference to a Municipality under Chapters IV to VIII of this Act shall include a reference to, as the case may be, the Cantonment Board or the railway authority, in respect of areas included within the jurisdiction of the Cantonment Board and the railway land, respectively.

3. The provisions of this Act shall have effect notwithstanding anything inconsistent therewith contained in the Employment of Manual Scavengers and Construction of Dry Latrines (Prohibition) Act, 1993 or in any other law, or in any instrument having effect by virtue of any other law.

CHAPTER II

IDENTIFICATION OF INSANITARY LATRINES

4. (1) Every local authority shall,—

(a) carry out a survey of insanitary latrines existing within its jurisdiction, and publish a list of such insanitary latrines, in such manner as may be prescribed, within a period of two months from the date of commencement of this Act;

(b) give a notice to the occupier, within fifteen days from the date of publication of the list under clause (a), to either demolish the insanitary latrine or convert it into a sanitary latrine, within a period of six months from the date of commencement of this Act:

Provided that the local authority may for sufficient reasons to be recorded in writing extend the said period not exceeding three months;

(c) construct, within a period not exceeding nine months from the date of commencement of thisAct, such number of sanitary community latrines as it considers necessary, in the areas where insanitary latrines have been found.

(2) Without prejudice to the provisions contained in sub-section (1), Municipalities, Cantonment Boards and railway authorities shall also construct adequate number of sanitary community latrines, within such period not exceeding three years from the date of commencement of this Act, as the appropriate Government may, by notification, specify, so as to eliminate the practice of open defecation in their jurisdiction.

(3) It shall be the responsibility of local authorities to construct community sanitary latrines as specified in sub-sections (1) and (2), and also to make arrangements for their hygienic upkeep at all times.

Explanation.—For the purposes of this section, "community" in relation to railway authorities means passengers, staff and other authorised users of railways.

CHAPTER III

PROHIBITION OF INSANITARY LATRINES AND

EMPLOYMENT AND ENGAGEMENT AS MANUAL SCAVENGER

5. (1) Notwithstanding anything inconsistent therewith contained in the Employment of Manual Scavengers and Construction of Dry Latrines (Prohibition) Act, 1993, no person. local authority or any agency shall, after the date of commencement of this Act,—

(a) construct an insanitary latrine; or

(b) engage or employ, either directly or indirectly, a manual scavenger, and every person so engaged or employed shall stand discharged immediately from any obligation, express or implied, to do manual scavenging.

(2) Every insanitary latrine existing on the date of commencement of this Act, shall either be demolished or be converted into a sanitary latrine, by the occupier at his own cost, before the expiry of the period so specified in clause (b) of sub-section (1) of section 4:

Provided that where there are several occupiers in relation to an insanitary latrine, the liability to demolish or convert it shall lie with,—

(a) the owner of the premises, in case one of the occupiers happens to be the owner; and (b) all the occupiers, jointly and severally, in all other cases:

Provided that the State Government may give assistance for conversion of insanitary latrines into sanitary latrines to occupiers from such categories of persons and on such scale, as it may, by notification, specify:

Provided further that non-receipt of State assistance shall not be a valid ground to maintain or use an insanitary latrine, beyond the said period of nine months.

(3) If any occupier fails to demolish an insanitary latrine or convert it into a sanitary latrine within the period specified in sub-section (2), the local authority having jurisdiction over the area in which such insanitary latrine is situated, shall, after giving notice of not less than twenty one days to the occupier, either convert such latrine into a sanitary latrine, or demolish such insanitary latrine, and shall be entitled to recover the cost

of such conversion or, as the case may be, of demolition, from such occupier in such manner as may be prescribed.

6. (1) Any contract, agreement or other instrument entered into or executed before the date of commencement of this Act, engaging or employing a person for the purpose of manual scavenging shall, on the date of commencement of this Act, be terminated and such contract, agreement or other instrument shall be void and inoperative and no compensation shall be payable therefor.

(2) Notwithstanding anything contained in sub-section (1), no person employed or engaged as a manual scavenger on a full-time basis shall be retrenched by his employer, but shall be retained, subject to his willingness, in employment on at least the same emoluments, and shall be assigned work other than manual scavenging.

7. No person, local authority or any agency shall, from such date as the State Government may notify, which shall not be later than one year from the date of commencement of this Act, engage or employ, either directly or indirectly, any person for hazardous cleaning of a sewer or a septic tank.

8. Whoever contravenes the provisions of section 5 or section 6 shall for the first contravention be punishable with imprisonment for a term which may extend to one year or with fine which may extend to fifty thousand rupees or with both, and for any subsequent contravention with imprisonment which may extend to two years or with fine which may extend to one lakh rupees, or with both.

9. Whoever contravenes the provisions of section 7 shall for the first contravention be punishable with imprisonment for a term which may extend to two years or with fine which may extend to two lakh rupees or with both, and for any subsequent contravention with imprisonment which may extend to five years or with fine which may extend to five lakh rupees, or with both.

10. No court shall take cognizance of any offence punishable under this Act except upon a complaint thereof is made by a person in this behalf within three months from the date of the occurrence of the alleged commission of the offence.

CHAPTER IV

IDENTIFICATION OF MANUAL SCAVENGERS IN URBAN AND RURAL AREAS AND THEIR REHABILITATION

11. (1) If any Municipality has reason to believe that some persons are engaged or employed in manual scavenging within its jurisdiction, the Chief Executive Officer of such Municipality shall cause a survey to be undertaken to identify such persons.

(2) The content and methodology of the survey referred to in sub-section (1) shall be such as may be prescribed, and it shall be completed within a period of two months from its commencement in the case of Municipal Corporations, and within a period of one month in the case of other Municipalities.

(3) The Chief Executive Officer of the Municipality, in whose jurisdiction the survey is undertaken, shall be responsible for accurate and timely completion of the survey.

(4) After completion of the survey, the Chief Executive Officer shall cause to be drawn up a provisional list of persons found to be working as manual scavengers within the jurisdiction of his Municipality and fulfilling the eligibility conditions as may be prescribed, shall cause such provisional list to be published for general information in such manner, as may be prescribed, and shall invite objections to the list from the general public.

(5) Any person having any objection, either to the inclusion or exclusion of any name in the provisional list published in pursuance of sub-section (4), shall, within a period of fifteen days from such publication, file an objection, in such form as the Municipality may notify, to the Chief Executive Officer.

(6) All objections received in pursuance of sub-section (5), shall be enquired into, and thereafter a final list of persons found to be working as manual scavengers within the local limits of the municipality, shall be published by it in such manner, as may be prescribed.

(7) As soon as the final list of manual scavengers, referred to in sub-section (6) is published, the persons included in the said list shall, subject to the provisions of sub-section (2) of section 6, stand discharged from any obligation to work as manual scavengers.

12. (1) Any person working as a manual scavenger in an urban area, may, either during the survey undertaken by the Municipality in pursuance of section 11, within whose jurisdiction he works, or at any time thereafter, apply, in such manner, as may be prescribed, to the Chief Executive Officer of the Municipality, or to any other officer authorised by him in this behalf, for being identified as a manual scavenger.

(2) On receipt of an application under sub-section (1), the Chief Executive Officer shall cause it to be enquired into, either as part of the survey undertaken under section 11, or, when no such survey is in progress, within fifteen days of receipt of such application, to ascertain whether the applicant is a manual scavenger.

(3) If an application is received under sub-section (1) when a survey under section 11 is not in progress, and is found to be true after enquiry in accordance with sub-section (2), action shall be taken to add the name of such a person to the final list published under sub-section (6) of section 11, and the consequences mentioned in sub-section (7) thereof shall follow.

13. (1) Any person included in the final list of manual scavengers published in pursuance of sub-section (6) of section 11 or added thereto in pursuance of sub-section (3) of section 12, shall be rehabilitated in the following manner, namely:—

(a) he shall be given, within one month,—

(i) a photo identity card, containing, inter alia, details of all members of his family dependent on him, and

(ii) such initial, one time, cash assistance, as may be prescribed;

(b) his children shall be entitled to scholarship as per the relevant scheme of the Central Government or the State Government or the local authorities, as the case may be;

(c) he shall be allotted a residential plot and financial assistance for house construction, or a ready-built house, with financial assistance, subject to eligibility and willingness of the manual scavenger, and the provisions of the relevant scheme of the Central Government or the State Government or the concerned local authority;

(d) he, or at least one adult member of his family, shall be given, subject to eligibility and willingness, training in a livelihood skill, and shall be paid a monthly stipend of not less than three thousand rupees, during the period of such training;

(e) he, or at least one adult member of his family, shall be given, subject to eligibility and willingness, subsidy and concessional loan for taking up an alternative occupation on a sustainable basis, in such manner as may be stipulated in the relevant scheme of the Central Government or the State Government or the concerned local authority;

(f) he shall be provided such other legal and programmatic assistance, as the Central Government or State Government may notify in this behalf.

(2) The District Magistrate of the district concerned shall be responsible for rehabilitation of each manual scavenger in accordance with the provisions of sub-section (1) and the State Government or the District Magistrate concerned may, in addition, assign responsibilities in his behalf to officers subordinate to the District Magistrate and to officers of the concerned Municipality.

14. If any Panchayat has reason to believe that some persons are engaged in manual scavenging within its jurisdiction, the Chief Executive Officer of such Panchayat shall cause a survey of such manual scavengers to be undertaken, mutatis mutandis, in accordance with the provisions of section 11 and section 12, to identify such person.

15.(1) Any person working as a manual scavenger, in a rural area, may, either during the survey undertaken by the Panchayat within whose jurisdiction he works, in pursuance of section 14 or at any time thereafter, apply, in such manner, as may be prescribed, to the Chief Executive Officer of the concerned Panchayat, or to any other officer authorised by him in this behalf, for being identified as a manual scavenger.

(2) On receipt of an application under sub-section (1), the Chief Executive Officer shall cause it to be enquired into, either as part of the survey undertaken under section 14 or when no such survey is in progress, within fifteen days of receipt of such application, so as to ascertain whether the applicant is a manual

scavenger.

16. Any person included in the final list of manual scavengers, published in pursuance of section 14 or added thereto in pursuance of sub-section (2) of section 15 shall be rehabilitated, mutatis mutandis, in the manner laid down for urban manual scavengers in section 13.

CHAPTER V

IMPLEMENTING AUTHORITIES

17. Notwithstanding anything contained in any other law for the time being in force, it shall be the responsibility of every local authority to ensure, through awareness campaign or in such other manner that after the expiry of a period of nine months, from the date of commencement of this Act,—

(i) no insanitary latrine is constructed, maintained or used within its jurisdiction; and

(ii) in case of contravention of clause (i), action is taken against the occupier under sub-section (3) of section 5.

18. The appropriate Government may confer such powers and impose such duties on local authority and District Magistrate as may be necessary to ensure that the provisions of this Act are properly carried out, and a local authority and the District Magistrate may, specify the subordinate officers, who shall exercise all or any of the powers, and perform all or any of the duties, so conferred or imposed, and the local limits within which such powers or duties shall be carried out by the officer or officers so specified.

19. The District Magistrate and the authority authorised under section 18 or any other subordinate officers specified by them under that section shall ensure that, after the expiry of such period as specified for the purpose of this Act,—

(a) no person is engaged or employed as manual scavenger within their jurisdiction;

(b) no one constructs, maintains, uses or makes available for use, an insanitary latrine;

(c) manual scavengers identified under this Act are rehabilitated in accordance with section 13, or as the case may be, section 16;

(d) persons contravening the provisions of section 5 or section 6 or section 7 are investigated and prosecuted under the provisions of this Act; and

(e) all provisions of this Act applicable within his jurisdiction are duly complied with.

20. (1) The appropriate Government may, by notification, appoint such persons as it thinks fit to be inspectors for the purposes of this Act, and define the local limits within which they shall exercise their powers under this Act.

(2) Subject to any rules made in this behalf, an inspector may, within the local limits of his jurisdiction, enter, at all reasonable times, with such assistance as he considers necessary, any premises or place for the purpose of,—

(a) examining and testing any latrine, open drain or pit or for conducting an inspection of any premises or place, where he has reason to believe that an offence under this Act has been or is being or is about to be committed, and to prevent employment of any person as manual scavenger;

(b) examine any person whom he finds in such premises or place and who, he has reasonable cause to believe, is employed as a manual scavenger therein, or is otherwise in a position to furnish information about compliance or non-compliance with the provisions of this Act and the rules made thereunder;

(c) require any person whom he finds on such premises, to give information which is in his power to give, with respect to the names and addresses of persons employed on such premises as manual scavenger and of the persons or agency or contractor employing or engaging them;

(d) seize or take copies of such registers, record of wages or notices or portions thereof as he may consider relevant in respect of an offence under this Act which he has reason to believe has been committed by the principal employer or agency; and

(e) exercise such other powers as may be prescribed.

(3) Any person required to produce any document or thing or to give any information required by an inspector under sub-

section (2) shall be deemed to be legally bound to do so within the meaning of section 175 and section 176 of the Indian Penal Code.

(4) The provisions of the Code of Criminal Procedure, 1973, shall, so far as may be, apply to any such search or seizure under sub-section (2) as they apply to such search or seizure made under the authority of a warrant issued under section 94 of the said Code.

CHAPTER VI

PROCEDURE FOR TRIAL

21. (1) The State Government may confer, on an Executive Magistrate, the powers of a Judicial Magistrate of the first class for the trial of offences under this Act; and, on such conferment of powers, the Executive Magistrate, on whom the powers are so conferred, shall be deemed, for the purposes of the Code of Criminal Procedure, 1973, to be a Judicial Magistrate of the first class.

(2) An offence under this Act may be tried summarily.

22. Notwithstanding anything contained in the Code of Criminal Procedure, 1973, every offence under this Act shall be cognizable and non-bailable.

23. (1) Where an offence under this Act has been committed by a company, every person who, at the time the offence was committed, was in charge of, and was responsible to, the company for the conduct of the business of the company, as well as the company, shall be deemed to be guilty of the offence and shall be liable to be proceeded against and punished accordingly.

(2) Notwithstanding anything contained in sub-section (1), where any offence under this Act has been committed by a company and it is proved that offence has been committed with the consent or connivance of, or is attributable to, any neglect on the part of, any director, manager, secretary or other officer of the company, such director, manager, secretary or other officer shall be deemed to be guilty of that offence and shall be liable to be proceeded against and punished accordingly.

Explanation.—For the purposes of this section,—

(a) "company" means any body corporate and includes a firm or other association of individuals; and

(b) "director" in relation to a firm, means a partner in the firm.

CHAPTER VII

VIGILANCE COMMITTEES

24. (1) Every State Government shall, by notification, constitute a Vigilance Committee for each district and each Sub-Division.

(2) Each Vigilance Committee constituted for a district shall consist of the following members, namely:—

(a) the District Magistrate—Chairperson, ex officio;

(b) all members of the State Legislature belonging to the Scheduled Castes elected from the district—members:

Provided that if a district has no member of the State Legislature belonging to the Scheduled Castes, the State Government may nominate such number of other members of the State Legislature from the district, not exceeding two, as it may deem appropriate.

(c) the district Superintendent of Police— member, ex officio;

(d) the Chief Executive Officer of,—

(i) the Panchayat at the district level—member, ex officio;

(ii) the Municipality of the district headquarters—member, ex officio;

(iii) any other Municipal Corporation constituted in the district— member, ex officio;

(iv) Cantonment Board, if any, situated in the district—member, ex officio;

(e) one representative be nominated by the railway authority located in the district;

(f) not more than four social workers belonging to organisation working for the prohibition of manual scavenging and rehabilitation of manual scavengers, or, representing the scavenger community, resident in the district, to be nominated by the District Magistrate, two of whom shall be women;

(g) one person to represent the financial and credit institutions in the district, to be nominated by the District Magistrate;

(h) the district-level officer in-charge of the Scheduled Castes Welfare— Member-Secretary, ex officio;

(i) district-level officers of Departments and agencies who, in the opinion of the District Magistrate, subject to general orders, if any, of the State Government, have a significant role to play in the implementation of this Act.

(3) Each Vigilance Committee, constituted for a Sub-Division, shall consist of the following members, namely:—

(a) the Sub-Divisional Magistrate—Chairperson, ex officio;

(b) the Chairpersons and the Chief Executive Officers of Panchayats at intermediate level of the Sub-Division, and where Panchayats at intermediate level, do not exist, Chairpersons from two Panchayats at Village level to be nominated by the Sub-Divisional Magistrate—member, ex officio;

(c) the Sub-Divisional Officer of Police—member, ex officio;
(d) Chief Executive Officer of—

(i) the Municipality of the Sub-Divisional headquarters—member, ex officio; and

(ii) Cantonment Board, if any, situated in the Sub-Division—member, ex officio;

(e) one representative to be nominated by the railway authority located in the Sub-Division—member, ex officio;

(f) two social workers belonging to the organisation working for the prohibition of manual scavenging and rehabilitation of the manual scavengers, or representing the scavenger community resident in the Sub-Division, to be nominated by the District Magistrate, one of whom shall be a woman;

(g) one person to represent the financial and credit institutions in the Sub-Division, to be nominated by the Sub-Divisional Magistrate;

(h) the Sub-Divisional level officer in-charge of Scheduled Castes welfare— Member-Secretary, ex officio;

(i) Sub-Divisional level officers of Department and agencies who in the opinion of the Sub-Divisional Magistrate, subject to any general orders of the State Government or the District Magistrate, have a significant role to play in the implementation of this Act—member, ex officio.

(4) Each Vigilance Committee constituted at district and Sub-Divisional level shall meet at least once in every three months.

(5) No proceeding of a Vigilance Committees shall be invalid merely by reason of any defect in its constitution.

25. The functions of Vigilance Committee shall be—

(a) to advise the District Magistrate or, as the case may be, the Sub-Divisional Magistrate, on the action which needs to be taken, to ensure that the provisions of this Act or of any rule made thereunder are properly implemented;

(b) to oversee the economic and social rehabilitation of manual scavengers;

(c) to co-ordinate the functions of all concerned agencies with a view to channelise adequate credit for the rehabilitation of manual scavengers;

(d) to monitor the registration of offences under this Act and their investigation and prosecution.

26. (1) Every State Government shall, by notification, constitute a State Monitoring Committee, consisting of the following members, namely:—

(a) the Chief Minister of State or a Minister nominated by him—Chairperson, ex officio;

(b) the Minister-in-charge of the Scheduled Castes Welfare, and such other Department, as the State Government may notify;

(c) Chairperson of the State Commissions for Safai Karamcharis, and Scheduled Castes, if any— member, ex officio;

(d) representatives of the National Commission for Scheduled Castes, and Safai Karamcharis—member, ex officio;

(e) not less than two members of the State Legislature belonging to the Scheduled Castes, nominated by the State Government:

Provided that if any State Legislature has no member belonging to the Scheduled Castes, the State Government may nominate the members belonging to the Scheduled Tribes;

(f) the Director-General of Police— member, ex officio;

(g) Secretaries to the State Government in the Departments of Home, Panchayati Raj, Urban Local Bodies, and such other Departments, as the State Government may notify;

(h) Chief Executive Officer of at least one Municipal Corporation, Panchayat at the district-level, Cantonment Board and railway authority as the State Government may notify;

(i) not more than four social workers belonging to organisation working for the prohibition of manual scavenging and rehabilitation of manual scavengers, or, representing the scavenger community, resident in the State, to be nominated by the State Government, two of whom shall be women;

(j) State-level head of the convener Bank of the State Level Bankers' Committee— member, ex officio;

(k) Secretary of the Department of the State Government dealing with development of the Scheduled Castes—Member-Secretary, ex officio;

(l) such other representative of Departments of the State Government and such other agencies which, in the opinion of the State Government, are concerned with the implementation of this Act.

(2) The State Monitoring Committee shall meet at least once in every six months and shall observe such rules of procedure in regard to the transaction of business at its meetings as may be prescribed.

27. The functions of the State Monitoring Committee shall be—

(a) to monitor and advise the State Government and local authorities for effective implementation of this Act;

(b) to co-ordinate the functions of all concerned agencies;

(c) to look into any other matter incidental thereto or connected therewith for implementation of this Act.

28. Every State or Union territory Government and Union territory administration shall send such periodic reports to the Central Government about progress of implementation of this Act, as the Central Government may require.

29.(1) The Central Government shall, by notification, constitute a Central Monitoring Committee in accordance with the provisions of this section.

(2) The Central Monitoring Committee shall consist of the following members, namely:—

(a) The Union Minister for Social Justice and Empowerment—Chairperson, ex officio;

(b) Chairperson of the National Commission for Scheduled Castes—member, ex officio;

(c) Minister of State in the Ministry of Social Justice and Empowerment— member, ex officio;

(d) Chairperson, National Commission for Safai Karamcharis— member, ex officio;

(e) the Member of the Planning Commission dealing with development of the Scheduled Castes—member, ex officio;

(f) three elected members of Parliament belonging to Scheduled Castes, two from the Lok Sabha and one from the Rajya Sabha;

(g) Secretaries of the Ministries of,—

(i) Social Justice and Empowerment, Department of Social Justice and Empowerment;

(ii) Urban Development;

(iii) Housing and Urban Poverty Alleviation; (iv) Drinking Water and Sanitation;

(v) Panchayati Raj;

(vi) Finance, Department of Financial Services; and

(vii) Defence, members, ex officio;

(h) Chairman, Railway Board—member, ex officio;

(i) Director-General, Defence Estates— member, ex officio;

(j) representatives of not less than six State Governments

and one Union territory, as the Central Government may, notify;

(k) not more than six social workers belonging to organisation working for the prohibition of manual scavenging and rehabilitation of manual scavengers, or, representing the scavenger community, resident in the country, to be nominated by the Chairperson, two of whom shall be women;

(l) Joint Secretary, Department of Social Justice and Empowerment in the Ministry of Social Justice and Empowerment, looking after development of Scheduled Castes—Member-Secretary, ex officio;

(m) such other representatives of Central Ministries or Departments and agencies which, in the opinion of the Chairperson, are concerned with the implementation of this Act.

(3) The Central Monitoring Committee shall meet at least once in every six months.

30. The functions of the Central Monitoring Committee shall be,—

(a) to monitor and advise the Central Government and State Government for effective implementation of this Act and related laws and programmes;

(b) to co-ordinate the functions of all concerned agencies;

(c) to look into any other matter incidental to or connected with implementation of this Act.

31. (1) The National Commission for Safai Karamcharis shall perform the following functions, namely:—

(a) to monitor the implementation of this Act;

(b) to enquire into complaints regarding contravention of the provisions of this Act, and to convey its findings to the concerned authorities with recommendations requiring further action; and

(c) to advise the Central and the State Governments for effective implementation of the provisions of this Act.

(d) to take suo motu notice of matter relating to non-implementation of this Act.

(2) In the discharge of its functions under sub-section (1), the National Commission shall have the power to call for

information with respect to any matter specified in that sub-section from any Government or local or other authority.

32. (1) The State Government may, by notification, designate a State Commission for Safai Karamcharis or a State Commission for the Scheduled Castes or such other statutory or other authority, as it deems fit, to perform, within the State, mutatis mutandis, the functions specified in sub-section (1) of section 31.

(2) An authority designated under sub-section (1) shall, within the State, have, mutatis mutandis, the powers of the National Commission for Safai Karamcharis as specified in sub-section (2) of section 31.

CHAPTER VIII

MISCELLANEOUS

33. (1) It shall be the duty of every local authority and other agency to use appropriate technological appliances for cleaning of sewers, septic tanks and other spaces within their control with a view to eliminating the need for the manual handling of excreta in the process of their cleaning.

(2) It shall be the duty of the appropriate Government to promote, through financial assistance, incentives and otherwise, the use of modern technology, as mentioned in sub-section (1).

34. No suit, prosecution or other legal proceeding shall lie against an appropriate Government or any officer of the appropriate Government or any member of the Committee for anything which is in good faith done or intended to be done under this Act.

35. No civil court shall have jurisdiction in respect of any matter to which any provision of thisAct applies and no injunction shall be granted by any civil court in respect of anything, which is done or intended to be done, by or under this Act.

36. (1) The appropriate Government shall, by notification, make rules for carrying out the provisions of this Act, within a period not exceeding three months from the date of commencement of this Act.

(2) In particular, and without prejudice to the generality of the foregoing power, such rules may provide for all or any of the following matters, namely:—

(a) the obligation of an employer, under clause (d) of sub-section (1) of section 2;

(b) the manner in which the excreta fully decomposes under clauses (e) and (g) of sub-section (1) of section 2;

(c) the manner of carrying out survey of insanitary latrine and publishing list thereof under clause (a) of sub-section (1) of section 4;

(d) procedure of giving notice and recovering cost of demolition of an insanitary latrine under sub-section (3) of section 5;

(e) content and methodology of the survey under sub-section (2) of section 11;

(f) the eligibility conditions for identification of manual scavengers and publication of provisional list of persons found to be working as manual scavengers under sub-section (4) of section 11;

(g) publication of final list of persons found to be working as manual scavengers under sub-section (6) of section 11;

(h) manner of application to be made to the Chief Executive Officer of the municipality, or to an officer authorised by him in this behalf, under sub-section (1) of section 12 or, as the case may be, sub-section (1) of section 15;

(i) provision of initial, one time, cash assistance under sub-clause (ii) of clause (a) of sub-section (1) of section 13;

(j) such other powers of Inspectors under clause (e) of sub-section (2) of section 20; and

(k) any other matter which is required to be, or may be, prescribed.

(3) Every rule made under thisAct by the Central Government shall be laid, as soon as may be after it is made, before each House of Parliament, while it is in session, for a total period of thirty days which may be comprised in one session or in two or more successive sessions, and if, before the expiry of the session immediately following the session or the successive sessions aforesaid, both Houses agree in making any modification in the rule or both Houses agree that the rule should not be made, the rule shall thereafter have effect only in such modified

form or be of no effect, as the case may be; so, however, that any such modification or annulment shall be without prejudice to the validity of anything previously done under that rule.

(4) Every rule made under this Act by the State Government shall, as soon as may be after it is made, be laid before each House of State Legislature, where there are two Houses and where there is one House of State Legislature, before that House.

37. (1) Notwithstanding anything contained in section 36 of this Act:—

(a) the Central Government shall, by notification, publish model rules for the guidance and use of State Governments; and

(b) in case the State Government fails to notify the rules under section 36 of this Act within the period of three months specified therein, then the model rules as notified by the Central Government shall be deemed to have come into effect, mutatis mutandis, in such State, till such time as the State Government notifies its rules.

(2) The model rules made by the Central Government under this Act shall be laid, as soon as may be after they are made, before each House of Parliament while it is in session, for a total period of thirty days which may be comprised in one session or in two or more successive sessions, and if, before the expiry of the session immediately following the session or the successive sessions aforesaid, both Houses make any modification in the rule, the rule shall thereafter have effect only in such modified form; so, however, that any such modification shall be without prejudice to the validity of anything previously done under that rule.

38. (1) If any difficulty arises in giving effect to the provisions of this Act, the Central Government may, by order published in the Official Gazette, make such provisions, not inconsistent with the provisions of this Act, as may appear to it to be necessary or expedient for the removal of the difficulty:

Provided that no such order shall be made in relation to a State after the expiration of three years from the commencement of this Act in that State.

(2) Every order made under this section shall, as soon as may be after it is made, be laid before each House of Parliament.

39. (1) The appropriate Government may, by a general or special order published in the Official Gazette, for reasons to be recorded, and subject to such conditions as it may impose, exempt any area, category of buildings or class of persons from any provisions of this Act or from any specified requirement contained in this Act or any rule, order, notification, bye-laws or scheme made thereunder or dispense with the observance of any such requirement in a class or classes of cases, for a period not exceeding six months at a time.

(2) Every general or special order made under this section shall be laid, as soon as may be after it is made, before each House of Parliament or each House of State Legislature, where there are two Houses and where there is one House of State Legislature, before that House.

P.K. MALHOTRA
Secy. to the Govt. of India.

Index

T

U

V

W